Oklahoma Memories

Oklahoma Memories
Edited by Anne Hodges Morgan and Rennard Strickland

University of Oklahoma Press : Norman

Drawings by Dick Gilpin

BY ANNE HODGES MORGAN

Robert S. Kerr: The Senate Years (Norman, 1977)
Oklahoma: A Bicentennial History (with H. Wayne Morgan) (New York, 1977)
Oklahoma Memories (with Rennard Strickland) (Norman, 1981)

BY RENNARD STRICKLAND

Speaker's Sourcebook Series (7 volumes) (Fayetteville, 1965–71)
Sam Houston with the Cherokees (with Jack Gregory) (Austin, 1967)
Starr's History of the Cherokees (editor) (Fayetteville, 1967)
Indian Spirit Tales Series: *Cherokee Spirit Tales, Creek-Seminole Spirit Tales, Choctaw Spirit Tales, American Indian Spirit Tales* (Muskogee, 1969–74)
Language Is Sermonic (editor) (Baton Rouge, 1970)
Hell on the Border (editor, with Jack Gregory) (Muskogee, 1971)
The Cherokee People (with Earl Boyd Pierce) (Phoenix, 1973)
How to Get into Law School (New York, 1974)
Avoiding Teacher Malpractice (New York, 1975)
Fire and the Spirits: Cherokee Law from Clan to Court (Norman, 1975)
Newcomers to a New Land Series: *The Indians in Oklahoma* (Norman, 1980)
Oklahoma Memories (with Anne Hodges Morgan) (Norman, 1981)

Library of Congress Cataloging in Publication Data
Main entry under title:

Oklahoma memories.

Includes bibliographical references and index.
1. Oklahoma—Biography. 2. Oklahoma—Social life and customs.
3. Frontier and pioneer life—Oklahoma. I. Morgan, Anne Hodges, 1940–   II. Strickland, Rennard.
F693.037   976.6   81-2777
AACR2

Copyright © 1981 by
the University of Oklahoma Press, Norman,
Publishing Division of the University of Oklahoma.
Manufactured in the U.S.A.
First edition.

*To Oklahoma's librarians,
the stewards of our
state's cultural heritage*

Contents

Preface / ix

Acknowledgments / xi

Editors' Introduction / 3

1 ALICE MARY ROBERTSON
  Christmas Time in Indian Territory / 7

2 MORRIS SHEPPARD
  A Slave's Remembrances / 15

3 EMMA ERVIN CHRISTIAN
  Memories of my Childhood Days in the Choctaw Nation / 25

4 J. H. BEADLE
  Indian Territory in the 1870s / 37

5 GENERAL R. A. SNEED
  The Reminiscences of an Indian Trader / 57

6 ARTHUR W. DUNHAM
  A Pioneer Railroad Agent / 67

7 EVAN G. BARNARD
  The Opening of Oklahoma / 83

8 CARL SWEEZY
  From Fighters to Freighters / 93

9 J. W. PRYER
  A Drummer's Early-day Experience / 105

10 MRS. TOM B. FERGUSON
   Picture of a Pioneer Town / 113

11 *A Great Race* / 127

12 SEIGNIORA RUSSELL LAUNE
   Clubs and I / 131

Oklahoma Memories

13 *A Creek Camp Meeting* / 141

14 ETHEL C. KREPPS
    A Strong Medicine Wind / 145

15 OSCAR AMERINGER
    If You Don't Weaken / 163

16 *What's The Latest From Europe?* / 175

17 GEORGE LEVITE
    At the Old Ball Game / 181

18 PERLE MESTA
    Father's 300-Room Hobby / 187

19 SADIE DUGGETT
    The Oil Field Cook / 197

20 MR. DILLINGHAM
    I Wish They'd Never Found Oil / 213

21 CAROLINE A. HENDERSON
    Letters from the Dust Bowl / 223

22 SERGEANT DON ROBINSON
    News of the 45th / 245

23 TOM RUCKER
    The Shakedown Cruise of the U.S.S. Oklahoma City / 259

24 GEORGE LYNN CROSS
    Guess Who's Coming to School? / 265

25 CLARA LUPER
    Behold the Walls! / 279

26 ROBINSON RISNER
    The "Humane and Lenient Treatment" Begins / 293

27 MICK HINTON
    First Impressions of Newcomers to Oklahoma City, 1978 / 297

Index / 305

Preface

THE IDEA for this book grew out of a conversation we had in the fall of 1977 about how often Edna Ferber's warning in the preface to her novel about Oklahoma, *Cimarron*, had proved correct. "In many cases," wrote Mrs. Ferber, "material entirely true was discarded as unfit for use because it was so melodramatic, so absurd as to be too strange for the realm of fiction."[1]

We know the truth of Mrs. Ferber's statement from personal experience. Often in our writing about Oklahoma we have confessed to one another that while we really wanted to use a particularly colorful anecdote to illustrate an event, we usually opted for a less vivid example if it seemed more "believable." Timid historians! That is what we were!

As the conversation progressed and each told of historical evidence not used, we became bolder. Why not bring together a collection of those selections that we thought so revealing of Oklahoma's history? Why not let the men and women who settled the last frontier tell of their own experiences, in their own words, without the apparatus of formal historical scholarship? So we did, in *Oklahoma Memories*. The selections we have chosen are memoirs and recollections. In most cases they are autobiographical or firsthand accounts. A few of the narratives are the work of children recording the events of their parents' lives.

We have elected not to clutter the text with footnotes or explanatory material. There are many good general histories of Oklahoma, including Arrell M. Gibson, *Oklahoma: A History of Five Centuries*, second edition (Norman: University of Oklahoma Press, 1981) and *The Oklahoma Story* (Norman: University of Oklahoma Press, 1978); Edwin C. McReynolds, *Oklahoma: A History of the Sooner State* (Norman: University of Oklahoma Press, 1954); and H. Wayne Morgan and Anne Hodges Morgan, *Oklahoma: A Bicentennial History* (New York: W. W. Norton & Company, Inc.,

1. Edna Ferber, *Cimarron* (New York: Doubleday Doran and Co., 1930), ix.

1977). Angie Debo's *Oklahoma, Footloose and Fancy-free* (Norman: University of Oklahoma Press, 1949) is a provocative and shrewd analysis of the Sooner character.

Many of the place-names and geographic designations that appear in these selections have changed or disappeared. The reader may wish to consult John W. Morris, Charles R. Goins, and Edwin C. McReynolds, *Historical Atlas of Oklahoma*, second edition, revised and enlarged (Norman: University of Oklahoma Press, 1976), and John W. Morris, *Ghost Towns of Oklahoma* (Norman: University of Oklahoma Press, 1977).

It is a pleasure to thank the people who helped us. The staffs of the Shleppey Collection at the University of Tulsa, the Western History Collections at the University of Oklahoma, and the Oklahoma Department of Libraries were consistently cheerful and cooperative. Bernice Jackson, Director of the Lawton Public Library, provided some elusive biographical material. Dee Ann Ray, Director of the Western Plains Library System, constantly encouraged us to prepare a book in which ordinary people told their own history and thus illuminated the history of the state. We are especially grateful to Rosemarie Spaulding and Margaret Murray for their patience and good humor while typing the numerous versions of this manuscript.

We owe a profound debt to H. Wayne Morgan. When we overcomplicated our task, he introduced simplicity. When we were discouraged and distracted, he buoyed our spirits. And when we had doubts, he gave us confidence.

Norman, Oklahoma   ANNE HODGES MORGAN
Tulsa, Oklahoma   RENNARD STRICKLAND

Acknowledgments

The authors and the publisher make grateful acknowledgment for permission to quote from the following works:

Alice Mary Robertson, "Christmas Time in Indian Territory," "A Great Race," and "A Creek Camp Meeting" are used with permission from McFarlin Library, University of Tulsa, Tulsa, Oklahoma.

Emma Ervin Christian, "Memories of My Childhood Days in the Choctaw Nation"; General R. A. Sneed, "The Reminiscences of an Indian Trader"; and Arthur W. Dunham, "A Pioneer Railroad Agent" are used with permission from the Oklahoma Historical Society, Oklahoma City, Oklahoma.

Carl Sweezy, "From Fighters to Freighters," © 1966, by Althea Bass, used with permission from Clarkson, N. Potter, Inc., New York, New York.

Mrs. Tom B. Ferguson, "Picture of a Pioneer town," used with permission from the Burton Publishing Company, Kansas City, Missouri.

Seigniora Russell Laune, "Clubs and I," used with permission from the Northland Press, Flagstaff, Arizona.

Ethel C. Krepps, "A Strong Medicine Wind," used with permission from the author.

Oscar Ameringer, "If You Don't Weaken," used with permission from Mrs. Oscar Ameringer.

Sadie Duggett, "The Oil Field Cook"; Mr. Dillingham, "I Wish They'd Never Found Oil"; and "What's the Latest From Europe?" are used with permission from the Western History Collections, University of Oklahoma, Norman, Oklahoma.

George Levite, "At the Old Ball Game," used with permission from Mrs. Molly Levite Griffis and the Levite Family.

Perle Mesta, "Father's 300 Room Hobby," copyright 1960 by McGraw-Hill, used with permission from the McGraw-Hill Book Company, New York, New York.

Caroline A. Henderson, "Letters from the Dust Bowl," Copyright © 1936 by the Atlantic Monthly Company, Boston, Massachusetts, used with permission of the Atlantic Monthly Company.

Sergeant Don Robinson, "News of the 45th," copyright 1944 by the University of Oklahoma Press, reprinted with permission from the University of Oklahoma Press, Norman, Oklahoma.

Tom Rucker, "The Shakedown Cruise of the U.S.S. Oklahoma City"; and Mick Hinton, "First Impressions of Newcomers to Oklahoma City, 1978" are used with permission from the Oklahoma Publishing Company, Oklahoma City, Oklahoma.

George Lynn Cross, "Guess Who's Coming to School?" reprinted with permission; © 1976 Oklahoma Monthly, Inc. All Rights reserved.

Clara Luper, "Behold the Walls," used with permission of the author.

Robinson Risner, "The Humane and Lenient Treatment Begins," used with permission of Random House, Inc., New York, New York.

Oklahoma Memories

Some memories are better than realities and are better than anything that can ever happen again.

—WILLA CATHER, *My Antonia*

Editors' Introduction

THE RECORDED HISTORY of Oklahoma begins with the explorers, adventurers, and traders who traveled here before the nineteenth century. They left trails and placenames and a few tiny settlements but little else. In the decades after the Louisiana Purchase, thousands of Indians settled in Oklahoma. Some came voluntarily, but most were forcibly removed from their old homelands east of the Mississippi River. From the 1820s to the 1880s Indian Territory existed behind the dike of a different culture, with the tide of white settlement constantly surging against it. Slowly the barrier eroded, then finally collapsed. Oklahoma entered the Union as the forty-sixth state in 1907.

Life in Oklahoma in the twentieth century has been as colorful as her earlier past. Successive booms in oil, mining, and agriculture have changed the economy. Radical political movements have flared, sputtered, and died. Even unpredictable weather, culminating in the drought of the 1930s has affected the state. In the early years thousands of new settlers periodically swept in, looking for homes and a chance to start over. During the depression, thousands of Oklahomans streamed out of the state, looking for work and new lives farther west. In the decades since World War II, Oklahomans have recaptured much of the optimistic spirit that marked the state's early years. Steady, diversified industrial growth has improved the state's general economic health and its fiscal soundness so that the trend of population loss has been reversed.

Within this broad outline of the story of Oklahoma there were countless human dramas that "history" passed by as part of broad generalizations. The events, the dates, and the political figures that dominate most state histories are only

Oklahoma Memories

the surface of the story. The selections here deal with significant events: the Civil War, the land runs, the coming of the railroad, statehood, oil booms, the depression. But they are primarily concerned with how historical events affected individual lives. They are about people—their feelings, reactions, and impressions—and reaffirm Ralph Waldo Emerson's dictum that after all "there is properly no history; only biography."[1]

The subject matter of the selections ranges from the bleakness of the Dust Bowl to the opulence of the Skirvin Hotel lobby; from a glimpse at growing up in the Choctaw Nation to the life of a pioneer newspaperwoman; from the bittersweet opening of the Cherokee Strip to the small-town boosterism of the Apache baseball team. Several themes unite the material and provide a comprehensive overview of Oklahoma's human heritage. The author of each memoir and recollection chronicles the social, political, economic, and cultural transition that occurred during a lifetime in Oklahoma. In "Letters from the Dust Bowl," Caroline Henderson tells how western wheat farmers battled soil and wind erosion in what seemed then a futile and endless struggle, and won. In "A Strong Medicine Wind," Ethel C. Krepps records the pathetic story of her Kiowa father, who gave up his tribal religion, lived in a house, farmed, and eagerly accepted a role in a movie. When the script called for a buffalo hunt ending with the triumphant hunter sitting atop his prey, he cheerfully complied. "Things were going good, he was laughing and smiling, and then he looked down, saw the buffalo, and started to cry." Memories of a vanished era had overtaken a man caught between two cultures.

A spirit of adventure, a willingness to risk, the desire for change, and new challenges emerge from these collected memories. Settlers burned buffalo chips for fuel, survived on meager and unusual diets, and tolerated the intestinal discomforts of "gyp water" for the chance to start over in Oklahoma. Several generations of adventurers planted crops in soil suited only for sparse grasses, found oil in the

1. Ralph Waldo Emerson, "History," *Essays* (New York: Franklin Watts, Inc., 1967), 10.

flinty, worthless-looking Osage Hills, built towns that were blown away the first year, flooded out the second, and passed up by the railroad the third. These people also feasted on chilled oysters at prairie picnics, discussed Shakespeare and philosophy in one-room sod schoolhouses, rode to the hounds at Ponca City, and kept the sacred fire alive in the Cherokee hills. Mrs. Laune in "Clubs and I" refused to accept the notion that frontier life must be always coarse and graceless. And Evan Barnard, the cowboy who became a prosperous farmer, apparently scoffed at the common wisdom that saw this transformation as unlikely if not impossible.

The telescoping of change that distinguished Oklahoma's history from that of other states is vividly illustrated in these selections. Carl Sweezy's record of the abrupt alteration in the Arapaho warrior's life from a free-roaming fighter to a government-employed freighter is one of the most dramatic examples of the rapidity and abruptness of change in Oklahoma. Sadie Duggett's account of various oil camps and boomtowns and farmer Dillingham's description of how wealth from the oil fields affected his family capture the spirit of this state where rapid transition predominates.

Contrary to the popular stereotype of Oklahoma as a land only of cowboys and Indians, oil derricks and millionaires, these selections reflect the complexity and variety of life in the Sooner State. Events, ideas, life-styles, and different cultures overlapped and interacted in daily life. Ideas formulated for the Indian state of Sequoyah dominated the constitution of the fledgling Oklahoma. A Jewish merchant from eastern Europe was an Indian trader and a baseball player on the frontier. And the daughter of generations of Presbyterian missionaries to the Indians won a term among the male-dominated United States Congress. Oscar Ameringer's memoir shows that Oklahoma farmers could espouse both private ownership of land and the doctrines of socialism with no troublesome contradictions. And Clara Luper's story of the black sit-ins in Oklahoma City in the late 1950s helps place the civil rights movement in its appropriate na-

Editors' Introduction

tional context. These memoirs confirm, as Edna Ferber intimated, that in Oklahoma the truth is both stranger and more interesting than the fiction that often passes for history. Collectively they reaffirm what every Sooner knows and what every outlander suspects—that there is nothing simple about Oklahoma.

Christmas Time in Indian Territory

¶ *Alice Mary Robertson was one of those rare souls whose life mirrored the life of her nation. Born in 1854 at Tullahassee mission in the Creek country, she lived long enough to become the second woman elected to the Congress of the United States. Miss Alice, as she was affectionately known, watched the land of her birth change from the Indian Territory to the state of Oklahoma. She saw the little tribal village of Tulsey Town become what boosters later called "the oil capital of the world."* ¶ *Alice Robertson was more than the passive observer that women of her day were supposed to be. She had intellectual and spiritual strength and also was a woman of action. Miss Alice was a child of the New England tradition, born of the frontier experience. In an ironic way, the life of Alice Robertson was the final secular flowering of the nine generations of Winthrop, Edwards, Worcester, and Robertson servants of God. Her grandfather, the Reverend Samuel Worcester, was the pawn in the great constitutional battle over Indian rights, which was fought between Andrew Jackson and John Marshall and climaxed in the historic case of Worcester v. Georgia. Her parents were the most influential white missionaries among the Creeks.* ¶ *"Christmas Time in Indian Territory" is the story of the mission family after their return to Tullahassee following the American Civil War exile. The Creek Indians, many of whom owned black slaves, were bitterly divided over the Civil War and suffered devastating warfare in their own land. Written as a newspaper feature more than fifty years after the war, Alice Robertson's evocative narrative says much about life in Indian Territory. The account tells even more about Miss Alice and what it meant to be a young girl in the world of Indian missions. While Alice's 1866 Christmas gift of "improving poetry" may have lacked the glamour of a china doll,*

From Alice Mary Robertson, "Christmas Time in Indian Territory," *Kendall Collegian*, College Files, Worcester-Robertson Collection, McFarlin Library, University of Tulsa, Tulsa, Oklahoma.

8

Oklahoma
Memories

the morality of this missionary world undoubtedly influenced a brave girl who was to become a truly remarkable woman.

IT WAS in the earlier Indian Territory days, away back in 1866, Father and Mother had only a few days before Christmas returned to their old missionary post at Tullahassee to find the large brick building which had been used for the boarding school almost a ruin. Through much of the war time this had been a hospital and rows of already grass-grown indentations showed the unmarked resting places of unknown soldiers of the Confederacy. Not a door or window remained in the building and there were great gaps in the walls where quantities of brick had been torn away for use by the Federal Army at Fort Gibson to build bake ovens for the post. The attic had been floored with wide, rough plank as a storage room in old times and some of this flooring yet remained.

So father went to work with saw and hammer, for in those days a missionary must toil with his hands unceasingly. Until windows could be boarded up and battened doors made we camped in the yard, occupying the tent which had been our nightly shelter during the overland journey of three hundred miles.

NECESSITIES WERE HIGH

Only the most meagre supply of household necessities could be brought with us and the sutler's store at Fort Gibson afforded little more. Mother priced a tiny cooking stove, but the cost, one hundred dollars, was prohibitive. However, an oldtime heating stove, broken and battered, was found down in the orchard where it had been gathering rust through the years of war, and on this we did most of our cooking. Bread we had to bake in a Dutch oven out of doors.

The cavalrymen who had last occupied the place had left several tons of hay in an old log barn and ticks filled with hay made very acceptable beds, though father and mother had a feather bed as well.

Christmas Time in Indian Territory

HOME-MADE FURNITURE

Father made table and chairs and bedsteads for us from sassafras saplings and planks and we children were very proud to help by smoothing the rounded pieces of sassafras with bits of broken glass. Father was in a hurry to get us all fixed as he was anxious to get out among his Indian "sheep without a shepherd," who in their days of famine and stress, returning to ruined homes and appalling poverty, surely needed him.

So Christmas eve found us, father, mother, myself, 12 years old—the oldest child at home—for one sister pitifully young to be so far away was at boarding school—a sister nine years old, a brother five, and the twins eight months old. Mother spread a fresh white cloth on the new table and each of us placed a plate to see what the morning might bring.

Sister and I whispered softly what we would like to have until the howling of a pack of wolves at the very door, which, accustomed though we were to the sound, never lost its horror to us and made us cling close together in shivering silence till we went to sleep.

CHRISTMAS MORNING

In the morning how gaily we awaited the lifting of the cover from the table and how bravely we rejoiced over the simple love tokens! Only the babies had new gifts from the store, but they flourished their bright tin rattles with a gleefulness that made up to all the rest of us. Mother had given to sister and me tiny, red morocco bound copies of "Young's Night

Thoughts," and "Pollock's Course of Time," valued treasures of her young lady days.

I hated improving poetry then as I hate it yet, but I knew it was all mother had to give and I tried to like it. After breakfast, which I cooked—fried venison, corn cakes raised over night and baked on top of the stove, with molasses for us all and coffee for father and mother, there were family prayers when father read, as always on Christmas, the wondrous story of the Nativity and mother played on her little old "melodeon," we all sang joyously "While Shepherds Watched Their Flocks by Night."

The babies wanted their rattles during prayer time, but mother thought that eight months was quite old enough for babies to be quiet in prayer time and they did not get them till we had all risen from our knees.

REAL MINCE PIE

Then the Christmas dinner was to come. What a grave responsibility rested upon me in following mother's directions about that dinner. We were going to have real mince pie!

Christmas Time in Indian Territory

True, the mysterious good things usually entering into the composition of mince pie we could not have but we were sure that venison must be as good as beef and long soaking and careful mincing and cooking of dried apples surely would make them indistinguishable from fresh, and a mixture of nuts—hickory and walnut and pecan—would surely be better than suet. From some secret hiding place mother produced a little package of raisins.

We could hardly wait for the pie to bake in the little Dutch oven out of doors. We were going to have raised biscuit, too, for the flour that cost ten cents a pound we could not afford on ordinary occasions. Nowhere nearer than the post at Fort Gibson was there a cow or chickens, and milk, eggs and butter were impossible luxuries to us. Game was so plentiful as to be secured almost without effort and the big wild turkey we had father bought for twenty-five cents from an Indian who killed it with his bow and arrow. Father never hunted any for he was too near sighted. We had boiled rice for dinner too that Christmas day.

OLD AUNT TENAH

Such a dinner it was and the twins sat in their little sassafraswood high chairs on either side of mother and pounded the cloth with their rattles and we were all sure nobody had so good a dinner as we. After we had eaten all we could and sister and I had washed up the dishes mother sent us with a little basketful to old Aunt Tenah, who had been cook at the mission when mother came there a bride but was bedridden now from rheumatism brought on by hardships of those refugee days of the war.

I remember our gay walk of a mile and a half through the dense forest and how the redbirds sang and what a gorgeous flock of brilliant green flame-crested paroquets we saw.

Good old Aunt Tenah was profuse in her expressions of gratitude, though she would not eat her dinner till we had gone, but she would not let us go until from the sacredly cherished Bible she owned but could not read, I had read to her the story of the coming of the Christ child.

LIGHT-HEARTED AND THANKFUL

Coming back we talked about how rich we were in comparison with poor Aunt Tenah, for she hardly ever could get anything but nuts and game to eat and we had twenty-five bushels of corn. We had heard father tell mother how far it had been hauled and how carefully we must treasure every ear for that must be the food for "Old Jim" the horse and ourselves until we could raise a garden in the spring.

We found it went farther in hulled corn than in meal ground in a handmill, so hulled corn served us that winter for our only vegetable and mostly our bread. We always had biscuit for a Sunday treat.

MISSIONARY WORK

Soon after Christmas father began his preaching tours, going horseback on "Old Jim" whose corn was carried in one side of the saddlebags, while on the other was his Bible, English and Indian, some hymn books, a little case of medicines, etc. Over them was strapped a roll of grey blankets, usually his only bed.

When he was gone there always seemed a specially heavy responsibility on my shoulders for I must take care of mother and the babies, and mother was not very strong.

Sometimes I thought I was as brave as any 12-year-old boy could possibly be, for one day I chased a big grey wolf away from the house with nothing but a stick and I often went away down to the old well for a bucket of water all alone in the dark.

Christmas Time in Indian Territory

THE NEXT CHRISTMAS

When the next Christmas came the battered little tin rattles with the tiny well worn shoes had been carefully hidden away among mother's most precious treasures. A summer of plenty had followed the famine time.

We had a cow and chickens and gifts for our Christmas. But in the autumn had come days of fever to all the family. Brave little sister and I had been the last to yield to it, but when father and mother both lay sorely stricken with it, first one and then the other of the twins slept in that waxen loveliness of purity that death brings.

Old Uncle John made little boxes from the rough boards of the attic floor which I covered and lined with one of mother's sheets. I remember helping Uncle John to close the lid for the last time shutting out the baby face, and then the fever seized me too and for many days the fever dreams left no memory.

TINGED WITH SORROW

So when the Christmas came again though we had much more of material comfort than the year before, father's voice faltered as he read the story of the Christ Child in morning prayer and mother's fingers trembled on the melodeon keys and when we thought of the little tin rattles laid away, we could not sing all the verses of "While Shepherds Watched Their Flocks by Night."

A Slave's Remembrances

¶ *The Five Civilized Tribes who were brought to Oklahoma during the 1830s and 1840s were slaveholders like their white neighbors in the Deep South. The number of slaves that the energetic mixed bloods owned varied from one per family to several hundred. One wealthy Choctaw planter reputedly owned more than five hundred slaves. Slavery was a cruel and debasing system whether the owner was Indian or white, and the Five Tribes adopted the South's harsh slave codes to control and subjugate their blacks.* ¶ *The Reconstruction Treaties of 1866 promised former slaves the same political rights that Indians enjoyed, plus an equal share in tribal annuities and land and other benefits. Yet in practice, life after the Civil War was as difficult for the Indian freedman as it was for the black Mississippi sharecropper.* ¶ *Morris Sheppard was a slave belonging to Joe Sheppard of the Cherokee Nation. Although he was seventeen at the end of the Civil War, his reminiscences were not recorded until he was eighty-five. The passage of years probably softened and smoothed the rough edges of his own history, but his recollections are important for the record of slavery in Oklahoma and as a glimpse of his life as a free man.*

MORRIS SHEPPARD
Age 85 yrs.
Fort Gibson, Okla.
Old Master tell me I was borned in November 1852, at de old home place about five miles east of Webbers Falls, mebbe kind of northeast, not far from de east bank of de Illinois River.

From Federal Writers Project, *Slave Narratives: A Folk History of Slavery in the U.S. from Interviews with Former Slaves*, vol. 6 (St. Claire Shores, Michigan: Scholarly Press, Inc., 1976), 285–99A.

Master's name was Joe Sheppard, and he was a Cherokee Indian. Tall and slim and handsome. He had black eyes and mustache but his hair was iron gray, and everybody liked him because he was so good-natured and kind.

I don't remember old Mistress' name. My mammy was a Crossland negro before she come to belong to Master Joe and marry my pappy, and I think she come wid old Mistress and belong to her. Old Mistress was small and mighty pretty too, and she was only half Cherokee. She inherit about half a dozen slaves, and say dey was her own and old Master can't sell one unless she give him leave to do it.

Dey only had two families of slaves wid about twenty in all, and dey only worked about fifty acres, so we sure did work every foot of it good. We git three or four crops of different things out of dat farm every year, and something growing on dat place winter and summer.

Pappy's name was Caesar Sheppard and Mammy's name was Easter. Dey was both raised 'round Webber's Falls somewhere. I had two brothers, Silas and George, dat belong to Mr. George Holt in Webber's Falls town. I got a pass and went to see dem sometimes, and dey was both treated mighty fine.

The Big House was a double log wid a big hall and a stone chimney but no porches, wid two rooms at each end, one top side of de other. I thought it was mighty big and fine.

Us slaves lived in log cabins dat only had one room and no windows so we kept de doors open most of de time. We had home-made wooden beds wid rope springs, and de little ones slept on trundle beds dat was home-made too.

At night dem trundles was jest all over de floor, and in de morning we shove dem back under de big beds to get dem out'n de way. No nails in none of dem nor in de chairs and tables. Nails cost big money and old Master's blacksmith wouldn't make none 'cepting a few for old Master now and den, so we used wooden dowels to put things together.

They was so many of us for dat little field we never did have to work hard. Up at five o'clock and back in sometimes about de middle of de evening, long before sundown, unless they was a crop to git in before it rain or something like dat.

When crop was laid by de slaves jest work 'round at dis and dat and keep tol'able busy. I never did have much of a job, jest tending de calves mostly. We had about twenty calves and I would take dem out and graze 'em while some grown-up negro was grazing de cows so as to keep de cows milk. I had me a good blaze-faced horse for dat.

One time Old Master and another man come and took some calves off and Pappy say old Master taking dem off to sell. I didn't know what "sell" meant and I ast Pappy, "Is he going to bring 'em back when he git through selling them?" I never did see no money neither, until time of de War or a little before.

Master Joe was sure a good provider, and we always had plenty of corn pone, sow belly and greens, sweet potatoes, cow peas and cane molasses. We even had brown sugar and cane molasses most of de time before de War. Sometimes coffee, too.

De clothes wasn't no worry neither. Everything we had was made by my folks. My aunt done de carding and spinning and my mammy done de weaving and cutting and sewing, and my pappy could make cowhide shoes wid wooden pegs. Dey was for bad winter only.

Old Master bought de cotton in Ft. Smith because he didn't raise no cotton, but he had a few sheep and we had wool-mix for winter.

Everything was stripedy 'cause Mammy like to make it fancy. She dye wid copperas and walnut and wild indigo and things like dat and make pretty cloth. I wore a stripedy shirt till I was about eleven years old, and den one day while we was down in de Choctaw Country old Mistress see me and nearly fall off'n her horse! She holler, "Easter, you go right now and make dat big buck of a boy some britches!"

We never put on de shoes until about late November when de frost begin to hit regular and split our feet up, and den when it git good and cold and de crop all gather in any

A Slave's Remembrances

ways, they is nothing to do 'cepting hog killing and a lot of wood chopping, and you don't git cold doing dem two things.

De hog killing mean we gits lots of spare-ribs and chitlings, and somebody always get sick eating too much of dat fresh pork. I always pick a whole passel of muskatines for old Master and he make up sour wine, and dat helps out when we git the bowel complaint from eating dat fresh pork.

If somebody bad sick he git de doctor right quick, and he don't let no negroes mess around wid no poultices and teas and sech things like cuppinghorns neither!

Us Cherokee slaves seen lots of green corn shootings and de like of dat, but we never had no games of our own. We was too tired when we come in to play any games. We had to have a pass to go any place to have singing or praying, and den they was always a bunch of patrollers around to watch everything we done. Dey would come up in a bunch of about nine men on horses, and look at all our passes, and if a negro didn't have no pass dey wore him out good and made him go home. Dey didn't let us have much enjoyment.

Right after de War de Cherokees that had been wid the South kind of pestered the freedmen some, but I was so small dey never bothered me; jest de grown ones. Old Master and Mistress kept on asking me did de night riders persecute me any but dey never did. Dey told me some of dem was bad on negroes but I never did see none of dem riding like some said dey did.

Old Master had some kind of business in Fort Smith, I think, 'cause he used to ride in to dat town 'bout every day on his horse. He would start at de crack of daylight and not git home till way after dark. When he get home he call my uncle in and ask about what we done all day and tell him what we better do de next day. My uncle Joe was de slave boss and he tell us what de Master say do.

When dat Civil War come along I was a pretty big boy and I 'member it good as anybody. Uncle Joe tell us all to lay low and work hard and nobody bother us, and he would look after us. He sure stood good with de Cherokee neighbors we had, and dey all liked him. There was Mr. Jim Collins, and Mr. Bell, and Mr. Dave Franklin, and Mr. Jim Sutton and Mr. Blackburn that lived around close to us and dey all had slaves. Dey was all wid the South, but dey was a lot of dem Pin Indians all up on de Illinois River and dey was wid de North and dey taken it out on de slave owners a lot before de War and during it too.

Dey would come in de night and hamstring de horses and maybe set fire to de barn, and two of 'em named Joab Scarrel and Tom Starr killed my pappy one night just before de War broke out.

I don't know what dey done it for, only to be mean, and I guess they was drunk.

Them Pins was after Master all de time for a while at de first of de War, and he was afraid to ride into Fort Smith much. Dey come to de house one time when he was gone to Fort Smith and us children told dem he was at Honey

A Slave's Remembrances

Springs, but they knowed better and when he got home he said somebody shot at him and bushwhacked him all the way from Wilson's Rock to dem Wildhorse Mountains, but he run his horse like de devil was setting on his tail and dey never did hit him. He never seen dem either. We told him 'bout de Pins coming for him and he just laughed.

When de War come old Master seen he was going into trouble and he sold off most of de slaves. In de second year of de War he sold my mammy and my aunt dat was Uncle Joe's wife and my two brothers and my little sister. Mammy went to a mean old man named Peper Goodman and he took her off down de river, and pretty soon Mistress tell me she died 'cause she can't stand de rough treatment.

When Mammy went old Mistress took me to de Big House to help her, and she was kind to me like I was part of her own family. I never forget when they sold off some more negroes at de same time, too, and put dem all in a pen for de trader to come and look at.

He never come until the next day, so dey had to sleep in dat pen in a pile like hogs.

It wasn't my Master done dat. He done already sold 'em to a man and it was dat man was waiting for de trader. It made my Master mad, but dey didn't belong to him no more and he couldn't say nothing.

The man put dem on block and sold 'em to a man dat had come in on a steamboat, and he took dem off on it when de freshet come down and de boat could go back to Fort Smith. It was tied up at de dock at Webbers Falls about a week and we went down and talked to my aunt and brothers and sister. De brothers was Sam and Eli. Old Mistress cried jest like any of de rest of us when de boat pull out with dem on it.

Pretty soon all de young Cherokee menfolks all gone off to de War, and de Pins was riding 'round all de time, and it ain't safe to be in dat part around Webber's Falls, so old Master take us all to Fort Smith where they was a lot of Confederate soldiers.

We camp at dat place a while and old Mistress stay in de

town wid some kinfolks. Den old Master get three wagons and ox teams and take us all way down on Red River in de Choctaw Nation.

We went by Webber's Falls and filled de wagons. We left de furniture and only took grub and tools and bedding and clothes, 'cause they wasn't very big wagons and was only single-yoke.

We went on a place in de Red River bottoms close to Shawneetown and not far from de place where all de wagons crossed over to go into Texas. We was at dat place two years and made two little crops.

One night a runaway negro come across from Texas and he had de blood hounds after him. His britches was all muddy and tore where de hounds had cut him up in de legs when he clumb a tree in de bottoms. He come to our house and Mistress said for us negroes to give him something to eat and we did.

Then up come de man from Texas with de hounds and wid him was young Mr. Joe Vann and my uncle that belong to Joe. Dey called young Mr. Joe "Little Joe Vann" even after he was grown on account of when he was a little boy before his pappy was killed. His pappy was old Captain "Rich Joe" Vann, and he had been dead ever since long before de War. My uncle belong to old Captain Joe nearly all his life.

Mistress try to get de man to tell her who de negro belong to so she can buy him, but de man say he can't sell him and he take him on back to Texas wid a chain around his two ankles. Dat was one poor negro dat never got away to de North, and I was sorry for him 'cause I know he must have had a mean master, but none of us Sheppard negroes, I mean the grown ones, tried to git away.

I never seen any fighting in de War, but I seen soldiers in de South army doing a lot of blacksmithing 'long side de road one day. Dey was fixing wagons and shoeing horses.

After de War was over, old Master tell me I am free but he will look out after me 'cause I am just a little negro and I ain't got no sense. I know he is right, too.

A Slave's Remembrances

Well, I got ahead and make me a crop of corn all by myself and then I don't know what to do wid it. I was afraid I would get cheated out of it 'cause I can't figure and read, so I tell old Master about it and he bought it off'n me.

We never had no school in slavery and it was agin the law for anybody to even show a negro de letters and figures, so no Cherokee slave could read.

We all come back to de negro cabins and barns burned down and de fences all gone and de field in crab grass and cockleburrs. But de Big House aint hurt 'cepting it need a new roof. De furniture is all gone, and some said de soldiers burned it up for firewood. Some officers stayed in de house for a while and tore everything up or took it off.

Master give me over to de National Freedman's Bureau and I was bound out to a Cherokee woman name Lizzie McGee. Then one day one of my uncles named Wash Sheppard come and tried to git me to live wid him. He say he wanted to git de family all together agin.

He had run off after he was sold and joined de North army and discharged at Fort Scott in Kansas, and he said lots of freedmen was living close to each other up by Coffeyville in de Coo-ee-scoo-ee District.

I wouldn't go, so he sent Isaac and Joe Vann dat had been two of old Captain Joe's negroes to talk to me. Isaac had been Young Joe's driver, and he told me all about how rich Master Joe was and how he would look after us negroes. Dey kept after me 'bout a year, but I didn't go anyways.

But later on I got a freedman's allotment up in dat part close to Coffeyville, and I lived in Coffeyville a while but I didn't like it in Kansas.

I lost my land trying to live honest and pay my debts. I raised eleven children just on de sweat of my hands and none of dem ever tasted anything dat was stole.

When I left Mrs. McGee's I worked about three years for Mr. Sterling Scott and Mr. Roddy Reese. Mr. Reese had a big flock of peafowls dat had belonged to Mr. Scott and I had to take care of dem.

White folks, I would have to tromp seven miles to Mr.

Scott's house two or three times a week to bring back some old peafowl dat had got out and gone back to de old place!

Poor old Master and Mistress only lived a few years after de War. Master went plumb blind after he move back to Webber's Falls and so he move up on de Illinois River 'bout three miles from de Arkansas, and there old Mistress take de white swelling and die and den he die pretty soon. I went to see dem lots of times and they was always glad to see me.

I would stay around about a week and help 'em, and dey would try to git me to take something but I never would. Dey didn't have much and couldn't make anymore and dem so old. Old Mistress had inherited some property from her pappy and dey had de slave money and when dey turned everything into good money after de War dat stuff only come to about six thousand dollars in good money, she told me. Dat just about lasted 'em through until dey died, I reckon.

By and by I married Nancy Hildebrand what lived on Greenleaf Creek, 'bout four miles northwest of Gore. She had belonged to Joe Hildebrand and he was kin to old Steve Hildebrand dat owned de mill on Flint Creek up in de Going Snake District. She was raised up at dat mill, but she was borned in Tennessee before dey come out to de Nation. Her master was white but he had married into de Nation and so she got a freedman's allotment too. She had some land close to Catoosa and some down on Greenleaf Creek.

We was married at my home in Coffeyville, and she bore me eleven children and then went on to her reward. A long time ago I came to live wid my daughter Emma here at dis place, but my wife just died last year. She was eighty-three.

I reckon I wasn't cut out on de church pattern, but I raised my children right. We never had no church in slavery, and no schooling, and you had better not be caught wid a book in your hand even, so I never did go to church hardly any.

Wife belong to de church and all de children too, and I think all should look after saving their souls so as to drive de nail in, and den go about de earth spreading kindness and hoeing de row clean so as to clinch dat nail and make dem safe for Glory.

Of course I hear about Abraham Lincoln and he was a great man, but I was told mostly by my children when dey come home from school about him. I always think of my old Master as de one dat freed me, and anyways Abraham Lincoln and none of his North people didn't look after me and buy my crop right after I was free like old Master did. Dat was de time dat was de hardest and everything was dark and confusion.

Memories of My Childhood Days in the Choctaw Nation

¶ The time between the end of removal and the beginning of the Civil War was a golden age for the Five Civilized Tribes. Each tribe owned land in common, and every citizen was protected in his occupancy. The full bloods who preferred the traditional way of the hunter and warrior withdrew to the woods and streams, while the mixed bloods adjusted to the new surroundings as farmers, mechanics, and entrepreneurs. ¶ Steamboats of shallow draft plied the Arkansas and Red rivers bringing farm implements, printing stock, china, and ladies' finery to exchange for the agricultural products of Indian Territory. Among the Choctaws, Cherokees, and Chickasaws there were large slaveholders with extensive plantations, who sold their cotton directly in Liverpool, England, for huge sums of gold. ¶ Interrupted at removal, tribal government flourished again in Oklahoma. Except for the Seminoles, the Civilized Tribes adopted written constitutions that were a curious blend of Anglo-Saxon usage and Indian custom. An orderly system of primary and secondary schools, some tribal- and some missionary-sponsored, were quickly reestablished. But the sons of the wealthy usually continued the preremoval tradition of finishing their education in the East. The missionary societies that had worked among the Indians before removal continued their ministries in Oklahoma. Church-owned printing presses soon began producing bilingual newspapers, religious tracts, almanacs, and tribal documents. The Park Hill Press published more than eleven million pages of materials for the Choctaw Nation alone. ¶ White settlers were forbidden to settle in Indian Territory except with permits from the resident tribes, so Oklahoma before 1860 was the sanctuary of the Five Civilized Tribes. But the Civil War brutally shattered Indian Territory's way of life. The decision to fight with the Confederacy provoked as much dissension among the Five Tribes as the removal question had a generation

From Emma Ervin Christian, "Memories of My Childhood Days in the Choctaw Nation," *Chronicles of Oklahoma*, 9 (June 1931), 155–65.

Oklahoma Memories

earlier. And when the fighting ended, most of Indian Territory was desolate and wasted. ¶ Slowly the recuperative process began to erase the sights of war, and it seemed for a time that the antebellum days might be recaptured. Unlike the southern planters who had lost both their slaves and titles to their lands with emancipation, the Indian aristocracy was only temporarily impoverished. Most were not ruined. Under the tribal system of common land ownership, ambitious mixed bloods worked their holdings with hired labor—usually white Civil War veterans unable to obtain homesteads in the West. Soon people rebuilt homes, planted gardens, and resumed social gatherings. Schools reopened with expanded curricula, trade quickened, and printing presses clattered once more. ¶ Emma Ervin Christian writes of these halcyon days. She grew up in the old Choctaw Nation where Indian boarding schools, funeral customs, and "doctorin' and cookin'" remained unchanged in spite of the war. Although this memoir was written when she was approaching seventy, her recollections are as simple and straightforward as a child's own account might be. She recalls the terrible racket of her father's water mill; her first trip away from home in a covered wagon; being lost within a mile of home where the wolves were "as plentiful there as the cottontail rabbits are here around my weedy place." There is no mention here of the railroads and cattle trails and highways and telegraphs that linked Indian Territory to the white world soon after the Civil war and forecast its demise. But then childhood is not concerned with the harbingers of modernization; nor does the little girl foresee the passing of her way of life.

MANY YEARS have passed over this hoary head of mine since I came into existence, in the early sixties on a farm three and one half miles west of old Doaksville; many years have flown, marking many changes as time swiftly passes by, yet youthful dreams often call me back to the grim past, to remind me of the many joys, pains, and sorrows I experienced in those by-gone days. The name of Doaksville may not be found on the map of Oklahoma today (1928) yet no town that has vanished so completely, ever kept itself so alive in the memory of the people who once knew it.

My earliest recollection of Doaksville gives a picture in my mind of a thriving village. In the days of its wealth, long before the Civil War, Doaksville was one of the important social and intellectual centers of Choctaw life. Here and in the neighborhood of Doaksville, on their big plantations, lived the Choctaw aristocrats, who owned many negroes that cultivated these plantations, while their masters the leaders of the Choctaw Nation indulged in sports of various kinds. At an early day, Doaksville was the Capital of the Choctaw Nation; here the Indian Legislature and courts were held, and all the important business of the time was transacted; but as the leading men began to move to the western part of the Territory our officials advocated the removal of the Capital to Armstrong Academy, now near Durant. Accordingly it was done and for many years the Choctaw council met here for the execution of our tribal laws. Fort Towson, the new town, has absorbed all that remained of Doaksville, but there is one thing that still survives and that is the cemetery.

No one now living knows when the clods first fell upon a coffin in that cemetery. It stands on a hillside fringed on the canyon's edge by a heavy growth of timber, while here and there among the graves stand somber pines. In spring and summer the place is bright with wild flowers; in the fall it is brown with withered grass, and yet the growth of aromatic weeds fills the air with sweetness, as if speaking of the good as well as the bad that lie buried in the old cemetery. Could one hear an old Choctaw patriarch tell the annals of Doaksville cemetery, it would make the blood curdle in his veins, for the victims of many a tragedy lie buried there.

Our farm home was not pretentious, the houses being built of large hewed logs, but such were most of the farm houses in those days, owing to the scarcity of lumber; but the farm was beautifully located on a level tract of land, with many thousand acres of giant forest trees to the north waving their stately branches toward the blue skies. To the

Childhood Days in the Choctaw Nation

south we had a beautiful view, over a smooth prairie for three miles, after which it gradually rose to a high point, and on the west end of this high point was a grove of large oak trees, where numerous prairie hens, or chickens as they were called, went for their nightly roost. We could hear them in the morning with their songs which seemed to say "Oh, goodin, goo." Hence this high hill was called Chicken Hill, but today there are no "goodin, goos" there.

I can remember just after the [Civil] war, when my father had the Post Office on this farm home of ours; how long he was Postmaster I do not remember but I never forgot the name of a boy, some seventeen or eighteen years of age that carried the mail from Clarksville, Texas, to our home, because he always spent the night at our home as it was a day's ride to Clarksville. We children were always glad to see him because he seldom failed to bring us candy which was a rarity to us, as my father did not approve of children eating candy. If this man is alive today, he is quite aged. His name was Alfonso Lane.

A mile and one half northwest of Doaksville was an Indian boarding school for girls. The name of this institution was Pine Ridge Seminary, deriving its name from the vast pine forest that traversed the entire country extending east into Arkansas. My older sisters, three in number, attended this school. It was managed by the Presbyterian Board, and Cyrus Kingsbury, a Presbyterian minister was the Superintendent. Ten miles northwest of Doaksville was another Indian boarding school, but this was for the boys. These schools were closed during the Civil War and Spencer Academy was used as a hospital and home for the soldiers. Many of them died there, for in a half mile of the Academy was a large grave yard and my father said that most of the graves were those of soldiers.

Childhood Days in the Choctaw Nation

My first memory of Spencer Academy was of a Presbyterian minister named Alexander Reed, who with his family, lived there, taking care of the place and property, as it was managed by the Presbyterians also. In 1868 my father was put in charge of Spencer Academy, to rebuild, recover and repair all damages which had been done during the war. One can well imagine how dilapidated and forlorn the place was after the ravages of the war had ceased. No one lived there for several months as A. Reed and family had gone back to New York from whence they came; he engaged an old colored man to go there and look after the things until some one was appointed to take charge of the place. So, as might be expected, numerous were the ghost stories afloat, about the old deserted place—so much that it took some persuasion to get my mother's consent to move there. She was superstitious and believed in all the old Indian signs and ghost stories, and really it was a haunted looking place, far from any neighbors.

Some people told that before the sun went down, the tables and chairs would begin to move around as if by magic, the windows would fly up or down and that it was an impossibility to keep the doors closed. My father did not believe in such bosh, as he called it, so in the fall of 1868 we moved into the haunted Academy and lived there for two years. The ghosts did not get any of us, but the wolves were as plentiful there as the cottontail rabbits are here around my weedy place.

Old Spencer Academy was east of the Kiamichi River; several years later they built a new Spencer Academy some thirty miles west of the Kiamichi River. The reason for moving the school was that it was so inconvenient about getting supplies; the roads were bad and often the river would get so high that they would not ferry any one across. There was only a small ferry boat at the Old Rock Chimney Crossing, which I suppose is known far and near. The two rock chimneys which marked this crossing on Kiamichi River were there as far back as I can remember. The houses were built and owned by an Irishman of name of Patrick. The houses were burned but the chimneys stood for years and years.

The old Spencer Academy was sold to an Indian preacher named Robert Frazier. He sold a great deal of the lumber out of the old buildings, and a store and postoffice were built there, but the place is known as Spencerville today. The new Spencer Academy in some unknown way, caught fire and burned down; that is, the largest building was consumed by fire and several boys were burned completely to ashes. I had a boy there and he barely escaped, just in his night clothes. One of the boys, who was more fortunate and had his clothes out, gave him a pair of great big overalls and that is what he had to wear home.

The first school that I attended was taught by a Chickasaw Indian lady named Selina Ayahkombee. Before the Civil War they owned a great number of negro slaves and had a large plantation one mile northwest of our home. They had an orchard of all kinds of fine fruit and berries, as the sandy soil was especially adapted to the growing of fruit. Though the negroes were free they continued to live in their old slave homes which were built on a sandy ridge not far from their old master's home. . . . There was a deep canyon between Sand Hill and the master's home and down in this deep gully was a spring of water as pure, cool and clear as crystal bubbling up through the white sand. Oh! how refreshing it would be if I could quench my thirst there this awful hot August day!

We had to go one mile beyond this place to our little log school house. The size of the house was 16 × 20 feet; one door to the east, one window (that is an opening, but no glass) to the west and one to the south. We had puncheon seats, that is what they called benches made out of a log split in the middle and smoothed off with an ax or a plane. We had a large play ground as there was only one home in half a mile of the place, consequently at noon time we would wander out of sight or hearing. Then Miss Selma would blow the great long cow's horn which she kept (and could blow) to bring us in to books. My studies were a reader and the old blue back spelling book which has long been discarded. The little log cabin was common and the seats were rough, but we had just as good a time then as the children do today.

Childhood Days in the Choctaw Nation

One of my greatest pleasures in my childhood days was a day spent at my father's old water mill which was two miles away from home on what was then called Cedar Creek, the boundary line between Towson and Cedar counties. I suppose that it would be a treat to the modern girl or boy to see one of those mills today, as I doubt of there being one in existence any where. The creek had a wall or dam across it which made a large lake of water above the mill building; about the middle of this dam was a water gate which was raised to allow the water to gush through onto the mill wheels with such force as to start them turning around and around. The mill was ready then to begin grinding. Oh! such terrible racket as it did make when it was in operation!

The next thing of importance to me was when the journey began to my next school which trip commenced in the latter part of August 1871, to old New Hope Seminary. My first trip in a covered wagon was quite a thrill to me . . . as I had never been any distance from home, and oh! horrors, such rough roads as we had to travel. Virtually speaking there were no roads across the mountains that we came over, until we struck the stage line running from Fort Smith to Stringtown and other points south. I went over these bad roads twice per year for five years. My father, Mrs. William Byrd (whose husband was in later years Governor of the Chickasaw Nation), an orphan girl by name of Carrie Stewart (who is still alive and resides in Caddo, Oklahoma), a hired boy and myself composed the party that traversed this rough, wild and unpopulated country. We saw wild game in abundance. We saw one bear, and at night we frequently heard the shrill squall of the panther which would send an icy sensation down our spines.

Arriving at New Hope about the 1st of September, we found there Rev. J. Y. Bryce, Sr., with a bevy of Indian girls. Some of the girls were fair, some very dark, some fat, lean, tall, short, some pretty and some monstrous ugly. After nine long months spent there [I took] my first trip home. . . . We had some hard luck on our trip, on crossing Kiamichi River where Tuskahoma is now, my horse lay down in the river and ducked me under. This was in the morning and that evening we became lost, the road was only a dim cow trail and when once off it we could not get out of a creek bottom.

It became darker and we wandered around and around and would come back to the same place. We were only ten or twelve miles from home and our aim was to get there two or three hours after dark, but try as we did, we could not find our way out of that creek bottom. I began to beg to stop for I was so tired that I could not sit upon my horse any longer. So we dismounted and they gave me the best blanket in the crowd for a pallet. I fell asleep the minute I lay down although the mosquitoes were there by the millions. My companions did not sleep at all. The mosquitoes were so bad that they put in their time building small fires to smoke them away. They might have killed me had they not built those little heaps of smoke, for I was too tired to awaken. We arose early to get home as we had nothing to eat, and lo! and behold, found ourselves just a mile from Spencer Academy.

I will now give some of the Indians' ways of doctoring . . . which were common when I was a child. The Indian doctors that I knew were mostly women and they made their medicines out of various kinds of weeds, the bark and roots of trees and herbs, and they also believed in witches. My oldest sister had a bad sick spell, and Mother sent for an Indian doctor. She came, examined Sister, then she went off to the woods to get her medicines. There was a room built off, separate from our bedrooms that the boys generally occupied. This room had a fire place and the floor was very near the ground. She demanded the use of this room and called for an old fashioned pot to cook her herbs and roots in. When she got them prepared, she took one or two planks out of the floor, then she dug a hole in the ground to fit this pot into, then she fixed a concern for Sister to lie on over this place and then she steamed her several times a day for three days in succession, and gave her teas to drink.

After the time of steaming was over she showed Mother a little ball, presumably made of hair and a clot of something like blood on it. She pretended that she drew this out of Sister's side by the steaming process. She said that Sister had been shot by an enemy with a poisoned ball; well she got well and lived to be seventy-seven years of age. No doubt she had pneumonia and the steaming was good for her, but the poison ball was a hoax.

We went to several Indian homes where they had the conjuror or witch doctor, where they served pachofa and had dancing while doctoring the sick which was a queer way of doing in case of sickness. I will give the particulars of one which I attended as the sick man was a brother of my first teacher; his name was Gipson Ayahkombee. Late in the evening Father, Mother and all of us children walked to the home of the sick man, as we had an invitation to come, and they expected us to come, or we were not good friends. They had a large yard, nicely grassed over, and each family was seated around on the grass in groups, then we were served with pachofa in large vessels, and all of one family had to eat out of this vessel. We had paddles made out of cedar and horn spoons to eat with. Some of the spoons were made of cow horns and some were buffalo spoons. The vessel we ate out of was made of cedar, and they used to call them keelers, the smaller ones with a handle were called piggin.

This pachofa was made of corn and fresh pork cooked together. When all were through eating, the weird music of the tom tom began in front of the room where the patient lay; we were not allowed to see in this room nor to pass around it, so in order to prevent any one from passing around this room, a rope was secured to the corner of the room and stretched out for a considerable distance. When the doctor began his queer noise in the room, all the young men and women lined up in two rows opposite each other to commence their odd way of dancing. I listened attentively to the whimsical noise the doctor was making in the room, which to me, sounded like a dried gourd, with shells, dried peas, beans or buttons in it, and her mutterings were a continued he, he, ho, ho, and something else that I could not understand. There was a sound that seemed like she was spitting on him. I can not describe the noise made by the tom tom man with all kinds of shells and everything that would jingle around his body and limbs. When all this was over and all starting for home, one of my mischievous sisters raised the rope and ran by the forbidden room; the guards chased her but it was dark and she got away. The man died and they blamed sister for his death. If the guards had caught her they would have stripped her clothing off and dipped her under cold water, thereby dispelling the evil spirit.

The custom of the Indians was to go and cry at the grave of the dead, with the wife or mother, once in a while until the final funeral was preached or you were not considered a true friend. The final funeral was preached from six to twelve months after burial. So many used to come to our home to cry with Mother after the loss of some member of the family. On one occasion I remember an old friend of Mother's had passed away, who lived about six miles from us on the west side of the Kiamichi River, owing to inclement weather Mother did not attend his burial, so not long after she was going to cry at the grave with the widow and took me along. I was small but could ride a pony and I was thrilled with joy over my trip, as I was going to a place I had not been to before. On arriving there a boy came out and tied our ponies, and Mother sent me to the house and she proceeded to the grave which was about 150 or 200 yards from the home. The family could not speak a word of English and as I could not talk the Indian language at the time, all my joy and thrills were gone. It seemed to me like they cried a half day, for I could hear them and felt like crying too.

Some would cut or bob the wife's hair when the husband died. They always buried their dead at home and sometimes under the house. I remember an instance where a wealthy Chickasaw Indian named Pitman Colbert, was buried (perhaps before I was born) but I knew the family and knew he was buried there. Some four or five years after I moved away from Doaksville some robbers went in to his grave and secured all the valuables that were buried with him, but in the dark they missed several pieces of coin which were found in the dirt the next day.

After I was ten or twelve years old, I asked Mother why did the Indians bury at home instead of taking them to the graveyard, as the white people did; she said that it seemed like you were throwing them away to take them away from home and bury them, so we had a family graveyard at our home too. The last Indian cry that I attended was over the Jackfork mountains. It was conducted similarly to those in my childhood days; they had a large brush arbor built and seats for all, they sang and prayed then preached the funeral sermon, after which all proceeded to the grave, where all are supposed to cry, but they do not. After this all were invited to a dinner of barbecued beef and various kinds of food.

Indian Territory in the 1870s

¶ *The quarter century from Appomattox to the first land opening was a time of dramatic economic, social, and political change in Indian Territory, with the railroad as the principal agent of that transformation. The first line into Oklahoma, the Missouri-Kansas-Texas system, or "Katy," followed the old Texas Trail and had crossed the Five Civilized Tribes' land into the Lone Star State by 1872. The railroads made a more sophisticated and complex economy possible and opened Indian Territory to communication with the rest of the world.* ¶ *As tracks crisscrossed Oklahoma, new industries arose. Lumbering developed in the southeastern forests to supply railroad construction needs and to build the towns that followed the steam engine's wake. The railroads also provided new markets for the Five Civilized Tribes' products. Stable, year-round transportation made it profitable to work the glistening black coal seams in the Choctaw Nation and to recover lead and zinc in the northeast corner near the Missouri border. Everywhere the rails went, telegraph and telephone lines followed, linking Indian Territory to the white world.* ¶ *The railroads stimulated economic growth, but they also increased lawlessness and disorder. The turbulence of railroad and mining towns attracted renegades and desperadoes. Hustlers, gamblers, drifters, bootleggers, and prostitutes all mingled with the law-abiding townspeople. Indian Territory became a kaleidoscope of the extremes and excesses in American society as industrialism burgeoned.* ¶ *To feed the insatiable Eastern appetite for information about "prospects in the West," various newspapers dispatched reporters to spy out the land. J. H. Beadle was the western correspondent for the* Cincinnati Commercial. *He traveled from Ohio to Oregon preparing a book "to give the facts in regard to lands opened for settlement." Beadle's chapter on Oklahoma pro-*

From J. H. Beadle, Western Wilds and the Men Who Redeem Them (Cincinnati: Jones Brothers & Company, 1881), 194–211.

Oklahoma Memories

vided a fairly comprehensive view of Indian Territory in the 1870s. An observant factual reporter, Beadle also enriched his commentary with reactions to what he was seeing. Although he was a seasoned western traveler before he reached Indian Territory, he was appalled at the alcohol-induced violence in the railroad town of Muskogee. The freedmen's plight stirred him, and he was saddened at the irony of mixed-blood Indian speculators scheming with whites to barter away their brothers' birthright.
¶ Beadle's prejudices and biases were also apparent and important because they reflected the pervasive white view of Indian Territory as a "place of stagnation" and of the white's private landownership system as "the only true fountain for a progressive society...." Yet in spite of his enthusiasm for the "rattle of commerce" heard in nearby Kansas and his contempt for the Indian land tenure system, J. H. Beadle was a man of conscience. His business was to attract settlers to the West. But where Indian Territory was concerned he warned that government action permitting white settlement would be a "shameful breach of faith." To the sodbuster and the town builder his advice was "go elsewhere," for there was still an abundance of good land to be settled. And for a little time longer they listened.*

THE YEAR 1872 opened with a revival of interest in the Atlantic and Pacific Railroad, otherwise known as the Thirty-fifth Parallel Route. This road was already completed from St. Louis to Vinita, in the Indian Territory, and was to run thence westward to the Rio Grande, and through a succession of valleys and passes, nearly on the line of the thirty-fifth parallel, to California, terminating at San Francisco. That city and St. Louis had struck hands on the project; thirty-five million dollars had been pledged; it was the era of speculative railroad construction, and we were promised an early completion of the line. I determined to traverse the proposed route—or as much of it as possible—on horseback, and give the world an impartial report.

Indian Territory in the 1870s

Spring was just tinging the prairies with a pale green when I entered the country of the Cherokees, and soon after was crossing Grand River passed a heavy wooded strip, and in the next prairie found the terminus town of Vinita. Here the Missouri, Kansas & Texas Railroad crosses the A. & P., and here we should naturally expect to see a place. In Kansas or Nebraska we should see a city with lots selling at from one hundred to two thousand dollars, dwellings and stores going up on every hand, one or two live journals blowing the place as the "future metropolis of the boundless West, the last great chance for profitable investment," etc, and a dozen streets lively with the rattle of commerce. Here, we see nothing. We feel the dead calm of stagnation; we breathe the atmosphere of laziness. There is one tolerable hotel, one stone store, and two frame ones, kept respectively by a Cherokee and a Delaware; and, besides the railroad employees, there is a population of perhaps a hundred—a few good men, more shiftless whites, average Indians, and suspicious-looking half-breeds.

For five weeks I wandered about the Indian Territory, a pleasant sort of half wilderness for a Bohemian to recreate in. Here are pure-blooded Aborigines who are something more than hunters and root-diggers; here are republican governments run on aboriginal principles, with aboriginal official titles, and such a mixture of races as affords a fine field for the ethnologist. One meets with some awkward surprises, with facts that unsettle a great deal we had considered settled. A region half as large as Ohio (excluding the sand-hills and deserts) has some 60,000 inhabitants: a people rich in flocks and herds, enjoying themselves in a simple, pastoral way, content with their mode of life, and indifferent to the rush and struggle of more artificial societies. One may travel for hundreds of miles on the public roads and never see a full-blooded Indian; yet such are in the majority, as shown by the census. They usually live off the roads and in the timber along the streams.

The mild warmth of a March Sabbath in that latitude led

me to make an excursion down Cabin Creek to a log church and schoolhouse, where I found a congregation of fifty-two persons. There were all shades, from African black to pure white with blue eyes and flaxen hair. There were families of half a dozen each, representing three or four types of the half-breed. One very intelligent gentleman told me he had a family of nine—of just nine different shades—from pure white to almost pure Indian. His first wife was half Shawnee, from Canada, and her first husband a full-blooded Cherokee, the three children of that union being rather dark. By this woman he had four children, only quarter blood, but varying greatly in complexion. After her death he married a blonde Irish woman; they had two children, one a clear-skinned, freckled, blue-eyed Celt, the other dark enough to pass for a "White Cherokee."

"It's singular how it will come back in this country," he explained. "I've known 'em to have regular Injun children after two generations of nearly white, and children of pure white people born here are often very dark. I know two White Cherokees, married, that you couldn't tell either of 'em from a regular white person, and they've a whole family of nearly half-bloods. Old Injuns say it comes back on 'em sometimes after people have done forgot they had any Injun blood in 'em."

Our preacher was a white man, but a citizen of the Cherokee Nation; and the society was Baptist, as are a majority of Cherokee Christians. The Methodists, Presbyterians, Moravians, and Episcopalians also have churches in the Territory. The Senecas alone, of all the located tribes, retain their aboriginal heathenism. That entire tribe numbered then but ninety persons, including one baby. They occupy a township in the north-eastern part of the Cherokee country, where sacrifices, incantations, and a separate priesthood are still maintained. They stroke their faces to the moon, and once a year burn a certain number of dogs to propitiate the spirit of evil. These, with offerings of fruits, serve them instead of incense and holy water.

Traveling northward through the Cherokee country, I

reached the Kansas line at Chetopa, and with amazing suddenness passed from a wilderness to a thickly settled country. From east to west, far as the eye can see, extends a marked line of division between State and "Nation": on the south an unbroken prairie, on the north farms, orchards, neat dwellings, and thriving villages. If one side of Broadway should utterly vanish, leaving a vacant plain, the other side remaining as it is, the contrast could scarcely be greater. It is a powerful argument, and one in constant use in favor of congressional action to open the Territory to white settlement. Thence, after a short visit, I took the southward train on the Missouri, Kansas & Texas Railroad, having meanwhile been joined by Mr. C. G. De Bruler, of the *Cincinnati Times*. The road was then completed but ninety miles into the Territory, and at midnight we stopped at the new town of Muscogee, in the Muskokee or Creek Nation.

Indian Territory in the 1870s

We opened our eyes next morning upon a long, straggling, miserable railroad town, the exact image of a Union Pacific "city," in the last stages of decay. Some two hundred yards from the railroad, a single street extended for nearly a quarter of a mile; the buildings were rude shanties, frame and canvas tents, and log cabins, open to the wind, which blew a hurricane for the thirty-six hours we were there. If Mr. Lo, "the poor Indian," does in fact "see God in the clouds and hear Him in the wind," as the poet tell us, he has a simple and benign creed which gives him an audible and ever-present deity in this country, for the wind is constant and of a character to prevent forgetfulness. The weather is mild and pleasant enough, but walking against the wind is very laborious, and the howling so constant as to make conversation difficult inside a tent. I have observed in my travels that windy countries are generally healthful, but a different report is given here. They say bilious diseases of all kinds prevail, and complain particularly of fever, ague, and pneumonia.

We ate in the "Pioneer Boarding Car," and slept in another car attached; five of them being placed on a side track,

anchored down, and converted into a pretty good hotel. Here, and about the depot, were the citizens employed on the road. Of the town proper, a majority of the citizens were negroes, formerly slaves to the Indians. Slavery here was never severe, and they are little more their own masters than before. They earn a precarious subsistence, the women by washing and the men by teaming and chopping, and were all sunk deep, deep in poverty and ignorance. All day the wenches were strolling about in groups, bareheaded, barefooted, half naked, stupid-looking, ragged, and destitute. But all around them was nature's wealth, needing only industry to create plenty. Fertile prairies, even now rivaling Ohio meadows in May, rolled away for miles to the north and east; beyond them the heavy line of timber marked the course of the Arkansas.

The records of Muscogee are bloody. During the five weeks the terminus business and stage offices were there and at Gibson, sixteen murders were committed at these two places, and in a very short time five men were killed at the next terminus. One man was shot all to pieces just in front of the dining-car at Muscogee, and another had his throat cut at night, almost in the middle of the town. It is ture, strangers, travelers, and outsiders are rarely if ever troubled. These murders are upon their own class, and new-comers who are weak enough to mix in, drink and gamble with them. But a few days before our arrival, a Texan reached Canadian Station with the proceeds of a cattle sale. He met these fellows at night, was seen at 10 o'clock with them, drunk and generous with his money; a few days after his body was washed ashore some miles down the Canadian. And yet I am assured, and believe it, a man with a legitimate business, who will let whisky alone, can travel through this Territory as safely as any other. . . .

After two days at this lively town, we concluded we had better see the Creeks at home, and started afoot for the Agency, traveling over a beautiful, rich prairie, gently rolling rising from the river into long ridges, which occasionally terminated in sharp bluffs, crowned with pretty groves.

The prospect was delightful by nature, and not a little enlivened by the numerous herds of cattle cropping the rich herbage. The tasty groves, the high prairie, and the slow-moving herds, with an occasional group of horses, produced the exact likeness of an old and wealthy estate, with pretty parks and stock grazing about the lawns and meadows. Eight or ten miles west of Muscogee, we entered a region of rude log-cabins and gaunt farm stock, where black faces peered at us through the cracks of "worm fences," and occasional "free nigger" patches showed something like civilization. A colored girl replied, in answer to our queries, "Agency over thar," and a mile further brought us to a beautiful grove, in which was an irregular square of log-cabins, including some three or four acres. We saw no signs of Government buildings, and but one neat, commodious house. There we were directed to a double log building, corresponding to those of the poorest farmers in Indiana, some distance from the square in a field, and that we found to be the Agency.

The place is overrun by freedmen. A continuous line of settlements, with "patches" rather than farms, extends for ten miles along the Arkansas, with a population of perhaps a thousand freedmen and a hundred Creeks. Only the poorest and lowest of the Indians live among the blacks, but there has been more amalgamation in this than in any other tribe. The pure Creeks differ noticeably from the Cherokees. They are shorter, broader, and rather darker; without the high cheek bones and solemn gravity of the others, and with a more cheerful and kindly expression. The white traders say they are more industrious than the Cherokees, but less intelligent.

The government of the Creek Nation is republican in form; the entire "constitution" and laws are printed in a small pamphlet of less than twenty pages. The law-making power is vested in a House of Kings and a House of Warriors; the members of each are elected for four years, by general vote of all the male Creeks over eighteen years of age. Each of the forty towns sends one member to the House of Kings; to the House of Warriors one, and an additional member for each two hundred citizens. The Kings elect their own President, the Warriors their own Speaker-in-Council; each house elects its own interpreter, and all speeches made in English are forthwith rendered aloud into Creek, and vice versa. The records are kept in English.

The Executive of the Nation is styled the Principal Chief, his Vice the Second Chief; they also are elected for four years each, and thus the entire Government is liable to a complete change at each election. The Judiciary begins with the High Court, which consists of five persons, chosen by the Council for four years. They have original jurisdiction in all cases involving over one hundred dollars, and appellate jurisdiction from lower courts in criminal matters. The Nation is divided into six districts, in each of which a judge is elected by the qualified voters; he has jurisdiction of all cases involving sums under one hundred dollars, and local criminal jurisdiction. Of course, in such a brief and simple criminal code, there is much left to the discretion of the judge, and, as far as a white man can see, he seems to have almost absolute power. The death penalty is often inflicted. Each district elects a "light horse company," consisting of one lieutenant and four privates; these act as sheriff and deputies under orders of the District Courts, and are subject to a general call from the Principal Chief to execute the mandates of the High Court, or suppress extensive disorders. In hundreds of instances these light-horse companies and the District Judge simply make the law as they go, calling court on each particular case, following the statute if there is one, and if not, assigning such penalty as in their judgment fits the case. The laws are singularly plain and unambiguous. No space is wasted in definitions, it being taken for granted, apparently, that every body knows the meaning of such terms as "steal" and "murder."

After a few days at the Agency, where we were handsomely entertained, and assisted in our researches by Major J. G. Vore and his assistant, Mr. A. S. Purington, who were in charge, we determined to visit the Tallahassee Mission, a sort of high school for the Creeks. Starting afoot, Mr. De Bruler and I soon reached the Arkansas, and, after half an hour's vigorous shouting the ferryman came over, with two negroes. A sudden storm drove us to the nearest hut. A bright mulatto soon appeared, who informed us that he was a slave to the Creeks "afoh de wah; run away and went off den, which I larnt Ingliss, sah." So, with him for interpreter, we succeeded in an hour in extracting half a dozen remarks from Charon the Silent, as we named the determinedly reticent Creek. The storm passed, and we were set across the river, for which Charon demanded "pahly-hok-kohlen hoonunvy, pahly osten"—rendered by our linguist to mean "twenty cents a man—forty cents all." This we disbursed, and footed it across the bottom over a road rendered very toilsome by the rain. At dark, splashed and weary, we reached the Mission, which is beautifully situated in an open grove, appearing to us a very haven of rest—fitting emblem of the faith and hope which planted it in this wilderness.

There we spent a most delightful Sabbath, entertained by the Superintendent, Rev. W. S. Robertson, and family. This mission has been thirty years in existence, and has educated all the leading men of the Creek Nation. The teachers are selected and paid by the Presbyterian Board of Home Missions; the material interests are looked after by the Nation, which sends a boy and girl from each of the forty towns, a new one being selected for every departure. Supper was called soon after our arrival; we took "visitors' chairs," and watched with much interest the orderly incoming of some seventy young Creeks, of every age from eight to twenty-two. Nearly all were pure bloods, and the whole scene was a revelation to me. I had seen the savage-painted Indian, and the miserable vagabond on the white frontier; but the civilized, scholarly Indian boy and girl presented a new sight. Supper over, a chapter was read, and the school united in prayers and a devotional hymn. Then we were invited to hear classes, who volunteered an evening recitation for our benefit.

Their natural talent is surprising, particularly in drawing and figures. Every Creek boy seems to know the law of outline by instinct. In figures they are very quick; in reading not so apt. Creek and English being the only languages used at the Mission, every Uchee, Natchee, or Alabama pupil has to learn a new language before his education proper begins.

Like the common school system of our own people, this school tends to break down tribal prejudice, and make the people homogeneous. Two Uchee boys, of the reading class, conversed awhile in that language at my request. It is entirely devoid of labials; for five minutes they touched lips together but once. It also rarely requires the dentals; and thus to a Uchee it is almost impossible to distinguish between b and p, d and t, or a and e. This inability produces most ludicrous results in spelling. Pronouncing the words to be spelled orally, the teacher can not possibly determine in the quick sound whether the spelling is correct or not—that is, with Uchee beginners. But, when they come to write it on the slate, bat becomes p-e-t, hat h-e-d, bad b-e-t, etc. The Creeks are lively and affectionate, but their original language does not contain a single term of endearment. Some have been adopted from English, others formed by combining primitive words in their own tongue. The word for sweetheart has eight syllables—a nice jawbreaker to murmur in a maiden's ear by moonlight. Love (between the sexes) is slem-lem-an-dah-mouch-wah-ger. A girl must be delighted to hear a fellow say he has a good deal of that for her.

Mr. Robertson, with the aid of an interpreter, has adapted our alphabet to the language, and published a series of books and translations of many of our hymns. These we heard at the Mission Sabbath School, which was also a delightful surprise in its way. I felt all the enthusiasm of the occasion when the seventy sweet voices, led by Miss Rob-

Indian Territory in the 1870s

ertson with an organ, took up the strain of "Shall we gather at the River?" in the Creek.

Thence we continued our survey of the Creek country by leisurely journeys among the farmers. The soil is generally fertile, while almost every dwelling is the center of a beautiful grove of fruit trees, at that season green with springing leaves, or white and red with blossoms, giving off the sweet scents of advancing spring. The people as a rule are simple, civil and hospital; the Nation contains several churches aggregating a thousand members. But the natural tendency, as with other Indians, is towards a sort of fatalism. Among all the races in the Territory conjurers are found, and the testimony is universal that they never fail to cure snake-bites. There is not a dissenting statement from white, black or red! If you ask the more intelligent how they explain it, the answer generally is: "I don't explain it; I don't believe in conjuration; I only know the cure is certain." The conjurer uses no medicine but a small leaf of tobacco or other plant, which he holds upon his tongue while pronouncing the charm. He applies it then to the bite, pressing it smartly with the ball of his thumb, and in less than twenty-four hours the patient is entirely well.

At noon of a bright April day we return to the railroad at Muscogee, to find matters worse than ever. As we sit down to dinner in the boarding-car, a half-blood Creek, crazy with smuggled whisky, is galloping up and down the row, brandishing a huge revolver, and threatening death to all opponents. At one moment he rides his horse into a shop, emerges the next, and gallops upon a group of wenches, who scatter with a chorus of screams. A file of soldiers from a detachment on the road appear on the scene, arrest and disarm him, and the town returns to its normal condition of listlessness and idle chatter. Severe penalties are prescribed against selling whisky in the Territory, and that which is smuggled in, is the vilest compound known to the trade, familiarly called "tarantula juice," from the deadliest insect in the country. . . .

Indian Territory in the 1870s

The railroad was pushing southward as fast as a small army could lay track, to meet the Texas Central, which was in like manner pushing northward toward Red River. From Muscogee we traversed the last section then built, to the main Canadian River. Between the two Canadians was the passenger terminus, near the Old Methodist Mission; and here we pause a few hours. Dusty and travel-worn pilgrims are coming in from all points in Western Texas, and spruce, clean looking people from civilization, starting out on long and toilsome journeys through the sandy plains between here and the Rio Grande. Thence to Main Canadian we traverse a dense forest; all the point between the two rivers is heavily timbered, and choked with underbrush. The main stream is now wide and rapid, apparently thick with red mud and sand; but after standing a few minutes, it is sweet enough to the taste, and close examination shows the stream to be tolerably clear, the red showing through the water from the bottom.

We observed, with some nervousness, that Brad Collins, a "White Cherokee" desperado, with a dozen of his retainers had come down on our train. Soon the smuggled whisky they brought began to take effect, and half a dozen young half-breeds were galloping about town, firing pistols in the air, and yelling like demons. My companion took a brief look, and suggested: "This is a devilish queer place, let's get out of it." I was glad I had waited for him to speak first, but promptly acquiesced; and we crossed the Canadian into the Choctaw Nation, and spent the day with Tandy Walker, Esq. This gentleman, nephew of Ex-Governor Walker of the Choctaws, is nearly white, and strongly in favor of throwing open the Territory to white settlement. Once a leading man, he is now politically ostracized for his opinions. And here I may as well present a view of the party divisions which have caused so much trouble and some bloodshed in this Territory. It is a "Territory" only in a geographical sense, not being governed under an organic act like Utah or Montana. It was set apart by Act of Congress of May 28, 1830, and each Indian nation has its own government. The proposition, before Congress ever since the war, is to organize it into the "Territory of Oklahoma," (a Choctaw compound signifying the "Red men's State") and throw it open to white settlers. Hence the three parties among the Indians:

First—the Territorial party: in favor of Oklahoma and white immigration, after setting apart, in fee simple, a considerable farm to each Indian.

Second—the Ockmulkee Constitution party: in favor of sectionizing the land, giving each Indian his farm and the two railroads their grant, keeping all the rest in common as it is now, and uniting all the tribes under one government of their own (the Ockmulkee Constitution), with American citizenship and local courts; but no territorial arrangement and no white settlement.

Third—the party in favor of the present condition.

On further examination I found that the first party was very small among all the nations, and that the members of it were regarded as traitors to their race; that the third party had as yet a large majority of the whole people, but that the Ockmulkee Constitution promised most for the Indians, and had the support of their most able men.

The Choctaws number 16,000, the Chickasaws 6,000; the two constitute one nation, the citizens of either tribe having equal rights in all respects. Their country lies between the Main Canadian and Arkansas, and is two hundred miles from east to west: an area equal to two or three New England States, the eastern third very fertile, the center good for timber and pasture, the western part running into the flinty hills and barren plains. The citizens are more advanced in civilization than the Creeks; they enforce their laws much better, particularly in cases where whites or half-breeds are concerned. With their sporadic population timber increases yearly, game is abundant and cheap, common pasturage is plenty, and cattle are grown at a cost of from three to eight dollars per head. The Choctaws were immensely wealthy before the war. Single herders numbered their cattle by thousands. The average wealth was twice as great as that of any purely agricultural community in the States, and golden ornaments of every sort were profusely displayed on horses, carriages, and the Indians' persons. The amount of fine clothes and jewelry sold by traders here at that time seems incredible. The war swept them clean; literally broke up and ruined them, leaving nothing but the land. Before the war Mr. Walker was accounted a millionaire. He began again, in 1865, with fifty dollars and one saddle-mule. He was ahead of his neighbors only in this: his fifty dollars were in greenbacks, theirs were in Confederate notes. Those who "went South" were even worse ruined than those who "took the Federal side." Some died of grief and despair, on returning home in 1865. But most went resolutely to work, and are once more prospering. But many years will be required for those vast herds of cattle to be renewed. This neighborhood has every sign of a prosperous community of civilized farmers. On the whole, I rather like the Choctaws.

Indian Territory in the 1870s

We soon returned to Muscogee, and on the afternoon of a sultry day set out to walk to Fort Gibson. Three miles brought us upon the old cattle trail from Texas to Kansas City, where we were soon overaken by a grizzled and weather-beaten old Texan, who politely asked us to take a seat in his wagon. Eyeing our valises suspiciously, he asked:

"Got any whisky in them?"

"No," was the answer, with expressed regrets.

"Ef ye had, ye'd walk, you bet; wouldn't have you get in here with one pint of whisky for five hundred dollars!"

This radical temperance platform in this latitude excited our astonishment, and we called for an explanation. He gave it: "A burnt child dreads the fire. One pint, yes, one dram o'whisky'd cost me this hull load. These deputy marshals—d—n the thievin' rascals, I say—they'll search y'r wagon any minit; and if they find one drop, away goes the hull load to Fort Smith, and d—n the haight of it d'y ever see again. One trip a nice lookin' chap enough asked me to ride. He got in, and pretty soon pulled a flask. 'Drink,' says he. 'After you,' says I. Well, in less'n ten minutes comes the marshals and grabbed us. If they find a drop even on a man as is ridin' with you, they take every thing, and nary dollar do you ever git. Why, that feller was in with 'em, of course. They seize every thing they can git a pretense for, and then divide. There won't any body but a scamp and a rough take such an office as deputy marshal in this country. They're all on the make, and in with these roughs. That's what I say."

Three miles with our slightly rebellious Texan friend brought us to the Arkansas River, and to a steam ferry-boat. At the mouth of Grand River, is the head of navigation on the Arkansas. Steamers run up the Grand River, which has backwater from the Arkansas, three miles or more, and land at Fort Gibson. By a series of dams and locks, like those on Green River, Kentucky, I am convinced the Arkansas could have slack-water navigation a hundred miles or more above this. The waters of Grand River and those of the Arkansas show like two broad bands, one misty blue and the other dirty red and yellow, in the main channel as far as we can see below their junction. The two streams, the clear and the muddy, run side by side for nearly twenty miles, when a series of riffles and sharp turns mingles them freely in a fluid of pale orange tint.

At Fort Gibson we found quarters at the usual double-log-house hotel, kept by a Pennsylvania Dutchman, with a "White Cherokee" wife; and there we met Judge Vann, Hon. A. Rattling Gourd, and other prominent Cherokees. This is a rather handsome town for the border, with several neat brick and frame houses. After a few days' study of local politics, we concluded more was to be learned at the capital, and started afoot for Tahlequah. The distance is twenty-two miles, which we must divide in two journeys. "Better stop at Widow Skrimshee's over night; got a good house and a white son-in-law; 'taint but fifteen miles there," said our new friends. So, valise on shoulder, we started for the widow's, through a beautiful and well-improved country for the first six miles. The log-houses here are superior in style to those in most new countries, being high, neatly squared at the corners, and well shingled. There are few frames. The improvements are much finer than among the Creeks, and about equal to those of the Choctaws. From rolling prairie we descended into a broad valley with heavy timber. From the open and windy plain to this grove was like going from pleasant April to sultry July. Our valises seemed to weigh a hundred each; our clothing dripped with sweat, and we were soon exhausted by fatigue. We turned aside to the residence of a "White Cherokee"—the usual double-log-house with porch between—where we lay prostrate in the passage, smoked a pipe of his "home raisin'," and "interviewed" him as to the situation. He had been a Union Cherokee; took a hundred men out of here by night in the fall of '61; went North and became a captain; came back after the war, to find his house and fences burned, and all his stock run off—some to Kansas, some to Texas. "Was rich afo' the war; derned poor now, but gittin' started again. Hated the loss of my sheep wass'n any thing else—fine bloods—couldn't get others like 'em."

At dark, fagged and heated, we reached the widow's. She was a bright, half-blood Cherokee, and entertained us till late bed-time with accounts of "the old nation in Geaugey," and their fights and troubles till they were sent here. Thence we traveled on to Tahlequah, the Cherokee capital, a pretty town of perhaps eight hundred people. Our first acquaintance was with William Boudinot, brother of the Elias Boudinot who has been so active at Washington pushing the Oklahoma Bill. William is editor of the *Cherokee Advocate*, official organ of the Nation, published in English and Cherokee, and a handsome, well-conducted sheet. The Choctaws also have a small paper called the *Vindicator*, these being the only papers published in the Territory. Tahlequah was for us rich in historic interest, and we spent three days most delightfully among the curious old records of the Nation, here preserved.

The Cherokees represent the best history and the highest hope of the Indian race. If they are a failure, the race can not be civilized—the aborigine is doomed. They have been an organized nation with constitution and written laws for eighty years; far back of that they were superior to all neighboring tribes.

In 1860, they were, as a commuity, the wealthiest people in the West. Single herders owned stock to the value of a hundred thousand dollars. In this mild climate and upon these rich prairies cattle multiplied rapidly. There was soon no land "running to waste," for all was utilized as pasture. Many white men sought citizenship or married Cherokee girls, and were adopted, and the advance of the Nation was healthful, natural and rapid.

In 1865 their country was almost a waste; the people in extreme poverty. But they came back from the war and sadly went to work again. Now it is proposed, because part of them joined the Confederates, that all shall lose their present title and take their chances under a new allotment.

The Choctaws and Cherokees have the greatest number of intelligent men, but the Creeks are just now doing the most for the rising generation. They have three Mission High Schools, under control respectively of the Baptist, Methodist, and Presbyterian churches. In 1872 there were in the whole Territory a hundred and sixty common schools—the high average of one to every four hundred of the population. The number now reaches nearly two hundred.

The present weakness of these [Indian] people is their imperfect land tenure. The land is held in common by the whole tribe, but whatever area any citizen incloses with a lawful fence is his while he occupies it. He may be said to own the improvements, but not the land. Any thing may be removed at the owner's will; hence there is practically no real estate, no conservative landed interest—the only true foundation for a progressive society and a stable civil structure. The herder, hunter or explorer, from Kansas or Texas, rides through a beautiful tract, and, when he asks who owns it, the only answer is: "The Injuns—it's Injun land;" that is, in his estimation, nobody's land, if he can by force or fraud get a foothold. If he were told that it was the property of John Johnnycake or William Beaverdam, or any other individual, with a patent title on which he could sue and be sued, the case would be very different to him. A strong party, therefore, is rising up, agitating for this reform, which is the distinctive feature of the Ockmulkee Constitution.

There are a score of reasons why a little time should be given the Indians, and why we should not now throw open this country to general settlement. In the first place, we have solemnly agreed not to do it, which is reason enough for any honorable man. Secondly, there is no present necessity for it. There are countless millions of acres lying idle in every State and Territory north of it, untouched by the cultivator, and even unoccupied by the herdsman. It is too soon by half a century to repeat to these civilized Indians the old order: "GO WEST." There is room in Nebraska for half a million farmers. There is a tract in Dakota about the size of Indiana, yet unappropriated, with a climate suitable for Northern people, and a most prolific soil. When these are filled, and our population really begins to feel crowded, it will be time enough to trouble the Indians. But with Kansas on one side and Texas on the other offering millions of acres of good land, it seems as if thousands are half crazy to get into the Indian Territory just because it is forbidden.

Our true policy is to secure these people their lands, assist them a little in their progress, and make them our agents to deal with the wild tribes. Half civilized and barbarous races can best be reached through the medium of their more advanced brethren. The nations here are already moving in the matter, and a little assistance only is needed to enable them to reach and negotiate with all the wild tribes of Northern Texas and New Mexico. I am hopeful enough to believe that, with a proper policy, all the tribes in the same latitude, except possibly the Apaches, might eventually be made citizens of this Territory. We have sent the

Indians, as a rule, our worst men and most destructive practices, and have systematically broken faith whenever it seemed profitable to do so. Here only has a policy something near sensible and just been pursued, and the results are not discouraging. Let it be improved and extended, and we may reasonably hope the Indians of the southern territories will be gathered here; than an aboriginal community of two hundred thousand will grow into a high civilization; and in due time we shall have a real native American State—a progressive and prosperous State of Oklahoma.

The Reminiscences of an Indian Trader

¶ *The trader, along with the missionary, the Indian agent, and the cavalry officer, is a legendary figure in the story of the frontier. Sometimes he is portrayed as a venal, crafty charlatan, cheating ignorant Indians with shoddy goods and growing fat on the profits. In other versions he is the all-wise guide and naturalist, skilled linguist and philosopher, merchant prince and part-time poet. Both versions, and their countless movie-inspired variations, distort reality.* ¶ *General R. A. Sneed, a licensed trader to the Comanche and Kiowa and Prairie Apache tribes at Fort Sill and Anadarko from 1885 to 1890, is representative of the men who supplied the necessities and later the luxuries that eased a harsh frontier existence. His recollections correct the trader mythology and are a virtual encyclopedia of the customers and commerce of the prairie near the close of the nineteenth century.*

FORTY-EIGHT YEARS have passed since I first visited the Comanche and Kiowa country, and forty-three years have elapsed since the termination of my first sojourn there. Great changes have marked the intervening era. It is not vouchsafed unto me to live to see the beautiful country as it will appear, forty-three to forty-eight years hence, though some of the people who now read these lines may do so. It was a land that was good to look upon when I first saw it. The Indians loved it then, as their children's children love it still.

A native of Mississippi, and long a citizen of Tennessee, I remember wondering if I would find life in a prairie country, tolerable, to say nothing of pleasant. Yet to my astonishment, I found it not merely tolerable but enjoyable. In-

From General R. A. Sneed, "The Reminiscences of an Indian Trader," *Chronicles of Oklahoma*, 14 (June 1936), 135–55.

deed, there was something about the primitive, unbroken prairie-land that was positively enchanting.

I arrived in what is now Comanche County, in October, 1885—forty-eight years ago. At that time, there was but one railway line that ran across the Indian Territory—the Missouri, Kansas & Texas, which passed through Vinita, Muskogee, McAlester and Durant. The town of Caddo, on this line of railway, had formerly been the nearest railway station to Fort Sill, the distance between the two points being 153 miles. There was regular traffic between Caddo and the military point at the eastern base of the Wichita Mountains—a stage line and freighting trains of wagons—until the construction of the Fort Worth and Denver Railway line reached Henrietta, Texas, in 1885, reduced the distance to rail connection to sixty-five miles, so that travel and traffic between the Fort and Caddo station soon ceased.

When I landed at Henrietta, I found that there was a daily stage line between that place and Fort Sill. This stage carried the mail and such passengers as might be going that way, together with light express. The Red River was crossed at Charley Station, about twenty miles out from Henrietta. The river was ordinarily crossed by fording, but when the current reached a flood stage, a small ferry-boat was brought into service. Another station known as "Grogan's" about 15 miles down the river was later chosen by the stage line as the official crossing place, Charley's being abandoned for the purpose. Midway between Red River and the Fort was what was commonly called the Snake Creek Station, it being located where a small stream of that name—a tributary of East Cache Creek—was forded. At the Snake Creek stage stand, I met the first white man that it was my fortune to come to know in the Indian Territory of that day, in the person of W. G. Williams, then better known locally under the cognomen of "Caddo Bill" Williams. He was driving through to Henrietta, accompanied by his wife, who was a member of the Caddo Indian tribe. He had already lived in the Washita Valley, in the Anadarko vicinity, for more than twenty years. He lived many years afterward, dying at his home in El Reno about 1912.

When I came to leave Henrietta by stage, I was surprised and delighted to find that the driver was none other than "Uncle Jeff" Griffith, a native of Lincoln County, Tennessee, who had been a stage driver throughout his life since his young manhood. He had been driving the stage between Canton, Mississippi, and Yazoo City when I was but a young boy. He was a man of fine character, gentlemanly demeanor and kindly disposition and was always deservedly popular among his patrons. He had never married. He continued to drive the stage between Henrietta and Fort Sill until the growing infirmities of age led to his retirement. He was a man of sixty-five or seventy, when I met him at Henrietta, the first time. The vehicle which he drove on that road was of a type known as a "mountain wagon," having four springs. It had three seats and was capable of carrying eight or ten passengers. It was usually drawn by a team of four mules of light or medium weight.

Uncle Jeff was retired as a driver during the time that I was living at the Fort Sill sub-agency, being assigned to keep the stage stand at the Snake Creek Crossing. Though stage stand-keepers, as a rule, did not attract much attention on the part of travelers, Uncle Jeff was an exception as to this. In his living quarters at Snake Creek, he kept a small "monkey" stove and, always, when the stage was due to arrive, he would have the water boiling hot and ready to make coffee which he gladly gave to all passengers who were invited to enjoy his hospitality. Needless to say, he was not less popular as a stand keeper than he had been as a stage driver. When he finally became too old to serve as a stand keeper, he took up his residence at the ranch home of Cal Suggs, a well known stockman of that region and there the closing years of his life were spent. Though many years have passed since he died, no one who ever knew him has forgotten him and though his place in the world's affairs was an humble one, he dignified it by his manliness and

Reminiscences of an Indian Trader

fidelity so that, even if this brief tribute may seem to be a tardy one, it is abundantly justified.

When I first arrived at Fort Sill, I stopped at a small hotel kept by Tolly Maupin, a Missourian. He had been called back to his old home by the illness of a relative, some days before my arrival, and he had left his hostelry in care of some Mexicans. These people baked big soda biscuits, served black coffee (without cream) and fried fresh beef so burned that it tasted bitter.

A day or two after my arrival at the Fort, I went on to the Comanche and Kiowa Agency, at Anadarko, thirty-five miles farther north up the trail. This agency, which was also the location of several trading establishments, was situated in the beautiful valley of the Washita River, adjoining the site of the present county-seat of Caddo County, which is still known by the name that had then been recently bestowed upon it—Anadarko. It had been so named out of compliment to the remnant of the Anadarko tribe of Indians, which was closely related to and affiliated with the more numerous and powerful Caddo tribe.

. . . In all, there were ten or a dozen families, including those of the agent, physician, clerks, teachers, mechanics, farmers and traders. There were no missionaries there then, but several of them came in within the next few years. There were two Indian schools—the Riverside School, on the north side of the Washita, which was maintained for the children of the Wichita, Caddo and affiliated tribes, and the Kiowa school on the south side, which was maintained for children of the Comanche, Kiowa and Apache tribes. I spent two or three days at the Agency. . . .

On my return to Fort Sill, I stayed only a day, or two, going from thence to my home in Tennessee, where I remained during the ensuing winter. Along in the latter part of the winter (February, 1886), I began to make preparations to move to Fort Sill. Most of the goods for the new store were purchased in St. Louis and Chicago and in Fort Worth. The Indian goods were bought in St. Louis and Chicago. Groceries, meats and provisions, and many other items for the stock were purchased at Fort Worth. The Indians were very fond of fruit, such as prunes, figs, dates, raisins, etc., and large quantities of these were purchased in nearly every consignment; also the best grade of canned goods.

The first stock of goods was opened out in an old building down near the East Cache Creek, on the bank of that stream. In fact, this structure had been built some years before, the material being what was known in those days as "raw-hide" lumber, i.e., native lumber sawed out of cottonwood logs. This was in March, 1886. At the same time, I was making preparations for the erecting of a new building near the old sub-agency and school, two and a half miles south of the military post. This building was occupied when completed, and the stock of goods being transferred thither on the 17th of July, following. It was commonly known as the "Red Store." It was two stories high, the upper floor being finished as a residence for my family. The lumber for this structure was hauled from Henrietta, Texas, a distance of sixty-five miles. My family did not join me until November, 1886.

The new business house was thirty-six by seventy feet in dimensions and, even at that, the stock of goods which was installed, used up the floor space to such an extent that only convenient passage ways were left open. The stock included staple and fancy groceries, canned goods, cured meats, etc. Of course the dry goods included robes, blankets, shawls, silk handkerchiefs, red flannels, blue broadcloth, etc. All had to be of the best quality, as the Indians would not buy cheap imitations or goods of inferior material. We also handled high grade saddles and bridles, and all kinds of harness. The hardware was all of good quality though the stock was not a large one. The hardware which was in demand among the Indians was chiefly axes, hatchets, saws, files, etc.; also kettles, frying pans and other cooking utensils, especially coffee pots. Most of the kettles were of the best grade of brassware and were sold at good prices.

One of the main articles of trade was tanned and dressed buckskins of which a large quantity was always carried in stock. This was in keen demand for making moccasins, leggings and clothing. Most of this buckskin was purchased in Chicago. It was listed as "black-tail" buckskin and was assumed to be from the Rocky Mountain country. Practically every Indian had a complete buckskin wardrobe which was kept for ceremonial and state occasions.

One item of hardware that was in more or less constant demand was a type of hatchet which was known as the "hunter's ax." It was of good metal and had a short handle. It was accounted as especially useful in trimming and making teepee poles. These poles were always made of red cedar. The trees from which they were made were always selected in the cedar brakes, in the northern part of the Wichita-Caddo reservation, and were carefully selected, each being tall and straight, with few, if any, large limbs. The Indians used to go in large parties for the purpose of securing pole timber. Only one pole was made from a tree. This necessitated a lot of trimming and shaving, the work being done by the squaws. When the poles were first brought in, they were green and heavy with sap, so that four to six of them were a load for any Indian pony to drag. Securing and bringing in these teepee poles and making them by the laborious methods and means in use among the Indians made them expensive and high-priced. An ordinary family domicile, or lodge, was twelve to fifteen feet high, with poles fifteen to eighteen feet long. Of these, there would be fifteen to eighteen or twenty. Some of the larger lodges, which were used for ceremonial or tribal gatherings, council meetings, etc., were as much as twenty feet high, with poles twenty-four feet in length and as many as thirty in number. These large teepee poles were valued at $4.00 or $5.00 each. When I came among the Indians, the teepees were mostly covered with 12-ounce duck, though some of the smaller lodges used 8-ounce or 10-ounce duck coverings. Down to a dozen years before I went among them, their lodges were covered with buffalo hides, with the flesh side out.

When a band of Indians moved their camp or village, before they began to use wagons, many of their movable belongings were transported in bundles which were fastened between the trailing lodge poles dragged by the ponies. This vehicle was called a "travois," among the northern Indians such as the Sioux. Naturally, a well traveled travois trail soon came to have its paths deeply worn in the soil. In driving across the country with a team and buggy or other light conveyance, if I overtook or passed a travois train, I always turned out of the road and gave it a wide berth, as most horses other than Indian ponies were easily frightened at the sight of that sort of transportation.

The Indian people were remarkable for their truthfulness and honesty. I seldom had occasion to go to their camps to make collections—they always came in and settled their own accounts. Their sense of honor and honesty and their regard for their word when they had made a promise were almost universally above question. If an Indian died owing a debt, his relatives always paid it. The lowering of their morale did not come until the white people came to live among them. They were keen traders and did not hesitate to take advantage of the other party to a deal if opportunity was afforded, but once they gave a promise, its performance was regarded as a sacred obligation. Though they were unable to read and write, many of them seemed to be skilled in the art of diplomacy.

When my family came out, in the fall of 1886, two of our old servants—a cook and a nurse—came along. In 1887, when I had been to St. Louis and Chicago to buy goods, I took a trip around by my home at Jackson, Tennessee, for a brief visit. When I left there on my return to the West, William Davis, a young negro, accompanied me. He had worked for me at various times before and was industrious and trustworthy, so I offered him employment around the store at the Fort Sill sub-agency. Of course the trip west was a great event in his life as he never traveled very much. After we had crossed Red River and the road led out across the unbroken prairie, I noticed that he appeared to be greatly interested in all that he saw. Finally, I asked him what he thought of the country, whereupon he said:

"Mr. Sneed, who cleared all this land? It sure must have been during slavery times—there hain't no stumps. It look like old fields that's been long turn out."

The fact is that, though he was thirty-five old, he had never before seen prairie lands, so he supposed that it had once been covered with timber.

Texas ranchmen used to bring watermelons from south of Red River by the wagon load, to the Agency and to Fort Sill. I used to buy many of them but was never overstocked. The Indians were as fond of melons as negroes possibly could be. One time, when an Indian payment was under way, I bought 1300 water melons, all of which I sold, mostly to the Indians, though some were sold to white people. Wild game was still plentiful. Deer and antelope were abundant. Feathered game, especially wild turkeys, prairie chickens and quail fairly swarmed. The Indians would not eat anything that had feathers or scales or fins but all was game to them that had its skin covered with hair. Beef from the Agency issue pen, of course, was the staple meat diet but it was varied with the venison of deer and antelope, as well as the flesh of smaller game animals. If a horse was accidentally injured or disabled, it was killed and skinned and its flesh was accounted a great delicacy. But all of the Indians of the Southern Plains region were deeply prejudiced against eating the flesh of birds. They would kill wild turkeys and bring them to the agencies, forts and trading establishments to trade or to sell to white men, whom they doubtless despised for eating the same. Turkeys, prairie chickens and quail were all accounted cowardly, hence it was "bad medicine" to eat their flesh. At first, they did not care for pork, so they used to throw away dry salt pork when it was issued to them but they subsequently overcame that dislike. Of fish, they knew nothing and consequently they paid no attention thereto.

Thus briefly have I tried to tell of the Comanche and Kiowa country, and especially of the settlements at and surrounding Fort Sill and Anadarko, as I found and came to know the same, nearly half a century ago. It has been a pleasure to live over again in retrospect the life of those years and the pleasant memories with which they were filled.

A Pioneer Railroad Agent

¶ *In 1888, a year before the first great land rush into Oklahoma, a sixteen-year-old Kansan stepped from the Santa Fe platform at Oklahoma Station to take up his duties as the railroad agent in the Unassigned Lands. Arthur W. Dunham's recollections illustrate the enormous impact of the railroad and the way it touched individual lives. The railroad provided the reliable transportation and the tools needed for settlement. It brought land-hungry settlers to their new homes, and the lumber for houses and towns, fences, schools, churches, and coffins. Until wells were dug, the railroad tank provided water. When crops failed, the Santa Fe and Rock Island distributed precious seeds to settlers, and with that seed came the chance to hang on for another season. The railroad acted as supplier, banker, and paymaster when there was simply no one else to do the job. Arthur Dunham was as important a pioneer as the man who farmed 160 acres. And as the railroad man he was literally an "agent for change."*

THAT YOU may visualize the past, I might mention that my father was a soldier in the Civil War, and after that memorable conflict was over, came west from the State of Michigan to settle on one of Uncle Sam's 160-acre tracts in Kansas, so you see I was an original "boomer." At that time I was about eighteen months old. The Santa Fe had been completed as far West as Emporia from which point we continued overland sixty miles further.

Someone has intimated that I am a railroad man, but my mother used to tell me the earliest evidence of that fact was shown on the way out to Kansas when I took great interest in transportation matters. Every time the engine would

From Arthur W. Dunham, "A Pioneer Railroad Agent," *Chronicles of Oklahoma*, 2 (March 1924), 48–62.

whistle I tried to imitate it, and the friendly passengers observed that I was destined some day to engage in railroad service.

There were hard times in Kansas. We survived the grasshopper year. We finally located at Florence where, at the age of five, I was placed in school. Later my spare time was spent as a boot-black, selling news papers, herding cattle, working as a bell-boy and lunch counter attendant in Fred Harvey's hotel and eating house. I was also a news agent on a Santa Fe train.

I first gained prominence in local railway circles in this way: we boys had two good swimming holes, one at Doyle Creek, the other at a bend in the Cottonwood River; both close at hand. There was not enough novelty or adventure, and as I had been around the railroad a good deal, I proposed that we climb up into the railroad tank for a swim, which was readily assented to. The tank was high and large. We stripped our clothes at the platform inside, near the top of the tank, and plunged into about fifteen feet of water. Somehow the railroad people got next to this—the tank supplied the Harvey House with water—they raised quite a disturbance over it. The result was I was placed on my good behavior—but all the same I got acquainted with the minor officials of the road. I was given an opportunity to apply myself to some of the fundamentals of railroad operation. I acquired some knowledge of telegraphy, and clerical work around the station.

The first big money I ever earned was acting as a guide for the famous Doctor Pierce, of Buffalo, New York (Dr. Pierce's Favorite Prescriptions, you know). It was on a hunting trip around Florence. He was so well pleased that he gave me a twenty-dollar gold piece.

The next large sum of money I earned was for riding a fast horse to the county seat at Marion, ten miles away, to file some legal papers at the court house within a limited time. This netted me ten dollars.

Shortly after this I was made Santa Fe agent at Burns. I had then reached the age of fifteen. I was soon promoted to other Kansas stations. A little later I was asked to go to Oklahoma.

On one cold night, February 20th, 1888, to be exact, and at about 2:00 A.M., as near as I can remember, I got off the southbound Santa Fe train at Oklahoma station, where this beautiful city now stands. I was accompanied by the traveling auditor of the railway, and the route agent for Wells Fargo & Company's Express. This was then the pretentious abode of one George Gibson, where he fed and housed what we used to term "Mule skinners" and "Tenderfeet" occasionally.

This building was made from rough lumber, a story and a half high, and had two or three sleeping rooms upstairs. The cracks were not closely battened, and the cold wind found its way through in unstinted measure. We knocked at the door, and soon made it understood who we were and what we wanted. George Gibson came down the steps holding a coal-oil lamp, to which was attached a tin reflector.

The light momentarily dazzled us, but we soon discerned a number of Indians on the floor, rolled up in their bright colored blankets. We had to step over one or two of them to get to the stairway, much to their disgust—and ours. They grunted and we passed on. Indians were no novelty to me at this early stage, as I had many times seen them in Kansas, and knew something of their habits. I was wondering whether there were still more Indians upstairs.

We were each given a blanket, and the bed had a thin cover, but it was so cold I kept my clothes on, and used my overcoat as well, my other companions did the same.

When we came down to breakfast we were seated on benches at a long pine table, and our bill-of-fare consisted of the usual sow-belly, black coffee, soggy biscuits, and molasses.

The man I had come to relieve had been hobnobbing freely with John Barley-Corn, but I was finally checked in as railroad agent, express agent, manager of the Western Union Telegraph Company, and stage agent. My duties immediately commenced. My force consisted of one night op-

A Pioneer Railroad Agent

erator. He was my only subordinate. I arranged my bunk in the depot, because I had to get up at 4:30 every morning to let the stage out and look after passengers, baggage and express. This took about one hour. I would then go back to bed and sleep a while longer.

There was considerable business transacted thru this office, even before the country opened up, as Oklahoma was the only reporting agency between Arkansas City and Purcell, a distance of one hundred fifty-four miles. It is true there were some telegraph offices like Ponca City, Wharton (now Perry), Guthrie, Norman, but they were established primarily to take care of train service. Freight could be sent to these places if fully prepaid and put off at the risk of the owners, but there were no regularly authorized agents to handle it.

After I was there a short time I moved the family down to Oklahoma, which consisted of my mother, two sisters and a brother. We occupied the cottage built by the railway company to accommodate the agent. It had four rooms, and while not a thing of beauty, it was at least comfortable.

Business was increasing rapidly, and I was permitted to employ my brother Van, as a helper. He was not an operator, and at that time had not been trained in railroad work, but we got along very well when we were not scrapping with each other. He was a year and a half younger than I.

The stage ran regularly between Oklahoma and Ft. Reno, the fare was $3.00 one way, or $5.00 for a round trip. Forty pounds of baggage were allowed free, anything over that took express rates. The old Concord style of stage was used—a boot in front and one behind, and as I recollect it, it was drawn by six horses.

We carried quite a few notables over the line, most of whom, however, were in government service. Sometimes it taxed our capacity to take care of the express. The government used Oklahoma as a distributing station in supplying a number of Indian Agencies, which included the Sac and Fox, Kickapoos, Mississippi Choctaws, Kiowas, and Comanches, Cheyenne and Arapahos, and some others. It was

also the government supply station for the soldiers quartered at Fort Reno. There was a Quartermaster Agent stationed at Oklahoma in the person of one Captain C. F. Somers, and the government furnished him his quarters, which consisted of a quite respectable frame building, located near the slope toward Maywood, not far from the railway. The Indian freight alone amounted to about one million pounds each month. It was not unuusal for freighters to haul supplies a distance of one hundred twenty-five miles.

Previous to my coming to the Indian Territory there had been an attempt made by the government to suppress the cattle men, but there were still numerous herds left. During my first year we shipped out of Oklahoma station over a thousand cars of cattle. We also shipped a car or two of buffalo horns, and a number of cars of bones which had been gathered by enterprising nesters.

There was quite an abundance of game in the vicinity, we frequently had venison and quail; at times prairie chickens and wild turkey were brought in. I had little time for hunting but did kill wild turkey along the North Canadian river, and had sighted deer not far away.

Frequent bands of friendly blanket Indians passed thru. Occasionally they camped several days. We could not converse with them freely but had a mutual understanding on some things. They gave us no trouble whatever, but we kept our eyes open to see that nothing of value was laying around loose to be carried off. We visited their camps to see them dance, a little of which was enjoyed for the novelty of the thing. I believe I can do some of their steps now.

There must have been a great many "sooners" in the country. We saw new faces all the time. They would come and go. No one knew where they were from or their ultimate destination.

Detachments of Cavalry from Fort Reno scoured the country to round up and deport the "sooners." We at the station generally knew about when a detachment was expected. We could tell by the scramble in getting to the depot. As many as a hundred tickets to Purcell for one train was sold. Purcell was the closest place of exit from the forbidden districts. When the raid was over they filtered back.

I believe the soldiers did their full duty on these raids but they had too much territory to cover. Some hardy persons defied the Cavalry but gained nothing by this. Those that did not take the railway were escorted out by the soldiers, if caught. I saw an old man (I'll not mention his name for obvious reasons) chopping wood near the postoffice as a blind. A Sergeant with a detail came after him. He tried to strike one of the soldiers with the axe, and was promptly knocked down by the Sergeant who used his fist only. He was carried away bodily and deported, but like the proverbial cat, he came back. As far as I could see no more force was used than was necessary.

Occasionally some timid fellow the boys called a "tenderfoot" would put up at one of our leading hotels, Radebaugh's or McGranahan's. The "mule-skinners" who happened to be in would start a "phoney" fight, or pretend to be shooting at each other to throw a scare into the new comer. They would adroitly engage the stranger in some trivial conversation. This would start a controversy and all would take sides, resulting in a make-believe riot.

I remember one such occasion when several of the boys came to me and outlined a little fun they intended to stage. The person they were after was the "runt," later christened "Insect"—I don't care to mention his real name as afterward he figured in Oklahoma matters, and became a citizen of the community. The plan was to run the victim over to the depot where I was to offer asylum, grab a gun and pretend to protect him. The play was carried out as scheduled, but it was a long time before the victim could be made to realize it was a put up job.

A Pioneer Railroad Agent

We had no banking facilities and the medium of exchange was good old United States currency. The Express Company was used freely for money-orders and in transporting money and valuables. Frequent transfers of money were necessary to supply a vast extent of country tributary to us. It was necessary to pay off the soldiers at Fort Reno, and money was needed for the Indian Agencies, and Post Traders. When Government money was handled it was usually met with an escort of Cavalry, but we received a good deal without such protection.

On one occasion at least the government failed with their escort. Evidently the cipher message was not received at the right time, or someone overlooked the matter. We had to hold thirty-five or forty thousand dollars for about a week, awaiting the escort. I knew the little safe we had offered no real protection, so I concealed the money in old rubber boots and rubbish underneath the counter, near where I slept. Not even the night operator knew we had it. All I can say is we were fortunate. The trains had been held up and robbed at other places, and it was known there were many bad men in the country.

The people for the most part were law-abiding and friendly, but there is no denying the fact that the Indian Territory then was a rendezvous for a vast number of criminals of every description. Some of them used to get supplies at Oklahoma, their names, of course, disguised. We received express addressed to Belle Star, and many such characters not locally known. (I have forgotten the names). Once an unknown person, well equipped with guns, inquired for certain packages, and after such identification as was necessary to prove ownership, signed up, then wrote

Oklahoma Memories

across the express book in bold letters "Texas Jack," saying "How are tricks Kid!" We greeted each other cordially and he disappeared never to be seen again by me. I always thought he was one of the desperadoes that infested the territory at that time.

Dealers in liquor from Kansas City and Texas did quite a business; they camouflaged the packages and shipped by express. Deputy marshals would raid us once in a while, and occasionally take some fellow before the United States Court at Wichita, but not often.

We bought most of our groceries at Arkansas City—but by reason of Purcell being close by, we would sometimes get supplies from that place. One day, I think it was in February, 1889, I went to Purcell on the afternoon train to make some small purchases, and expected to return on a freight train leaving about 8:00 P.M. I had forgotten something. The conductor told me I had plenty of time to go back for it. After I was gone he received orders to get out of town immediately.

I reached the depot as the tail lights of the train were fading away in the distance. I was certainly in a dilemma, there were no other trains until sometime next day. There were two or three trains of cattle to load at Oklahoma, and I had to be there. I tried to find someone who would take me back. It was very cold, and the ground covered in spots with fine sifting snow. I finally secured the service of a man by the name of Shepherd. He agreed to make the trip for twenty dollars. We started about nine o'clock. He had a buggy and two good horses. At intervals one of us would drive while the other walked. We had to do this to keep from freezing.

We got along pretty well until just after we crossed the Santa Fe tracks, about where Norman now stands, we lost the road. Some one sang out sharply, "Who are you, where you going—don't come this way or I will shoot." We said we were on our way to Oklahoma. We were directed how to find the road, which was not very distant. Sometimes we would get down on our hands and knees to be sure we were on the road. When we got to the North Canadian we had trouble in finding a suitable ford where we could get across. We arrived at daylight. I thawed out, drank some coffee, and went to work. The Superintendent who came in with first train to take stock, never knew I had been out all night.

A Pioneer Railroad Agent

Just before the country opened for settlement, there were many news writers gathering material for the press, some of which was highly colored. We hadn't many wires, and it taxed our capacity at times to handle these stories. The night operator and myself were kept busy sending copy—many times I worked way into the night helping the night operator clear this "trash" as we called it.

Shortly before the opening of Oklahoma there were four companies of Infantry stationed on the military reservation, in command of Lieutenant Colonel Snyder, and while the town was not placed strictly under martial law, Captain D. F. Stiles, at the opening of Oklahoma, acted as a sort of provost marshal. It was a wise provision of the government to afford us some military protection, as it served to restrain the lawless element and prevent riots and shedding of blood.

We were at the time without adequate laws for the proper control of the situation, and while in my opinion, there is hardly a parallel in the world's history for the restraint and self control exercised by these early settlers as a whole, there was at times great excitement and the people were under a constant strain. Sporadic instances of disorder did occasionally occur, and it was necessary for some arbitrary power to intervene.

With the permission of the War Department Mr. G. A. Biedler, commenced the erection of a small building near the railroad, about where Main Street now is, a day or two before the opening. He used this structure for the post-office, which he took over at that time.

Immediately after President Harrison's message was issued, March 23d, 1889, providing for the opening of the country on April 22d, everything commenced to take on a different aspect. There was plenty of excitement, and preparations were hurriedly made by the railroads to meet the expected abnormal conditions, and provide adequate facilities for handling the increased business. A new freight house was provided, and additional forces were being arranged. The bridges were guarded, watchmen were put on, and trains were policed. Mr. George L. Sands was general superintendent, and Mr. Avery Turner, division superintendent. On Sunday, the day before the opening, Mr. Sands was at Oklahoma a short time. We discussed the situation. He found that his suggestions had already been carried out and many other arrangements made of my own volition. Everyone was on his toes for the Grand Rush.

The day before the opening the Santa Fe Railway had just completed a well at the agent's cottage; also, arrangements were made with the drillers to put down a well at the intersection of Main and Broadway and one on Grand Avenue, to supply the needs of the people. These were the first wells established after the opening.

On that memorable day, April 22d, in order to get a better view, I stood on a box car along side the depot at the zero hour of 12 o'clock noon. My astonishment was complete—people seemed to spring up as if by magic as far as the eye could reach. I could see them racing in very direction, some on horses, some in vehicles, and a greater number on foot. They were carrying all sorts of impedimenta—some had spades, some stakes, some clothing, some had hand-bags, some had pots and pans, or other cooking utensils. My words are not adequate to describe the scene. I then commenced to realize that history was in the making.

About 2:10 P.M. the first train arrived from the South. It was loaded down—people were on the platforms—on top—and seemed to be everywhere. I believe there were two thousand persons on that train. The big rush was on in full. Other trains came and deposited their loads of human freight. A city was made in a day—tents sprang up everywhere, and that night as the stars were shining and some wary souls were going to rest, the sound of a distant voice rang out on the still air "Oh Joe, here's your mule." Another would take it up, and then another, until the whole world seemed to know that Joe's mule had been found.

Charles Chamberlain, with a corps of surveyors, was on the ground and at 12:00 o'clock noon commenced laying off the townsite. Such a scramble for town lots can hardly be imagined.

As a single townsite entry was restricted by law to three hundred twenty acres, there were not enough lots for all. This coupled with the fact that several townsite companies made surveys which had to be reconciled with each other, accounts for jogs and offsets in some of Oklahoma City's streets. Here was paved the way for disputes and almost endless litigation. In some cases there were several claimants for the same lot. Others ultimately found themselves in the street. There was all manners of trouble. I can't begin to describe the situation.

Although I had not reached the age of manhood, my work was strenuous. My force had been greatly increased. I had no legal rights to land, so why should I worry. I will leave to others the telling of the early struggles between the "Kickapoos," "Seminoles" and other factions. I was, however, acquainted with the principal actors in that drama.

I witnessed several near riots over the city organization and election matters. I saw the infantry troops under Captain Stiles, charge the crowds. A few were clubbed with guns or jabbed with bayonets, but none seriously hurt.

The water supply was a problem. We furnished all the water we could gratis from the railroad tank, but had to place a guard over it to keep the water from being wasted, even then the supply was exhausted. We had to haul water in our cars for a while.

The early days of Oklahoma City were little different from those of other frontier towns, with respect to gambling and its attendant evils. The "sure thing" men and "Knights of the Green Cloth" were on the job. They were open for business early and late. Their field of operation was not restricted. They seemed to have preempted all that territory along the railroad from Main Street to Reno Avenue, with a few places on Grand and California.

The soap man, the "chuck-a-luck" game, fan-tan, faro, roulette, three card monte, stud-poker, and even keno were much in evidence.

Dance halls and "honky tonks" were well patronized. The bright lights were burning and joy was unconfined. Bootleggers were there; booze, White Mule and Choctaw beer with a kick could be had, although the troops were active and did suppress a great deal of this traffic.

I don't know how many people came to Oklahoma City. Many thousands came and moved away in every direction. I believe we had a town of ten thousand when the sun went down that day.

The excitement continued at fever heat. Gradually order was brought out of chaos. People had to have supplies; household goods, furniture, stoves, building material, vehicles, farm implements, live stock, groceries, clothing, etc. Everything had to be brought in by the railroad. There was an urgent demand for freight, as you might well know. While the railroad had fully anticipated this, and did all possible to expedite shipments, the facilities for the time being were inadequate. There was not enough track room to hold the cars. The volume of business was only limited by the number of cars we could release from their lading each day. By the time one lot of cars was unloaded another would take its place. This state of affairs continued quite a while.

One of the principal commodities handled was lumber. If my memory serves me right we released one hundred five cars in one day. The lumber was disposed of as fast as it came from the cars. Dealers did a rushing business and could not supply the immediate demands. Many would buy it by the stick and by the arm full. They retailed lumber from cars.

The regular lumber dealers who early established themselves were fine fellows. We got along splendidly with them, but there were several "wild cat" outfits who were taking advantage of the peculiar conditions.

While we had watchmen patroling our yards, some one got away with four cars of lumber. We did not discover it until checking up at night. I had to have the bills of lading and the freight money amounting to several hundred dollars. The case looked hopeless.

I remembered a certain party who had been at the office several days before making inquiry as to his shipments of lumber. Early next morning I got hold of a deputy United States marshal and we started a search of town. After spending several hours, we were about to give the matter up for the time, when in going into one of the tents we found our man. I immediately recognized him. He at first denied all knowledge of the matter; we told him the United States commissioner was a friend of ours and would he mind accompanying us before that official; that the commissioner took a great interest in strangers and would no doubt give him the opportunity to recite some of his life's history. Well, he produced the bills of lading and peeled from his roll enough bills to satisfy my demands, and the transaction ended. He had enough money to start a bank. I never saw him again.

There were many other trying incidents during this formative period, wihch if I attempted to describe would take up too much of your time.

The early business men were honest and capable. They wanted only what was right and were willing to co-operate for the best interests of the town. It was a pleasure to know and do business with them.

Pimm & Banks, I believe had the first furniture store. They were also engaged in the undertaking business. One of them came to me and said he was preparing for shipment the body of a person who had been killed near Council Grove. He had no suitable place to keep it, and asked permission to let the casket rest in our freight house until train time the next day. I reluctantly assented and it was placed in one end of the building. It was quite impossible to find

A Pioneer Railroad Agent

suitable lodging, so a few of our force slept on cots and improvised bunks in the freight room. I came along with a lantern just before daylight, and to my surprise found these fellows had put one end of the bed springs on the box containing the casket, the other end rested on some smaller boxes. Their astonishment and chagrin was complete, when it was found they had been peacefully slumbering with the dead.

I must say something about the first railroad built into Oklahoma City after the opening. It was the Choctaw, Oklahoma and Gulf, afterward absorbed and now a part of the Rock Island. It was promoted by E. D. Chadick, who was, I believe, its first president. Preliminary surveys were made before the opening of Oklahoma, and Mr. Chadick left sums of money with me to pay the surveyors at intervals. Its first agent at Oklahoma City was Roll H. Dorsey, who had worked under me at the time of the opening.

The townsite board and land office was kept busy, and furnished most of the excitement. After a while a re-action set in and Oklahoma City saw several dull years. Contests and litigation, I believe, was partly responsible for this. It was a big drain on the purse of the people. Large sums for permanent improvements were not available. Titles had to be perfected to get money for large enterprises.

Everyone took an interest in the several capital fights and there were indeed some hot times. I remember once when it was proposed to send a train load of our citizens to Guthrie to protect our legislators, but cooler heads prevailed. It would only have led to trouble and possible bloodshed.

It is surprising how people under adverse circumstances got together for the common good. Churches, schools, societies of all kinds, and organizations for public benefit, were functioning. They soon commenced to make preparations for the first Fourth of July celebration. It was advertised far and near, and the trains brought in good crowds. The citizens attended en masse. A large grand stand was erected on the military reservation, bordering on what was later Maywood. There were horse races, roping contests,

Indian dances, and some athletic stunts. Public speakers were provided, in fact, the plans contemplated a first class celebration.

A Pioneer Railroad Agent

The grand stand was crowded to the limit. As the crowd had just gotten comfortably seated, the whole structure collapsed without warning. A good many were hurt. Dr. Ryan's child was killed. I was sitting near the top with two other companions. All three of us were covered with wreckage. I suffered no injury, but had my coat badly torn, the one next to me wearing a Derby hat, had the top cut off, causing his black bushy hair to show thru the top of the hat. The other was one of the boys from my office. He was injured so badly that we carried him to a dray. I took him to my home where his injuries were examined by the doctor; recovery, however was rapid, as no bones were broken. The next day several of the injured were taken out on the train. One poor fellow occupying a cot, was put in the baggage car. He had both legs broken.

The opening of Oklahoma came so late that the first year afforded little opportunity to prepare the ground and raise crops, and many had come from places where crops were poor. The second year saw a crop failure. This left some of the settlers in a deplorable condition; they had a hard time. They displayed a fortitude, courage and tenacity of purpose, worthy the best traditions of our time.

Appeals were sent out for aid. The Santa Fe and the Rock Island furnished seed wheat to the farmers at actual cost on notes given, requiring payment the following year. I was custodian of these notes in the Oklahoma City district, and looked after their collection. Let it be said that most of the notes were paid. I feel sure the makers of the unpaid notes would have met their obligation had it been at all possible for them to have done so.

I lived in Oklahoma City for some years after this, I saw the city grow in size and importance. I saw peace, prosperity and happiness all around. Many of those who bore the hardships and weathered the storm were abundantly rewarded. All honor to the old settlers who blazed the way for the making of this great commonwealth. They had the same love of country, the same ideals, and are worthy descendents of those heroic souls who carried the banner of civilization across the continent to the golden West. In this day and age, when all of Europe and most of the world is in the throes of trouble, when discord and strife is the order of the day, where money is worthless, suffering and starvation on every hand, it is well for us to pause and reflect on our own state of affairs.

The Opening of Oklahoma

¶ *In the 1870s and 1880s Oklahoma was a Cattle Kingdom in an Empire of Grass, but its lifespan was brief. Each time settlers on the Great Plains began to feel crowded or experienced hailstorms or grasshopper plagues their eyes turned toward Indian Territory. And with each glance, the antagonism between the cowman and the nester that characterized the history of America's westward movement flared again.* ¶ *By the time this old struggle centered on Oklahoma, the seemingly endless frontier was almost gone. The Indian could move no farther. There was no great green pasture left where ranchers could escape with their herds. Without new land, collision between the conflicting life-styles of the sedentary homesteader and the wide-ranging cattleman was inevitable. The homesteaders eventually overpowered the cattlemen numerically and politically. Although some cowboys stayed around for the excitement of the land openings, and some took up claims, most of them drifted on.* ¶ *Evan G. Barnard was one who stayed. The son of a Presbyterian minister from Pennsylvania, "Parson" Barnard grew up in Muscatine, Iowa, an avid reader of "yellow backed novels of the Wild West." When a neighbor purchased the Circle J H Ranch near Seymour, Texas, Barnard signed on as a line rider. Over the years various jobs, each offering better pay or in a new setting, took him throughout western Indian Territory. When the Unassigned Lands were opened in 1889, Barnard and some fellow cowboys decided to join the race for a claim "as a chance to make a little easy money." His memoir reveals a freewheeling cowboy who suddenly comprehended the point of view of the man who had a family and "knew what a home meant."* ¶ *Most of Barnard's friends secured claims in that famous land rush but quickly sold them for a profit and moved on. He remained and became a successful farmer, then was agricultural*

From Evan G. Barnard, *A Rider of the Cherokee Strip* (Boston: Houghton Mifflin Company, 1936), 138–48.

agent for the railroad, and finally became an organizer for the Grange.

AFTER YEARS of trying to settle Oklahoma by Captain David L. Payne and his boomers and Captain Couch, a bill passed Congress in 1889 opening it for settlement on April 22 of that year. President Cleveland signed the bill, and it was decided to open the country under the homestead laws; all people entering Oklahoma with a view of selecting locations before that time would be considered "sooners," and have no right to homestead any of the land. It was decided to let the people gather at the border around Oklahoma. The first man on the land was the one to homestead it. Soldiers were scouting the country all the time to keep out sooners, or anyone trying to locate on the land.

Thousands of people gathered along the border during the month of April and camped, waiting for the opening day. Soldiers were on guard, and brought sooners out now and then. The cowpunchers had worked the country for years and knew where they wanted to settle. They had good horses and knew how to ride them. As the day for the race drew near, the settlers practiced running their horses and driving carts, and every kind of rattletrap vehicle that could go.

The people grouped up in bunches, and each bunch thought it had someone to guide them who knew where to find the best land in Oklahoma. Any evening after supper one could go for miles along the line of the north border, south of where Enid now stands, and find people holding meetings in groups, discussing the manner in which they would take their claims. As soon as a stranger came near they talked about something else. We cowpunchers had much amusement watching these people who had never been in Oklahoma before, as we listened to them tell how they were going to take their claims.

We were bunched in a group by ourselves like the others,

and had decided before the country was to be opened where we would locate. This was on Big Turkey Creek, northwest of Red Fork Branch, now called Dover. We knew every trail and just where we wanted to go. We knew our horses would take us there as quickly as anyone could go. So we were having a good time watching the other people make their preparations.

One of our number, called "Ranicky Bill," said, "Fellows, if we can't outrun that bunch of nesters and haymaking horses, I go back to Old Mexico."

While watching some of the people running their horses, he remarked: "By golins, look at that old hill-billy nester riding a string-halted-dray-horse over there. His only trouble will be that when he gets started, that 'ar horse will never stop. He'll just run clear through Oklahoma."

The morning of the twenty-second, the people hustled around camp making arrangements for their wagons to follow them with their camp outfits, in order that they might have their supplies. As the hour drew nearer, the people gathered along the line held by the soldiers. They rode the border lines and kept the people from crossing into Oklahoma. Now and then we saw some soldier scouts bringing sooners out of Oklahoma who had slipped into the country the night before, and many faces that had been seen the day before the race were missing. We know that many sooners were already there.

Our plan was to stick together, and to stick after we got our claims. We knew where we wanted to go, but knew nothing whatever about the number of the sections or quarter-sections, township or range. That was Greek to the cowpunchers. We wanted bottom land on the creek where we would have wood and water and pasture. We wanted no wells to dig, and no wood to haul, at least for any great distance. But the cowpunchers knew about as much about the markings on the cornerstones as a nester would know about a totem pole in Alaska.

At ten o'clock the people lined up along the line ready for the great race of their lives, racing for a home of one hundred and sixty acres of land. We cowpunchers had never farmed, and looked at settling down on a farm just as a chance to make a little easy money. Consequently, we were not as much excited as some of the other people, who had families and knew what a home meant. All tried to get as near the front line as possible and the soldiers were kept busy holding the people back.

The starting signals were to be given by the soldiers by firing their six-shooters at twelve o'clock, noon. As far as the eye could see east and west, people were lined up and soldiers rode back and forth. The minutes were counted by these thousands of people, who were to take part in the greatest race of all time.

The men on horses were lined up in front, then the wagons and buggies and carts. Supply wagons followed behind. At twelve o'clock the soldiers fired the volley all along the lines and the race was on. The noise made by so many horses and wagons and rattletraps bumping over the prairies, and the yelling of the crowd, made a rumbling noise which sounded very much like ten thousand head of cattle on a stampede.

Gradually the noise died away as the people scattered. The men riding horses were soon far in the lead. We cowpunchers, riding as if we were trying to head off a wild steer, had nine or ten miles to go to get to our claims. Many others rode as fast as we, but we knew that it took the best of cow-horses to stand the pace we were going.

Ranicky Bill on his great Mexican pony "Blue Dog" was setting the pace, and we were sure our horses would hold out. Most of us had been over the ground many times before.

After the first three miles the riders were much more scattered. Many had stopped and taken their claims. We had our stakes marked and ready to drive into the ground as soon as we jumped off our horses. We followed the old Kiowa Trail until we got to Big Turkey Creek; then some of the boys stopped and staked their claims. This was some eight miles from the line, and from there on we left the trail and went down the creek bottom. As each cowpuncher came to the location he had selected as a spot where we would like to settle, he fell off his horse and staked his claim. We took fifteen quarter-sections of land. Then the real trouble of holding our claims began.

Just staking a claim did not hold it. We had to let many others, who claimed they had done the same thing, know we were the first ones on the claims. Hundreds of people were passing, and we kept busy riding like the devil seeing to it that others did not stop on our claims.

The creek ran through the claim I took and men came from the west side of the creek and claimed they settled there. I stopped on the east side of the claim, which was all prairie; the west side was timber. It was necessary to out-talk the other man, and if we thought he was a sooner, we told him so, and stayed with it.

One old man, riding a big gray mule, came through the brush about five minutes after I settled on the claim, and I saw him driving a stake. I rode up and asked him what he was doing. He said, "Staking this claim."

I jumped off my horse, pulled up the stake, and called Ranicky Bill, who was near. He came over and I gave him the stake. Ranicky Bill asked the man what country he was from, that he thought he could ride a damned old mule bareback and beat cowpunchers in a ten-mile race.

"Hell," he said, "I bet you have to get a guide to find your way back to where your wagon is."

We told him to look some other place for a claim and he left. Just then another man came up to me and said he had seen me when I got off my horse and that he was on the claim as soon as I was. He said we would have to divide it up, he to take eighty acres and I to take eighty. I told him it was a hundred and sixty acres or six feet, and I did not give a damn which it was. One of the boys told the man that if he fooled with that kid he would get punctured, that I had a Winchester pump shotgun, and it was loaded with buckshot. I also had a six-shooter. Everyone was armed. The man soon left.

Then I saw two men near the creek and rode down to them. One man with a Winchester rifle across his arm said, "I'll stay with you till hell freezes over."

I told him he would have plenty of company, there or any other place, and he and his partner left. I was kept busy telling people to move on; that there was bottom land ten miles wide and twenty miles long just over the ridge. We told them anything to keep them going and get them away from our claims. And away they went, riding big farm-horses with pots and pans tied to their saddles. I felt sorry for some of the poor devils, and did not have much time for others. It was necessary to watch our claims, stay with our partners, and make the "buffaloes" we ran, stick.

Two men had already built a dugout right on the line between my claim and Ranicky Bill's, the line running through the center of the dugout. One slept on his claim on the south side of the dugout, and the other on the north side of the other claim. These men stayed around several days and thought I was not old enough to take a claim. I convinced them that I was, however, and when they saw the backing I had among the cowboys, they left.

The first place I stopped, I just pulled one of my saddleblankets out from under my saddle and threw it over a small bush. After some hours there, I moved my stake some three hundred yards down the creek, and by four o'clock I moved it three hundred yards still farther down the creek where there was a great big burr-oak tree, with a great bushy top, some seventy feet across and trunk six feet thick. Here I started to dig my dugout. As I was digging, I saw four men crossing my claim on the south, between me and Ranicky Bill's place, I jumped on my horse and rode up to where they were and asked them what they were doing. I saw they had a tapeline and compass. They said they would not bother me, and that they were just trying to locate school land. They ran the line to the creek and went on west.

All the boys were kept busy keeping people off their claims. Some of them had company that said they would stay with them. Ranicky and I dug two holes near the line of his claim and mine as though we were starting to dig wells. We dug these four feet deep and had the dirt piled up all around the edge. We intended to use these for rifle-pits if we got into a hot scrap.

Ranicky said, "By godlins, if they get me out of there, they'll have to shoot me out like they would shoot a prairie dog out of his hole."

People in great numbers traveled down the Big Turkey Creek valley during the twenty-second day of April, the day the country opened for settlement. The grass was six to eight inches high, and there was not a sign of a trail in the bottom. By night there were ruts a foot deep worn down by the wagons and by people passing down the valley. At sun down they were still passing in great numbers.

I was getting terribly hungry, and looked for a small sack that I had tied behind my saddle which contained some jerked beef and bread, but it was gone. I had lost it, and

Ranicky had eaten his. I saw a light south of Ranicky's place and we rode down there. I asked the lady there who was washing supper dishes if she could give me something to eat. It was not long until I had a good supper. These people were from Nebraska, and their name was Vance.

Lights flickered all over the country from the campfires of the settlers. It was a great change for the cowpunchers to see this great cattle country transformed in a day from a region with thousands of cattle to one with thousands of people moving about. We wondered what they would do to make a living.

The night of the twenty-second we all got together and talked over the conditions in regard to the claims, and those who had others on them who were also claiming them. We decided to select from our members a committee to look after claim-jumpers.

On the south line of the Cherokee Strip, just southwest of the old town of Bison, where Big Turkey Creek enters Old Oklahoma, we cowpunchers had gathered to make the race. Pawnee Bill, the famous Indian Scout and frontiersman, was close to us and had organized quite a band of home-seekers, and was to lead them to the most desirable claims in the big bottom since he was very familiar with the country. It presented a most bewildering situation for those unfamiliar with the country, because before them lay over fifty miles of raw prairie land without a road or path, or a fence or landmark of any kind. Almost everyone had the erroneous idea that the best land was just a little farther down in the country. I understood that Pawnee Bill was most successful in locating his followers on choice claims. Anyone having a knowledge of that country at that time possessed a very valuable asset, and his services were at a premium and he was in demand. Pawnee Bill happened to be one of those lucky fellows.

A man by the name of Van Buskirk, in some way, was a little slow in getting a claim on the twenty-second, on Little Turkey Creek. Another man was camped there too, and declared he was the first one there by two hours. Perhaps he was right, but we wanted Van Buskirk to have that claim. We held a council and arranged a system of calling on the gentleman.

Two of us rode up to the man's camp and inquired for stray horses. He told us he had not seen any. Then we asked him which way he was moving. He told us it was his claim that he had staked it.

We said, "Partner, you are a stranger to us, but if we were called as a witness, we would be compelled to swear that that man camped down the creek was the first man we saw on the claim."

This method was followed until fully a dozen men had called on him and told him the same thing.

We all said, "You men are both strangers to us, and we have no interest in the land one way or other, but the truth is we know which one of you we saw on the claim first."

This man was from Kansas, and knew he was right in his claim, but what could he do with such odds against him?

Finally he told Van Buskirk that he would sell out to him for seventy-five dollars, which sum was paid.

"If I had half the backing that you have, I would stay with you until hell froze over," he said to Van Buskirk, and personally I'll bet he would.

He left the claim and Ranicky Bill remarked, "Hit's sure hell to get things regulated in a new country."

From Fighters to Freighters

¶ *Carl Sweezy, the Arapaho painter, witnessed the disappearance of the "buffalo road" of his ancestors as white settlers flooded into the Indians' domain. One of the first native American painters to use watercolor paints and paper as a way of preserving tribal memories and legends, Sweezy created a matchless pictorial record of the Arapaho way. Although a catalog of Arapaho dress, religious life, games, burial customs, and even household equipment, his paintings are much more than ethnological curiosities. Their artistic vitality transcends the act of merely recording an exotic subject matter.* ¶ *Whatever in Arapaho life Sweezy failed to capture in his paintings, he preserved in his memoirs. He evoked the affection and security that an Indian child felt as a part of a large, extended family. His word portrait of the Arapaho housewife who combined the skills of architect and builder, gardener, cook, laundress, seamstress, and hostess erases the white man's stereotype of the Indian squaw. As Sweezy's scribe, Althea Bass skillfully allows the Arapaho painter to speak directly and simply. And his words are indeed "a link between the old, free-roaming buffalo days and the modern Arapaho who lives much as his white neighbors."* ¶ *In this selection, Sweezy shows how Arapaho warriors used their natural talents to adjust to the restrictions of reservation life. He also explores the life of Indians embarking on the "corn road," designed by white policymakers to transform migratory Indian hunters into settled dirt farmers. Sweezy's account is poignant. It is the story of a way of life coming to an end and of a people drawing upon their traditions to survive. "Neither we nor our dogs nor our ponies understood this new way of white people," Sweezy begins. "To us it seemed unsociable and lonely, and not the way people were meant to live."*

From Althea Bass, *The Arapaho Way: A Memoir of an Indian Boyhood* (New York: Clarkson N. Potter, 1966) 38–48.

WHEN WE first sat down on the Reservation, the Agents and those who directed them in Washington expected all the Arapaho men to become farmers. There was plenty of rich land, and they expected each man to choose ground wherever he wanted it within our boundaries and settle down. But the Arapaho had always lived in bands, with their tipis side by side, their horses grazing together, and with hunting and fighting and feasting and worship all carried on by the group. It took years to learn to settle down on a farm and work alone and see one's neighbors only once in a while. Neither we nor our dogs nor our ponies understood this new way of white people. To us it seemed unsociable and lonely, and not the way people were meant to live.

Even our tribal leaders, great men at hunting and fighting and conducting social gatherings and religious ceremonies, knew nothing about how to prepare ground or what seed to plant and when to plant it, or how to plant and cultivate the harvest and store the crops. Those of us who were boys and were taught farming and dairying in the schools had a better chance to learn than our fathers had. We could grow up with the new idea. But even we had some problems in our education as farmers, for the country was new to the Agents and the teachers and the other employees. Sometimes all the corn failed, because of heat and drought; sometimes grasshoppers and locusts swept in and ate up everything. After a few years, the Agents and the Agency farmers were ready to admit that cattle raising and dairying were better, on most of our land, than raising corn and oats.

Some of our boys and men were learning other things besides farming. Mr. Seger had built a brick plant, where some of the men of both of our tribes learned to mix and mold and fire brick. Once in a while, some fellow who was good at molding would challenge the others to a public contest, with a prize put up for the winner by the editor of the *Cheyenne Transporter* or by one of the traders. That made a good game out of a hard job, and was great sport. We had always had contests of skill and strength in the old days, and we enjoyed them. And we made good bricks. Some of the buildings still standing, on the old Agency grounds and at the Mennonite Mission, are built of them.

We learned to cut and store hay, too. We had always moved our horses from one place to another, summer and winter, for good grazing; now we learned to move the grass to the horses and to store it in stacks or in bales. This was new to us, but we saw how it worked. Our ponies no longer grew weak and lean in winter, when snow and ice covered the dried grass. If there were good rains, the prairies and the hay fields could be cut not once but several times during the season. It was something we could hardly believe. We saw that the men who taught us were smart, and had a new kind of power. Brinton Darlington himself had begun putting up hay on the Agency farm, and showing us how and why it should be done. He taught us to prepare for a hard winter every year, instead of hoping and making medicine for a mild one.

What astonished us more than anything else was learning that the white man cut and stored ice in winter, for use in summer. That was before he had gone still farther and invented machinery to make ice the year around, instead of storing it. At the Agency they built a thick-walled storage house, and when the ponds and streams were frozen solid they sawed the ice into blocks, hauled it in, and packed it in sawdust from the Agency sawmill. We never heard of ice in summer before. It would have seemed like strong medicine, if we had not seen for ourselves how it was done. But when the next summer came, and some of the Indians drank the white man's iced lemonade, and when we tasted his ice cream, we knew that the white man had more schemes for comfort and good living than we had ever dreamed of.

Gradually, a good many of us, especially older boys and young men, came to be employed at the Agency, if we had learned to do some kind of work that was needed there. A few who had gone to Hampton or Carlisle, or later to Haskell Institute, and were good at the kind of learning that comes from books, interpreted for one tribe or the other, or worked in the commissary or in the brickyard or at the

From Fighters to Freighters

sawmill. I worked in the dairy at Darlington and later at other Indian schools, for I liked livestock and I had learned from the Mennonites in the mission school at Darlington and later at Halstead, Kansas, how to feed and care for them. Now and then, for some of the men not working regularly, there were jobs like cutting hay on the prairie, or building and mending fences, or cutting firewood and fence posts.

I have always been glad that as a boy and a young man I had the kind of schooling I had. It brought me back to the Reservation again, each time after I had been away, and gave me employment at one place or another among my own people. When my school days and my travels as a young man were over, I came to Rainy Mountain to take charge of the livestock at that Government school. It was there that I met Hattie Powless, a Oneida who was a matron there. Like the Arapaho, the Oneida like to sing, and have many beautiful songs. We became friends, and later we were married. We never had a permanent farm home of our own, or even a permanent home in town somewhere, because we lived at whatever school or mission employed me and where she, too, was sometimes employed as matron or housekeeper. Our four children, three sons and one daughter, though they were half Oneida, always thought of themselves as Arapaho, or at least as Plains Indians, because it was among these Indians that they grew up.

After we left Rainy Mountain we went to Saint Patrick's, the Roman Catholic Mission near Anadarko. Father Isidore was in charge there, and the children and the employees all liked him very much. Sometimes in the evenings, the Episcopal minister from the church at Anadarko would ride out for a visit with him. These two spent long evenings together, and one of the things they liked to talk about was horses and horse racing. That kind of talk was enough to please any Indian.

My wife came from the country around Green Bay, Wisconsin, and like most of the Indians there she was an Episcopalian. Years after we were married, we went back to visit her relatives at Green Bay. There were doctors and lawyers and businessmen among those Indians there, and I was proud of her people and of what they had accomplished, just as I am proud of the Arapaho. We went to the Episcopal church there, and the singing was fine. Since her death I have had no real home of my own, but I always find some place where I can live and paint and keep in touch with my family and my Indian and white friends.

All this was a long way from the buffalo road we had once traveled. But much of it was beyond us at first, and without training and time enough to learn to understand it we could not follow it. I have heard of groups of white people who have gone to Mexico or South America to take up a new road of their own and have failed in it and come back to their old homes to start over again. But we had no home to go back to; we could only follow the old road as long as it lasted, while we learned the direction of the new one.

Buffalo herds still roamed on the Reservation during our first few years there; and twice a year, as in the old free days, the Cheyenne set out on their buffalo hunt and we on ours. Both tribes held their buffalo dances before they set out, and got their bows and arrows and knives and guns ready for use. The women struck the tipis, packed the lodge poles and robes and kettles and parfleches on travoises drawn by the gentlest of our horses, and "went to buffalo." It was not an easy life, but it was a fine one: men, women, children, dogs, and horses moving together across land that had no roads or fences; temporary camps set up where grass was fresh and water plenty; hunting along the way, for deer and quail and turkey and prairie chicken and wild fruits and nuts to live on until they came to buffalo.

When a herd was sighted, the real action began. Men in breechcloths and moccasins jumped on their fastest, smartest horses, and all of them, circling and yelling, made the big surround. Heavy as they were, the buffalo were fast and hard to kill. When a herd was on the run, it was like thunder rolling over the ground too fast and furious to stop. If a man's horse stumbled, he might be trampled to death by the running herd. But the men could ride like the wind, and their horses, without the extra weight of a saddle and a man's heavy clothing, were as quick and smart as their riders. It was more of a game than football or polo is. It covered more ground and brought bigger results. Everything we were to have to eat and wear and shelter us for the next six months depended on it.

Every hunter, picking his buffalo, tried to circle in such a way as to send his arrow or his bullet just back of the buffalo's left shoulder, so as to reach his heart. But the hide was tough, and the animal was running and plunging and pawing, and the whole herd was running with him, getting into the hunter's way. Often the best a hunter could do was to send an arrow into the animal's hide, between the hump and the shoulder, crippling him. Then another arrow, or a bullet, could be sent to the heart. When the buffalo that had been shot were down and the rest of the herd had thundered away, the women and children moved in, and skinning and butchering and feasting began. It was the women who were busy then, while the men rested and ate and told stories of this and other hunting days.

We never killed more buffalo than we could use, to eat and to bring back in the form of hides and robes, dried meat and pemmican and tallow. So, we believed, the Indians and the buffalo would hold out together as long as grass grew. It was white men who slaughtered buffalo without limit, and brought our long-traveled buffalo road to an end. Some of them killed whole herds, for no reason except that they wanted to be rid of them. Men who built railroads and those who wanted to establish farms and towns had no use for them. A good many of these men had no use for Indians either, and the Indians and the buffalo were disappearing together.

The last of our hunts, before Reservation days began, were fights with white men as well. We hated the white men who slaughtered bulls and cows and calves alike and left them to rot on the prairies, and whenever we found them at it we attacked them. They had wagons and mules and camp gear to set up as barricades, and more ammunition than we had. But our horses were better trained than theirs, and we were better riders and sometimes better marksmen. Still, there were too many white men crossing the country to get to California, settling on the land to farm it, and building railroads and bridges. Each year the herds grew fewer and smaller, and our scouts went farther in search of them. By the time of the Medicine Lodge treaty, we had seen signs that the day had come when there would be no more buffalo. We wanted to believe what we had always believed, that the buffalo came up out of a hole in the ground somewhere out on the western Plains and that if we held our dances and used the buffalo as we had been taught to do, there would always be more. But our medicine was gradually losing its power.

After we came to the Reservation, we could not hunt beyond its boundaries. For a few years we still had good hunts, and came in with plenty of meat and robes and hides. The white people at the Agency thought we were irresponsible and lazy, when we left our gardens and field crops to go on the summer hunt, or when we took our children from school to go in winter time. But buffalo came first, in our minds, as long as any were left; we "went to buffalo" when buffalo were plenty, not when crops were laid by or schools dismissed. And since the promised Government issues of food and calico and lodge cloth were often delayed, so that we went cold and hungry while we waited, it is small wonder that, among the older people especially, the buffalo road seemed the one to follow. When I was growing up, old people on the Reservation still remembered those last buffalo hunts as the best thing they had ever known. Sometimes the Indians found white people within the Reservation boundaries, illegally shooting deer and antelope and turkey and prairie chickens, cutting our timber, stealing our horses and cattle. Even then we could not make war on the trespassers because we had pledged ourselves to peace, and the Agents reported that, considering the situation, the crimes we committed were very few. The last good buffalo hunt on the Reservation was in 1874. The next winter was very cold; the hunt was a failure; our lodge skins were worn out and our ponies thin for want of grazing; our annuity goods were long delayed; there was much sickness and hunger and death. Even the Cheyenne, most of whom had refused to send their children to school until then, began to see that they must take the new road. The old one had come to an end.

The white people at the Agency were learning something too. They were learning that we could not become farmers overnight because we were told to, and that we had strength and energy that must be used. Strong men, once horsemen and hunters and fighters, could not sit down in idleness without becoming sullen and discontented. Then Agent Miles, with some of our leaders, worked out a plan for the Cheyenne and the Arapaho to become freighters. There were no railroads to bring in what was needed at the Fort and the Agency to stock the traders' stores; there were no wagon roads that could properly be called roads. The freighting of goods and food from Kansas had always been a slow, hard, risky job, carried on by men driving teams of mules or oxen. The freighter had to be ready to stand all kinds of weather, summer or winter, eating camp food, fording rivers, fighting prairie fires. We Indians were used to bad weather and camp life, and we had hundreds of ponies that were idle. Mr. Miles believed that we could become freighters. Many white people understood us so little that they thought we would run away with the freight, or lose or damage it on the road, or use the time away from home to start an uprising. But we were honorable and responsible, and we hadn't lived by hunting and trading over the Great Plains for hundreds of years for nothing.

The trail the freighters followed could not be called a road. It was over the old Chisholm Trail for most of the way. This was a cattle trail, wide and dusty or muddy most of the time, and slow for wagon travel whenever cattle were being driven along it. About thirty miles of our route, from Darlington north to Dover, ran a few miles west of the

Chisholm Trail and was known as the Traders' Trail. From Darlington, it was one hundred and ten miles to Caldwell, one hundred and thirty-five to Arkansas City, and one hundred and sixty-five to Wichita. These were the points in Kansas where freight for Darlington was loaded. Sometimes Arapaho made the trip and sometimes Cheyenne, but we never combined. Usually one of our village chiefs was in charge of a train, because he was a leader and knew the men under him. At least one member of the Indian police went along with each train, to act with the chief as leader and to be in authority when they reached the town where they picked up their loads. They were off the Reservation then, and someone in authority must be responsible for them. Sometimes there were only five or six teams to a train, and sometimes there were thirty or forty, depending on the amount of freight to be hauled. A train in ordinary weather could cover from twenty-five to thirty miles a day; but if there was mud or snow or trouble with wagons or horses or flooded streams to cross, no one could tell how long a trip might take. The Government furnished wagons and harness, until the men driving the teams had earned enough to pay for them; after that, each man owned his outfit. He had furnished his own horses from the beginning.

These horses knew how to race and turn on the track of a steer, or how to draw a travois on the march, but to most of them freighting was new. They had never hauled a wagon, and they didn't like harness. Four horses, hitched two and two, made a team; the two ahead were called leaders and the two behind were called wheelers. They were not guided by lines fastened to bridles, the way a white man's workhorses were; instead, the drivers rode on other horses at the sides of a team to guide them. By yelling and cracking their whips and pushing the horses along, they kept them going forward over the trail. Usually, too, the wives of the drivers went along, sitting on the wagon seat or in the wagon itself in their fine, bright clothes, yelling at the horses and visiting with one another as they moved along. Even the horses were decorated for the trip, with bright red or yellow or

From Fighters to Freighters

green cloth braided into their manes and tails. Altogether, it was a busy, noisy, good-natured undertaking, which everyone enjoyed because it was a little like the old marches when a village moved or a party went out to hunt, and because when the freight was brought safely in to Darlington or Fort Reno there was money to spend afterward.

Everybody went into action when there was a stream to ford. The horses hated to go down the slippery banks into the water, and a good deal of yelling and shoving was needed to keep them going and to bring them up the grade on the other side. If the river was in flood, the driver and the women and children as well as the horses had to swim; and if the horses balked at the high water, everybody yelled and whacked and pushed and pulled till they were in up to their shoulders and had to swim. The goods in the wagon bed, high up above the wheels, were almost never damaged by water, but they would have been if the drivers hadn't kept the horses under control and known just where to make the best crossing. Anybody that couldn't swim or handle frightened horses or camp in cold and rain until ice melted or floods went down, had no business on a freighting trip. But there were wonderful days and nights on the road, as well as bad ones; sometimes there was a fine supper of turkey or quail or deer or land terrapin around the campfire; and always there was the good feeling of being outdoors with the sun and the moon and the changing seasons and the woods and grass and streams.

Once, when I was a little boy, I went on a freighting trip with my father, who was one of the Arapaho police. This was a short trip that took a little less than four days, to Oklahoma City where there was then a railroad and where some of the goods once hauled from Kansas could now be shipped. I remember the canvas-covered wagons bumping along, and the men riding and visiting by the side of the wagons, and the women and children tumbled together inside. Even the prairies between Darlington and Oklahoma City looked big to me then, with the sun shining high overhead and the North Canadian River turning and winding like a wide green band through the country. I remember a spot near Banner where there were big trees for shade, and grass and water for our ponies, and wood for fire. We made our nooning there. On the return trip, when we had camped for the night by the side of the trail, a summer storm came up, with thunder and lightning and heavy rain. The horses were frightened and plunged around in their hobbles, and the men worked for hours tightening up the canvas covers on the wagons and shifting the goods around to keep them from getting wet. I was inside one of the wagons, lying on a big box, and I was as badly scared as the horses were. I lay quiet and kept my fears to myself, as any Indian boy knew how to do, but I thought what it must be like to go on a trip, two weeks or more, to Wichita and back, with wider rivers to ford and with no warm lodge walls to shelter me for many nights. Anyhow, we got our loads in to Darlington the next day after the storm, without any damage to any of the goods. It was fine to pull in to the Agency with ponies running, wagons creaking and swinging, drivers yelling, and everybody running out from buildings to hear the news of the trip. I never went with the freighters again, for by the time I was old enough to go as a driver the railroad had been built to El Reno and freighting was about over.

There were more than two hundred and fifty wagons hauling freight when the business was at its height. Sometimes, in a year of freighting, with over a million pounds hauled, there was a perfect record of no damage or loss. The pay was not much, a dollar a hundredweight. Divided among the heads of all the families that had had a part in the hauling, I suppose that might be considered very poor pay. But we needed less then than people need today, and money bought more. Even a penny bought something then. And besides, we weren't freighting just for the pay we got, but for some of the kind of satisfaction that we once got out of hunting and fighting. The Agents began to trust the Cheyenne and the Arapaho then, when they saw what we could do year after year as freighters. There was almost no drinking and gambling on those trips, though the white people in Kansas put plenty of chances for those things in our way. The influence of Little Raven, even after his death, was strong against drinking and gambling, and men like White Cloud had the same kind of influence among the Cheyenne.

Sometimes the freighters had a load both ways. Some of the Arapaho cut fence posts to haul up to Kansas to sell, for fencing was being done everywhere up there, and there was always a sale for posts. Sometimes the women took along handwork that they had done to sell—embroidered shirts and moccasins and children's toys. Traders and travelers in Kansas had begun to ask for these things, and they sold well if we had an interpreter along to help us understand what kind of bargain we were making. Now and then, a group of Indian boys and girls on the way to school in Kansas or in the East, with interpreters and school matrons and parents, rode up in the wagons to some point where they could take the train. This was slower travel for them than by the Darlington stagecoach, but it was more sociable and there was no fare to pay.

Once in a while, we were cheated in what we bought or sold, and on a few trips some of our ponies were stolen while we were in town loading our wagons, but we got through without any fights. We kept out of trouble and we brought our freight in. We had given our word.

A Drummer's Early-Day Experience

¶ *The drummer was the frontier's equivalent of the modern traveling salesman. Enterprising and fearless souls, these men usually represented the great mercantile houses of Kansas City, Chicago, or St. Louis that supplied their samples and expense money and gave them a small percent of the profit. The drummer was the crucial link between the small, often isolated merchant, the railroad, and the wholesaler. A romantic figure singing the praises of the latest cure-all, displaying the daring fashions in ladies bonnets, or demonstrating the newest labor saving device, his very presence helped relieve the monotony and drabness of pioneering.* ¶ *J. W. Pryer, a patent medicine salesman for a Topeka, Kansas, firm traveled throughout the Twin Territories in the last decade of the nineteenth century. He seems to have encountered every aspect of Oklahoma's changeable weather as well as some of her more undesirable, though colorful, early residents. Through it all he kept his humor and realism.*

TIME, summer of 1875; place, the old farm school house at Brown's Corner, Eagle township, Clinton county, Michigan.

The tall red complexioned youth excitedly makes this statement, "As soon as I am old enough I shall go there and fight Indians and kill buffaloes." "I'll not," says the small freckled faced boy, and these two chums took a decided issue on the subject in hand. The cause of this youthful difference of opinion was an article in Monteith's Geography on the Indian Territory, describing it as a part of the Great Desert, subject to cyclones and sand storms, inhabited by Indians and outlaws, buffaloes and wild beasts.

From J. W. Pryer, "A Drummer's Early-Day Experience." *Strum's Statehood Magazine*, 6 (March 1908), 51–56.

Oklahoma Memories

How little we really know at the age of thirteen years what life holds in store for us. Before the year 1900 rolls around, I find myself toting a grip for a well-known Missouri river house, casting my lot with the makers of history in this same wild country, and this same chum remains in old Michigan, instead of living up to his boast of exterminating poor Lo.

In the early summer of 1889 I left Topeka, Kansas, and started south representing a large wholesale house on the Missouri river, authorized to pick a territory in which I could sell drugs. My contact was simple, "We will furnish you expense money and pay you a small percent on what you sell," said the manager. It simply meant, can you "make good?" and this I proceeded to do.

It was a beautiful moonlit summer night when I started south from Arkansas City to Oklahoma. I stopped first at Orlando, thence the next day to Mulhall and on the following day I engaged a rig from Zack Mulhall and drove across the country, as the crow flies, to Stillwater. There were no fences and scarcely any roads at all. In one place we unconsciously drove very near to the dugout of some claim holder, which seemed to incense him terribly, and he came at us with a pitch fork. . . . We passed the cabin used by the Dalton boys, the then most dreaded desperadoes of the territory, but the driver would not let me look back so I could not see whether or not they were at home, but in after years I came to know them well and often saw them at this rendezvous. From Stillwater we drove to Perkins, and thence to Guthrie. Here I established headquarters in the old Springer Hotel. This house was then the home of Governor Steel, and later became headquarters for the members of the legislature.

We were treated to a great deal of political news, and oh, the scheming of that legislative body! Here I was taken suddenly ill and remained for three days, meeting then for the first time Dennis Flynn, who was postmaster at Guthrie.

I was certainly a very blue and discouraged drummer when I finally took the train for Oklahoma City. How can I depict the happenings of that terrible night. No sooner on the train and well settled in my seat, than I discovered that the train was absolutely in control, and practically being run by some forty to fifty desperate drunken creatures— not women—I can't call them that, for they were Imps of the Darkness. If Hades is anything like the scenes and beings about me that night, then I certainly feel sorry for any poor creature whose ticket reads that way. If anyone now living deplores the change and loss of saloons, I wish it were possible for him to spend about five minutes amid such scenes as I witnessed that night.

A Drummer's Early-day Experience

Just how we reached Oklahoma City alive is still a mystery. Sick and faint I spoke to some man near me and asked him for the best hotel. He replied the "Grand Avenue." Upon alighting from the train, it being quite light at the depot, I noticed just across the street a large sign over an old frame building, that read, "Grand Avenue Hotel," supposing this to be the "best place" referred to, I walked across and into the building.

I was very faint and took a chair just inside the door. A very beautiful woman came to me and asked if I were ill. I told her I should like to be shown to a room at once; she turned to the colored porter and said, "take him to 15, it is the most quiet room in the house." Upon reaching the room I lay on the bed for some minutes unable to notice anything, but gradually I began to realize from what I could hear what I had run into. Beer corks were popping on all sides and such "language," it was terrible. While down below some man suffering with delirium tremens, was calling on both God and the Devil to take him away. I quite agreed with him on the latter proposition, and made up my mind to effect my escape as soon as possible.

About 3 o'clock when things had settled down somewhat, I took my grip and noiselessly groped my way down the dark stairway and out onto the street. Looking for sometime, I located a hotel and was overjoyed to meet "Bill Gage," the old Topeka colored boy, whom I had known for years (now porter at the Lion Store). He took me to a room

Oklahoma Memories

and I spent the next twelve hours trying to forget the strange things I had seen.

While in Oklahoma City, I was in a drug store when they brought in a man so badly pounded up, I doubt if his own wife would have recognized him. It proved to be Dr. Higgins and it took a good supply of court plaster and bandages to hold him together. I was told that was the way they fixed people who dared to contest a "sooner." I then resolved I did not care for any claim, if I had to contest them.

I made Norman and Purcell and then returned to Oklahoma City and drove to El Reno. Things went well until I came to spend Sunday at Kingfisher. A friend of mine and I resolved to go fishing and take our customers with us. Getting a good lunch and a livery rig we drove out on Kingfisher Creek to the home of John Dalton, a brother of the famous "Dalton Gang." Here we met the mother of the boys as well as the sister and two younger brothers, both of whom afterwards became famous, the younger for killing a man at Kingfisher, and Emmet of Coffeyville fame. Our companions on this trip were C. P. Wickmiller, the jolly druggist, and Mr. Hockaday, a hardware man. My "drummer friend" took the ice and the remainder of our lunch up to the Dalton home and presented it to them. Our catch of fish was not heavy, but the other things were. It developed the next morning that I, at least, had taken a fine crop of red bugs, chiggers, and by evening when I had reached Caldwell, I was about crazy. Someone said ammonia was good to kill them so I sent the porter out for a supply at once. He brought back something stronger than ammonia. This I managed to rub on pretty thoroughly and then the fun began. A doctor was sent for and he rubbed me with glycerine. This killed the ammonia and it killed the chiggers, but I came near being killed also.

From here I went into Topeka for a few days, and then started south for Indian Territory. In Vinita a deputy marshal spent a half-day watching a russia bound tin paint bucket of mine to place me under arrest for introducing whisky. He was surprised when he examined that bucket and said, "Why I can't even get a drink."

I then made Muskogee, back to Wagoner and then out to Claremore. Here I met a hardware man by the name of McEachin. He, too, was trying to make good on a trial trip, and we formed a partnership to travel together for economy and protection.

Stopping at Nowata, I overheard a native say that a certain "Doctor Allen" was going to buy an opening stock of drugs. Investigating, I found the doctor was married to a full-blood Delaware, and lived fourteen miles from Nowata, down on what my informant called "Jim Creek." I promptly hired a liveryman and started for "Jim Creek." This we finally reached, but not until ten o'clock that night. I will never forget that ride over stumps, down ravines, through timber and as dark as pitch. Finally the dogs announced some sort of stopping place, for no Indian ever has less than a dozen mean cur dogs. Arriving at the cabin I found the old doctor seated on the ground before an open fireplace and thumbing over an old Myer Brothers drug catalogue. "How are you Doc," said I. "As fine as a wooden hen," he replied. "How in Hell did you ever get here tonight," said he. "That's up to you," I answered. For two straight hours I hammered and talked, persuaded and begged, but the only impression I made on him was a promise to come into town next day and "make talk."

There was nothing to do but go back, and this we did reaching town about daylight. I now tried a little diplomacy; finding that the old doctor was a great friend of Mr. Rodgers, who owned the main store, I went to Rodgers and told him I was very much in need of that order, that I was young with my house and an opening stock would do me a great deal of good. He promised to see.

Just as he saw the old doctor driving up, he motioned to me to get out my order book. I did so and Mr. Rodgers began to give me an order for some patent medicines. When the old doctor came in he found us very busy.

A Drummer's Early-day Experience

"What!" says he, "Rodgers, do you buy goods of this young fellow?" "Yes," answered Rodgers, "He is a good boy, with a fine house to back him."

The old doctor changed his tobacco to the other side of his mouth, squinted one eye, and said, "Say, young fellow, you are made of the right stuff, if you can drive to my house in the dark for an order. Now look here, I am an old man, and don't know how to order a drug stock; sort up $1,200 worth of drugs and send them to me, and turning to Rodgers he said, "Rodgers give him $1,200 when goods are at the depot, and dang my buttons, young fellow, you stay by me and I'll stay by you." "Now, here, take this card, go to that fellow in Sapulpa and tell him Doc Allen sent you and you can sell him."

I went and sold a new stock as I did also at Claremore, and when I arrived in Coffeyville for Sunday with three complete new stock orders, I knew I had "made good."

Thirty days later I asked the house for, and obtained a half-car load of samples, which I opened in the Bamford Building in Guthrie, the first wholesale sample rooms ever opened in the new country. Soon after getting permanently located, Joe McEachin and myself concluded to take another trip to the eastern part of the Territory. We made the towns on the railroad and then engaged a team at Talala to drive to Sequoyah and Ringold. At Sequoyah we both sold to Mr. Carter, the merchant.

As we were about to leave he said, "Boys, be very careful about the crossing, the river is running very full." This stream was the Big Caney. Mr. Carter came and stood on the bank and showed us where to drive, and we went through all right, but it was just about swimming point.

We made Ringold on the opposite side and started to drive to Bartlesville. There were two roads, one a rough mountain road, and the other crossed the river twice and followed the lowland. We chose the lowland. Meeting a farmer we asked him how the river was, he replied, it was down and showed us on his wagon wheels where it came too, which was indeed encouraging, and disarmed us of suspicion. We drove into the stream only to go plumb out of sight the first thing and come up in fully fifteen feet of water. Joe and the driver both jumped and came ashore, but I, who cannot swim at all, did not feel much like jumping.

Now, it happened that after the farmer had crossed, a great flood coming down the Little Caney had just arrived. It came bearing great upturned trees and logs with its fearful rush. One of these great cottonwood trees struck our wagon and drove wagon, horses and myself high and dry on the bank, where we would have been out of trouble but for the foolhardiness of my companion. All our blankets, halters, grips and robes were swept away and lost. Looking out in the rushing waters Joe suddenly shouted. "Oh there goes my trunk!" and sprang into the stream. In vain I called to him to come back but he seemed intent only upon that trunk. He reached it, getting hold of it with his left hand, began to paddle with his right for the shore. It was nip and tuck, for the trunk weighed 150 pounds, and besides was rapidly filling with water. I saw he was getting exhausted, and ran to a point somewhat in advance of him at a bend in the river. Here were some willows and beyond them no living thing could ever get out of that river, as the banks were at least twenty-five feet straight up, and of slippery clay. Twisting my left hand into these willows and digging my feet into the roots, I leaned out as far as possible, and as my chum swept by I succeeded in catching him by the lapel of his coat. I now begged him to let go of the trunk but he seemed to have lost all reason. His eyes were set. I told him I could not lift him and the trunk both, and then realizing that he did not hear me and could not understand, with almost superhuman strength I pulled him up against the bank, where we both lay exhausted. After some time he realized his position and with my assistance got up the bank, where we lay and eyed each other, and although cold and wet we were glad to be alive. Our driver all this time lay on the bank overcome with nausea and unable to help us. In fact we had to help him into the wagon and drive ourselves the remainder of the way. We arrived in Bartles-

A Drummer's Early-day Experience

ville late that night, after traveling many miles over a rough mountain road, almost frozen and sick from exposure.

Dressed in a pair of the landlord's pants three or four sizes too large and wearing a pair of his old carpet slippers, while his wife was superintending the drying and pressing of our clothes, we called on the trade, and sold goods, too.

It is needless to say there were no oil wells in those days, and Bartlesville had only about twenty-five people, and a town pump which was a dip bucket and rope.

I must now tell you of the next trip to Oklahoma City, where I went to spend Sunday. Broadway at that time was badly littered with stone and all kinds of building material. They were, I think, just starting to build the stone building now occupied by the Security National Bank. On Sunday evening I tried to find someone at the hotel to go to church with me. Not many seemed inclined to go, but finally another young man and I started out to find the place where the Methodists were holding meeting. We finally located a small frame shack on First street. The place was very small and the thirty or forty people who were present nearly filled the house. Benches ran around the sides of the wall, too high for me to touch my feet to the floor. The preacher was quite eloquent in his remarks, and finally came the important feature, the collection. They passed the hat, my companion and I each dropped in fifty cents and the amount collected was announced as $6.85, for which the preacher thanked the audience. The preacher was the Reverend Murry, and a brother of the present Presiding Elder of the North Methodist Church. He has since told me that the money that night found him broke, and relieved him wonderfully.

The people at that time in Oklahoma were very poor, but very energetic, and outside the larger towns (where great wickedness abounded) were kind and obliging, ever ready to do anything to make the way easy for a poor heartsick drummer.

Picture of a Pioneer Town

¶ *The pioneering experience in Oklahoma and throughout the West is usually reported from the masculine point of view. But women also participated in the opening and settling of the nation's last frontier. Any woman over twenty-one could homestead in Oklahoma.* ¶ *Life on the frontier was not easy for anyone, but seemed especially harsh for women. Husbands were often away for weeks at a time harvesting crops or working on railroad construction crews to earn cash for a few necessities. These long periods of loneliness could become nightmares for women if children sickened, animals were injured, food stocks ran low, or a baby arrived suddenly.* ¶ *The half-tamed prairies held unexpected terrors for women reared in more settled regions. Yet in spite of the thousands of resolutions "to return to civilization" made that first night when bone weary, dirty, and homesick women drifted off to sleep, most stayed. The pioneer mother learned to cope with solitude, wind, and isolation. She brightened a dreary dugout with a few perennials growing in an old coffee can, a song bird in a delicate cage, or a few pieces of wedding china displayed on a high shelf safely out of harm's way. She transformed wild sand plums and sorghum into tempting desserts when sugar ran out and cooked the hardy turnip a dozen different ways when everything else in the garden shriveled in a drought. She dosed feverish children with nineteenth-century home remedies, trusted to nature's healing powers and saw many christening dresses become burial shrouds.* ¶ *Women who survived those early years coped with homemaking and child rearing under the most primitive conditions. They also joined husbands in the fields or in a business. Elva Shartel Ferguson combined the duties of a pioneer mother, housewife, and newspaper editor long before the women's liberation movement assured women that there were "alternatives."* ¶ *Born in Kansas in 1867, Elva Shartel married a young news-*

From Mrs. Tom B. Ferguson, *They Carried the Torch: The Story of Oklahoma's Pioneer Newspapers* (Kansas City, Mo.: Burton Publishing Co., 1937), 30–42, 63–67.

Oklahoma Memories

paper man, Thompson Benton Ferguson, in *1885*. When the Cheyenne-Arapaho country was opened for settlement in *1892*, the Fergusons joined the rush to Oklahoma. Settling in Watonga, they established the Watonga Republican. The newspaper was truly the joint enterprise of Elva and Tom, just as the masthead declared. The Fergusons and Oklahoma seemed destined for one another. As the state prospered so did they. In *1901*, President Theodore Roosevelt appointed T. B. Ferguson as territorial governor, and the small-town newspaperwoman became an accomplished and popular first lady as well as a shrewd and influential politician. After her husband's death, Mrs. Ferguson edited the newspaper until *1930*. ¶ Mrs. Ferguson's memoir recaptures the drama and color of early pioneering without idealizing the past. The most striking feature of these recollections is the underlying sense of humor which surely eased her path from pioneering to politics. Yet in spite of her prominence in the new state and her career as an editor, Mrs. Ferguson's experience in Oklahoma was not markedly different from that of thousands of other women. Although Edna Ferber immortalized this pioneer woman as Sabra in her novel Cimarron, Mrs. Ferguson's recollections illustrate once again the significance of the cliché that "truth is stranger than fiction."

THE PRESENT generation can hardly comprehend what a town or community could possibly be like without telephones, radios, paved streets, sidewalks, automobiles and picture shows. Blanketed Indians roamed over the prairies on spotted ponies and lived in wigwam villages; outlaws hiding in the range of hills north of town; no roads or bridges, no communication with the outside world except the daily mail and passenger coach from the nearest railroad point, and yet this is what Watonga looked like in 1892, and it was this spot which was chosen for the birthplace of the Watonga *Republican* and where it has been printed once a week for over forty years.

Picture of a Pioneer Town

The first issue of the *Republican* is before me as I write, not perfect typographically, but every sentence ringing with truth and the vigor of a young man looking with clear vision into the future. The sight of that paper brings back many memories, the struggle of winning the West, the hardships we endured together, the triumphs and heartaches of many years.

The Cheyenne and Arapahoe Indian reservation was the third of Indian land openings, and came on April 19, 1892, under a proclamation issued by President Harrison. Approximately four million acres were thrown open to settlers for homestead purposes and three thousand and three hundred allotments of one hundred and sixty acres each were given the Indians of these two tribes.

This reservation, bounded on the north by the Cherokee strip, was divided into counties consisting of parts of Kingfisher and Canadian, and of Blaine, Dewey, Day, Custer, Roger Mills and Washita. Later a change in lines made Ellis and Beckham counties.

Little could be grown that first year upon sod, and settlers had a hard time in providing for their families. Cutting cedar posts in the gyp hills, hauling them many miles to El Reno and Kingfisher, was resorted to although forbidden by the federal government. Many were fined for this practice, but the courts were lenient because of the extreme conditions and in most cases the fines were remitted. Considerable cedar of high grade from these hills was purchased and shipped to Germany for use in manufacturing lead pencils. Many years later cement mills were established in these hills for the purpose of using the vast deposits of gypsum in the manufacture of building material.

The homesteaders were to pay $1.50 an acre when final proof was made at the end of a five-year period. An extension of time was given the settlers and later the Free Homes Bill, through the efforts of Dennis Flynn, delegate to Congress, was passed and they were given the land with but the

small cost of making final proof. Droughts had come during the early period of settlement and it would have been impossible for many of the settlers to pay for their land. Flynn was regarded as their best friend, and his name is still honored in this part of the state.

The first religious service to be held in the new town of Watonga was on Sunday following the opening in the unfinished store building of W. H. Munger. It was held by a preacher who had been a missionary in Siam, who was home on a vacation and had drifted to the new territory. It was a queer crowd of folks who attended, but an orderly one, no shots fired and no one killed.

Soon the Missionary Baptists erected a little church with services twice a month held by Rev. Job Ingram, of Kingfisher. This was the only church building for several years and other denominations also held their services there. It was used for funerals, socials, Christmas trees and school entertainments.

It was an exciting experience, that of unpacking and setting in motion the small printing outfit from the wagon in which it was hauled overland from Sedan, Kansas. The Washington hand press had been sent by freight to Kingfisher, the nearest railroad point, to be brought to Watonga in the wagon. This process took two days because the road thirty-two miles between these points was scarcely more than a trail through the sand. An unpainted wooden building, which had been hurriedly erected during the first few weeks of the town's existence and which had been used as a hotel, had been rented for ten dollars per month for a printing office and also living quarters for the family. The largest room, containing the best light, was chosen for an office, and the other three rooms served as a home.

Picture of a Pioneer Town

En route to the new location, we had stopped in Wichita, adding a few necessary articles to the equipment, also a bundle of ready prints for the first number of the paper. The type had been left in the cases. Sheets of heavy cardboard were carefully nailed over the top to keep the type from jolting out and becoming mixed. After each case had been made secure, they were stacked one on the other, half a dozen in the pile, and crated together, then placed in the bottom of the wagon bed. The case racks had been knocked down for economy in packing space. The hand job press was crated and miscellaneous articles of equipment in boxes and bundles were all carefully packed into the covered wagon to which was hitched a team of strong, young horses for the long trip across the new territory, from southeastern Kansas. Long it seemed then with no roads across the territory and with horses, but now less than a day's travel with an auto over paved roads will carry us back to our starting place.

A light wagon with bedding and camp equipment was driven by myself. I held a young baby on my lap and a small boy rode by my side. After nightfall we drove into the little new town of Watonga through a muddy street. The town was brilliantly lighted from the open doors of many saloons. Drunken revelry from these places made me shudder and I looked at the sleeping baby on my lap, and at the small boy on the seat by my side, resolving that I would not rear my boys in such a wild place and that I would start back to Kansas the next morning. So much for resolutions. My family are all gone now and I am still here. The homesickness of that night was enough to make any woman regret the thought of becoming a pioneer and the lofty ambition of wanting to be a state builder. Now I wonder whether my boys even in those days were in greater danger from the liquor menace than are my grandsons in this day of high school pocket flasks filled with deadly bootleg stuff.

It took considerable persuasion on the part of my husband, who assured me that things would look brighter in the morning, to prevent my being a quitter before becoming fairly started. However, I can truly say that never again did I have the temptation to quit, for I stuck like a soldier, ready for anything. Early the next morning, while cooking breakfast with our camp outfit in the little kitchen, I was startled by a grunt of greeting, and there within a few feet was a blanketed and painted Cheyenne Indian. I gave out a yell that brought my husband from his work in the printing office to my side. The Indian stalked off muttering to himself, "Ugh, white squaw heap 'fraid." The Indian had heard of the new venture in journalism and was merely making a friendly call and later became one of our best Indian friends. In fact this Indian chief became so attached to the blue-eyed baby of the family that he once insisted upon trading his dearest possession, a beautiful spotted pony, for my "white papoose." Many years later, when this boy in the uniform of his country, was brought home for burial with military honors, this old Indian with many members of his tribe were among his sincere mourners.

A paragraph in the first issue, October 12, 1892, described the party policies of the editor better than anything I can write:

> We will in business matters endeavor to give our readers a paper which can be read and appreciated by all. In politics the paper will be uncompromisingly and aggressively Republican. We make but one promise and that is that the politics of this paper will never be questioned. We support the Republican party because it is the party of progress, truth and immortal history, the party of bravery, patriotism and justice.

And that was truly the political standing of the paper during his editorship. And as his successor I made every effort to carry out his policies. As time passed, party lines were not so strongly emphasized and leaders were more charitable toward each other, but the paper remained loyal to its political party as long as he lived and until its sale nine years after his death. He always denounced in no uncertain terms, graft and dishonesty wherever he found them, making no exceptions of members of his own party, when they strayed from honesty. It was because of his fearlessness and integrity that one of our greatest presidents sought him out and elevated him from the humble editorship of a country weekly to the governorship of the territory nine years after the paper was established.

How well he justified President Roosevelt's judgment is now state history and one of the outstanding pages of its annals.

Some of the great events taking place in the world during those early months of the *Republican*:

> Lord Alfred Tennyson, poet laureate of England, with great honors, was laid to rest in Westminster Abbey.
> A world's fair was being launched amid brilliant scenes at Chicago.
> Mary Ellen Lease was advising Kansas farmers to "raise less corn and more hell." Kansas had smashed her long-established reign of Republicanism by electing Lewelling, a Populist, governor.
> "Sockless" Jerry Simpson had defeated brilliant Chester I. Long for the U.S. Senate.
> John J. Ingalls' matchless oratory was to be heard in the land.
> Count Tolstoi was calling attention to distress in Russia.
> The famous Dalton raid in Coffeyville, Kansas, was occupying first page positions in daily papers.
> France was in the throes of a national scandal concerned with the Panama Canal project, the United States purchasing the rights from France and Panama to complete the canal.

Grover Cleveland was elected president for the second time.

I cannot resist the impulse to write of our first Christmas among our new surroundings. You have often heard of a "white Christmas," and if you were an Oklahoma pioneer you have no doubt also heard of a "blue Christmas."

Less than three months after our arrival, Christmas morning dawned cold and blue. Watonga certainly was a funny little place on that Christmas morning forty years ago—a strange town full of strange people—a little pioneer town, a mudhole in the middle of the street, with seven saloons, and was not calculated to cheer the homesick feeling of a woman with boys who had always lived in Kansas and had never seen a saloon.

One of these boys was a baby of only a few months, while the other was a wide-awake boy just old enough to believe in and expect a visit from Santa Claus. The outlook was gloomy for such a visit, and not particularly promising for anything resembling a real Christmas dinner. If there is a time in the history of a new country when a woman has a right to be homesick, it is on Christmas while thinking of the folks back home who are all together to celebrate that day. However, those who have the courage to go pioneering, usually have the courage to meet and cope with almost any situation, and it now affords me considerable satisfaction to look back at those pioneering days and think that I had the courage to stay with it.

And here let me say that if any skeptically inclined person tells you that there is no Santa Claus, don't you believe him, because there is. I spent that Christmas morning telling Christmas stories to the small boy and wondering how it would be possible under the circumstances to prepare anything resembling a Christmas dinner. While making a heroic effort to keep back tears of homesickness a knock at the door demanded my attention. When I opened the door, for a moment it seemed as if the stories I had been telling were really coming true, for there where the doorstep should have been was Santa Claus with a basket on his arm, smiling and bowing in such a friendly manner that my heart grew warm just to look at him. He wore a fur cap, had funny little side whiskers, was round and fat, with a wonderfully real Christmas look on his ruddy old face. It was hard to understand some of his words but his meaning was certainly plain as he put down the basket, patted the little boy on the head and said something about strangers in a strange land, Merry Christmas, and vanished, not up the chimney, but across the bleak street to his little bakeshop, the home of our patron saint.

But the Christmas spirit remained, the tears and blue atmosphere had disappeared as if by magic. The basket, when unpacked, revealed many treasures for small boys and first aids to a Christmas dinner. But best of all it was the genuine cheer of having been remembered that made the day a happy one.

Many years have passed since that Christmas day that began so sadly and ended so pleasantly. Many, many happy Christmas days have come and gone, but it is a pleasant thing to remember the jolly old German baker, long since gone to Heaven, who was so kind to us when we needed cheer more than any time I had known before or since.

In the days that followed, I became so absorbed in the adventure, and in making friends with the other women who, like myself, had left home and kin to go pioneering, that I ceased to long for the old home and friends back in the states. We made earnest and successful efforts to bring into our lives the things enjoyed in our old homes. Many happy busy days followed for all of us and the new town soon became "home" to us.

In the meantime our newspaper was beginning to attract notice not only in the west but over old Oklahoma, now arrived at the age of four years, with an organized government, a legislature, a state capitol location fight, city government, daily papers, railroads, and an active campaign toward statehood.

It took about as much genius during that period to be a

successful housewife and mother as it did to edit a paper. For the first year there were no meat markets, no home-grown vegetables, and although there were many cattle ranches, few milk cows. Everything must be freighted thirty-two miles by wagon from Kingfisher through sand trails, taking two days for the round trip. Having grown up on a farm in Kansas in times of plenty, I found that I must learn to adopt altogether different methods in providing palatable meals for my little family. A small cook stove fed with cedar wood was used. The smell of burning cedar even now brings back to me those pioneer days most vividly.

Some of my ventures in cooking were rather amusing. Canned goods were primitive in those days, compared with present articles. I smile when I recall the result of my attempt to make cream gravy from a can of condensed milk and canned corn beef, which sticky, sweet mess did not go down very well with the family. I was reminded of this mess four years ago while eating in a Chinese restaurant in Shanghai. Canned beef, tomatoes and corn, evaporated (dried) apples and sorghum, without butter, formed the basis of our food supplies at first. Later I learned how to make palatable preserves from watermelon and jam from the wild plums which grew in abundance. If I could not get sugar, I just used sorghum.

As time went on we were able to obtain better food supplies, but the necessity of inventing something out of nothing was pretty good training and I can still prepare a good meal out of things wasted by many cooks. Perhaps the recent depression will have a wholesome effect upon some of the cooks of our land in teaching them to be resourceful and more economical in the use of food. I learned to make shirts for my husband and clothes for my boys, and my best dress was of calico, sprigged with pink rosebuds and for which I paid eight cents a yard, making it myself. I got a lot more pleasure out of it than one I bought in Paris not long ago. A rag carpet for which I colored and sewed the rags to be woven on a hand loom by a neighbor, was more beautiful to me than anything I now possess. The feeling of achievement was a wonderful thing and led me on to more pioneer conquests.

During this time the *Republican* was printed with the assistance of but one printer and members of the family, so in order for both my husband and myself to be absent more than a day at a time took some planning.

One day a letter came telling of the serious illness of his father, who lived at Emporia, Kansas. The letter stated that he was very ill, the end seemed near, and if my husband wanted to see his father while he still lived he must come at once. For some reason he decided that the best connections could be made by driving to Fort Reno to take a train. It was a forty-mile drive and had to be made with a team and wagon. A basket of food together with several blankets was placed in the wagon and we started, taking the two small boys along. I was to drive home after my husband had taken the train for Emporia. After traveling but a few miles on the homeward trip one of the horses became sick and it was necessary to drive very slowly. At that time there were almost no settlers near the road we traveled, as much of the land was Indian allotments, and the Indians, most of the time, lived in wigwam villages. Some time after dark we passed one of these villages where there were at least five hundred of the plains or blanket Indians in camp. They were holding one of their tribal dances and as usual under such circumstances they had abandoned all traces of civilization and had reverted to the savagery of their ancestors. In an open space lighted by huge camp fires, men of the tribe, almost naked, their bodies glistened with paint, wearing the feathered head-dress of their tribe, chanting their ritual, danced to the weird music of the tom-toms until exhausted they fell to the ground. The dance and the chant were taken up by other Indians continuing many hours without ceasing.

Although we were told that since the settlement of the country the Indians were friendly to the whites and perfectly harmless it was entirely too much like a scene from the pages of "The Last of the Mohicans," for comfort, and,

Picture of a Pioneer Town

too, I recalled that it had not been very many years since the Battle of the Washita. To be truthful I was badly frightened, but Walter and Trad were good little pioneers, and if they were frightened they did not say so. We drove as quietly as possible past this savage scene, but less than a mile away it became evident that the sick horse could go no farther. I drove to one side of the road and got out to see what I could do. The horse lay down in the harness and could not be persuaded to get up. So I decided that we would have to spend the rest of the night there. After unharnessing the horses and tying their halter ropes to the wagon I gave the boys some food and we lay down in the wagon wrapped in our blankets to wait for daylight. I did not sleep, but the children did. I had hung a blanket over the front end of the covered wagon to shut out the glare from the camp fire and as much of the noise as possible from the Indian celebration, wondering how soon our presence would be discovered, which I knew was inevitable. After several hours of suspense, during the darkness of the long night, some of the younger Indians discovered our wagon. They had been drinking fire water, and fired by that and the tribal dance rode around and around our wagon with their savage war whoops. In my fright, I thought the end had come, and then all at once I realized that the Indians had received a check of some sort, and had been driven off, perhaps only temporarily. Suddenly the blanket over the opening was thrust aside, and a Cheyenne Indian peered in at us. To my joy he was the Indian who had made the friendly visit to our print shop some months before. He had recognized the horses and made me understand by signs and the few words of English he knew that he had been sitting in his wagon not far off for several hours watching, and that he had driven away the young savages, and was our friend. He told me that he would remain near until daylight. He helped me harness the horses, giving them corn from his own wagon, and helped us get started toward home. The sick horse had recovered sufficiently to travel and we reached home in safety, where I wrote the last necessary news for the weekly edition and then set it up in type by hand. Because we were used to strange and unusual experiences in this new land, I did not feel that there was anything extraordinary about it and when my husband returned I did not remember for several days to tell him about it. When I did he had a very grave look upon his face and must have been thinking as I have since thought, that while the adventure ended well, yet it might have had a far different finish. A young woman and two small children among such surroundings might have been subjected to most unpleasant experiences.

It happened that my husband and I were some months later able to do this Indian a great favor and thus repay him in a small way for his friendship in a most trying time. We were warm friends until the Indian's death many years later.

Picture of a Pioneer Town

A Great Race

¶ *The Cherokee Outlet, opened to settlement in 1893, contained some of the most desirable land available outside the domain of the Five Civilized Tribes. As desperate land-hungry men, many ruined in the drought of 1892–93 on the Great Plains, competed for the dwindling public domain, violence often flared. ¶ The confusion and lawlessness in the Cherokee Strip was greater than that of previous openings. Soon after the run one successful settler reported stumbling over the body of a man with a slit throat and crushed skull hidden in a hollow. Another told of meeting a man, who appeared demented, wandering around in a circle crying helplessly, "Where can I stake a claim? I want to get a home!" ¶ The inspired pictures taken by the frontier photographer W. S. Prettyman captured all the vigor and turbulence, the sense of desperate exhilaration as men tried to claim the future. Success determined history; the losers were forgotten in short order. ¶ A twelve-year-old Indian boy who helped many settlers find good claims that fateful day wrote his recollection of the event. Although more than a decade passed before he wrote down his memory of that day, his word picture is as accurate and evocative as any photograph of the time.*

ABOUT TWELVE YEARS ago it was my privilege to participate in one of the most exciting events that has taken place in our country since the civil war. . . . On this day the Cherokee strip was to be opened to settlement. The people were gathered all around the border in order to make the race.

I, being well acquainted with the country from working with cattle in that part, and a fairly good rider for a lad of

From "A Great Race," *The Kendall Collegian* (May 1906) College Files, Worcester-Robertson Collection, McFarlin Library, University of Tulsa, Tulsa, Oklahoma.

twelve, concluded I would spend the day with the multitude. I got up early in the morning, saddled my horse and proceeded on my day's journey. I lived about three-fourths of a mile from the line, and the first people I met were from Ohio. They saw from the looks of my horse and dress that I must be a native, so they began to ask me questions. I answered as well as I knew and went on. I saw people from all the states. I saw them in all shapes and in every kind of vehicle that our country produced at that time. I saw cripples and old women afoot, families in ox carts drawn by oxen, men on bicycles, in wagons, buggies, and men and women on horse-back, some of those big feathery legged horses with a blind bridle to guide them, and in every way you could imagine, to enter the great race. The signal was to be given at twelve o'clock. The U.S. government had soldiers stationed all along the line to keep the people back until the time came. The closer the time grew, the wilder the people got. While riding along I saw an old man who was trying to control a young horse. The animal was too vigorous for the old fellow and jumped over the line. A soldier came up and told the old man if he got over that line again he would put him back to stay. I thought I would stop and watch the proceedings awhile. Pretty soon the horse jumped over the line again. The soldier raised his rifle and cast a bullet through the old man just below the arm and killed him instantly. This old fellow's son was located down the line about fifty yards. He saw the performance and up with his revolver and killed the soldier. There, in less than five minutes lay the two dead bodies. The people were so excited about the homes they were going to get that they did not take much notice of the dead bodies. The two bodies were placed in a wagon and covered with some hay which had been brought to feed horses. I being somewhat excited from the bloody conflict, journeyed on west.

It was now about one hour until the signal was to be given.

There was a ridge about five miles in my lead that I wanted to reach before the race took place.

On gaining the top of the ridge I was about ten minutes ahead of time. I found the people were just as wild as they were at other places. They were all standing now, and each one trying to get as close to the line as he could. I was situated where I could see fifteen miles to the east, and as far as my eye could reach to the west, and as far as I could see there were nothing but people, people by the thousands.

I looked to the east and saw soldiers about one mile apart start from the base line southward in the strip. The time had come now for every one to run. When the soldiers got about one-half mile down in the strip, they halted their horses, turned facing the north, raised the stars and stripes, emptied their revolvers into the air and made a rush for the base line. This was the signal for the people to go, and they went with all the force and fury that excitement could lend them. I went too, and we had a grand race.

The soldiers had a very hard time to keep from getting run over by the multitude. I began to see things and realize the power of the greatest excitement.

I had not gotten more than two hundred yards until I saw a horse step into a badger hole and fall, throwing two women out of a buggy, to let the stampeded crowd rush over them. I know not what became of the women, I could not stop on account of the rush behind. I went right on with the crowd, looking first to the right and then to the left, and all the time seeing men and women thrown from their conveyances and crippled in many ways. After going about five miles watching the destruction of vehicle, horse and man, I looked to the right and about two miles away I saw a great mass of people wailing like a bunch of mad cattle. I determined to see what it was all about. The little streams in that country are narrow and deep, and you cannot cross them only at old trails. This mass of people were in the forks of two of those streams, and others were coming in so fast that those who were in could not get out. When I arrived they had their spades, shovels and picks trying to make roads to cross.

A fellow came galloping up to me and said, "Kid if you

will show me a crossing on this stream I will give you a ten dollar bill."

I knew all about the crossings and told him to follow me. I guided him up the stream about four miles and showed him an old cow trail. He and I took the lead and the rest followed. I would glance back and the stream of people looked like a twine string unrolling from a large ball.

The mob was so anxious to get across that they fought, swore and trampled on each other to make the crossing first. I watched them for about two hours and got tired and concluded I would go home. On my way I saw men quarreling, and some fighting, each claiming he was on the place first. Every now and then I would come upon a crippled horse, a torn up buggy, wagon, or crippled men and women. I found one little boy who had been thrown from a wagon and hurt pretty badly, but was still conscious. He told me how it came about and I took him up behind me to take him home. I got about two miles and by accident met his uncle, to whom I gave him. I never saw the little fellow afterwards.

It was getting toward night now and as I drew near the base line I saw people building houses, plowing, digging wells, and everything that goes to improve a farm.

I reached home about eight o'clock that night. My horse and I were tired from head to foot. I unsaddled, sat down to a supper that had been waiting for me for two hours.

Mother asked me many questions and she, noticing I was worn out, sent me to bed. I obeyed her command and this ended the great race.

Clubs and I

¶ *In the mid-1890s "Nonie" Russell, a young school teacher, left her family on the high plains of Texas to marry Sidney Laune, an energetic attorney, in Woodward, Oklahoma Territory. The inconveniences of mere daily living in Woodward were enormous. The streets were unpaved, the blowing sand and wind ceaseless. And just when folks began to take life easy, a tornado, dust storm, or flash flood reminded them of their precarious existence.* ¶ *But Mrs. Laune was a pioneer and a builder, no matter the perils and nuisances of frontier life. She and her husband helped bring paved streets to early Woodward. They worked to secure electricity, a water system, a public library, and to encourage in the community a tolerant spirit that allowed all classes of persons to enrich frontier living.* ¶ *Along with the necessities, people in frontier towns had their share of the luxuries too—music, poetry, and intelligent conversation were their staple pleasures. Mrs. Laune's recollections of social life in Woodward at the turn of the century help dispel the misconception that good manners and an interest in music and things literary stopped at the Mississippi River.*

THE LADIES of the town, dressed in the height of fashion, leaving engraved calling cards and in every detail following the social customs of metropolitan society, had been prompt to call when I first arrived and invite me to all the parties and receptions. We were quickly drawn into the Shakespeare Club that Mr. Laune had helped to organize almost as soon as he washed his hands after driving the stake on his lot, and I was asked to become a member of the Coterie Club. This was the second federated club in Oklahoma Ter-

From Seigniora Russell Laune, *Sand In My Eyes* (Flagstaff, Arizona: Northland Press, 1974), 145–54.

ritory. Most of the members were older than I, and were so competent, so gaily determined that Woodward should be a cultural center, and—I thought—so intellectual, that I was overwhelmed by the honor of being asked to become a member. I hesitated about joining, as I didn't see how I could find time to spare, but Mr. Laune insisted I needed the stimulation that this club offered.

It was, and is, a remarkable organization in ways beyond its constitutional definition of "a literary, charitable, and sociable" association. It really set the standards and formed the social policies of the town. The rigid rules that forbade gossip of any kind, politics in a partisan sense, and religion from a denominational standpoint, though "unwritten laws," were so consistently observed that the closest harmony has prevailed right up to the present time. No words of mine can express what a factor this club has been in the enrichment of my life.

We met in alphabetical order and, as the houses were so small, it was frequently necessary for the hostess to move beds and other large pieces of furniture out into the yard to make room for the meetings. Some of us were obliged to sit on the floor; I, with a baby on each side of me. Years later, I heard one of our sons say that the reason he did not attain a desired height of six feet, was because his growth was stunted from having to sit on the floor at Coterie meetings, unable to stretch out his legs or even take a deep breath.

For some time, Coterie had felt the necessity of a library in the town, and with eighty dollars, earned by a Fourth of July celebration, in the treasury it seemed like a good time to start one. Mrs. Patton, the doctor's wife, said she would write Mr. Andrew Carnegie who, she had read, was founding libraries all over the country. And she would write to Mr. John D. Rockefeller, who had a lot of money, too. She thought they would be glad to furnish Woodward with a library if they were asked. The other eighteen members thought this was a good idea, and it was moved, seconded and carried, that Mrs. Patton write and tell these wealthy gentlemen that the Woodward Coterie Club would appreciate it very much if they would furnish sufficient funds to open a circulating library in Woodward.

She wrote, and the club members waited impatiently for a reply. It came. Mr. Carnegie, or the committee that received requests in his name, had received our letter and noted contents, but respectfully begged to advise the club that it was not the policy—and so forth. It was a nice letter, but, briefly, Woodward was too small for a Carnegie library fund. Mr. Rockefeller wrote and said he was not giving out libraries at all.

Coterie was not discouraged. With eighty dollars, we would just go ahead and start the library ourselves. Margaret Gerlach rose in meeting and said she thought it was time to stop talking about it, and go to work on a real problem. She contributed a book by Richard Carvel and then each of us gave a book, so the library had eighteen books right away.

Our county clerk offered to let us use the rear shed room of the shack that was his office. This room, unfinished except for a floor, and with only two small windows, was on the west side. In summer the sun beat down mercilessly on the sloping roof, and in the winter it was freezing cold.

With our eighty dollars, we sent away for more books. The members of Coterie "took turns alphabetically," in keeping the library open for the patrons who paid a dollar for a membership card. We began a series of pie-suppers, food sales, chicken dinners, and such things to make more money to buy more books. Citizens of the town became interested and a number of books were donated.

After a while, the city decided that the library should be a municipal affair, and bought it from us. We were happy to turn it over to them. After another while, Mr. Carnegie came through with his help and the town acquired a Carnegie Library.

The study program of Coterie for those years was enough to stagger busy mothers and housekeepers. We studied every country in the world, beginning with the very first records that we could find. When our third child was a

nursing baby, I read two thick volumes of Greek history aloud to him because I had to give a paper on the subject, and this was a way to satisfy the other children's cry, "Read to us!" at the same time. Mr. Laune said he suspected that no other baby had been nurtured on Greek history at such a tender age.

Our own country was studied carefully from the discoveries, on down through the colonizations to the Revolution. Then we read aloud at the meetings every word of the Constitution and Amendments, and such controversial writings as we could find. These included writings of the Adamses, Franklin, Washington, and others. We invited lawyers and teachers in the town to come and give us more intelligent interpretations than we could form of some of the questions involved.

Once a year, we rewarded our husbands for the help that they so willingly gave our every endeavor, with a banquet. This was the high point in the year.

At that time, there were no fast refrigerated cars, automatic refrigerators, or even many iceboxes. We were forced to send away to Wichita, Kansas—the nearest market—for fresh fruits and vegetables, such as head-lettuce, artichokes, mushrooms, and alligator pears. We gave one of the banquets at the hotel, on Washington's Birthday. We sent away for ice cream molded in the form of George and Martha. Huge chrysanthemums were favors for the ladies, and there were small button chrysanthemums for the men's lapels. We had hand-painted place cards and menus, music and speeches and toasts. It was the last word in epicurean elegance.

At about the same time I became a member of Coterie, I was asked to join the Social Club, which met for the sole purpose of having a good time. We took our embroidery, darning, or other hand work. We had no charitable obligations and did nothing for the "uplift of the town." We simply relaxed and remembered that we were young. Later, the club was turned into a card club and so remains to this day.

The people of the town were seldom bored. For one thing, unusual musical talent was discovered almost as soon as there was a town. Len Stine, who ran a wholesale liquor business, recognized the need for something that would provide entertainment for the town and interest for some of the young men. So he invested $450.00 in instruments for a town band, and acted as leader until he found someone he thought more competent. In no time at all, concerts were being held on Main Street corners, and the band played for all public occasions. If the band lacked something in the way of harmony and technique, it made up for all deficiencies in volume of sound. Anyway, people were not critical, but appreciative. It was wonderful to see the young men tooting and blowing and puffing, their cheeks swelled to balloons and their eyes bulging. Quartettes, male, female and mixed, were formed and sang cheerfully for every kind of entertainment as well as for church and the rare funeral services. A music club was formed that included those who loved to listen as well as those who participated. But even in a music club where nearly everything is donated, money is necessary. At least, a little money.

The club therefore voted that each member should give a dollar to defray unavoidable expenses. Since not everyone could afford to give a dollar right out of her husband's pocket, it was decided that the dollar must be earned. Some husbands declared that the earning of the dollar cost them far more than that amount, and pled with their wives just to give the dollar and forget it.

A certain woman's husband—you guess which one—broke forth in plaintive verse which his wife found pinned to her pillow one morning:

> Oh, please just take a buck from me,
> I do not want again to be
> Compelled to earn some money.
>
> I'll gladly give a dollar now,
> That I will steal, or get somehow;
> But let's don't "earn" it, honey.

Hank O'Brian was not one of the husbands who protested. He had turned so many ice-cream freezer cranks, had driven so many miles collecting and returning so many dishes and chairs and tables, had wiped so many dishes after the parties, that a little thing like helping his wife, Stasia, earn a dollar for the music club was duck soup for him. When Stasia explained the matter to Hank, he was ready.

"What about that melon patch I have across the track?" he asked, lazily. "Why not peddle watermelons? They're wonderful watermelons. Everybody likes watermelons. Y'oughta make a dollar."

"Will you help me?" asked Stasia, guilefully. Stasia knew, and everyone in town knew, that Hank would help Stasia do anything, if she asked him. He would help, he agreed, by driving the wagon to the field, by gathering the ripe melons, by loading them into the wagon, and driving to the customers that Stasia solicited, and dumping them on porches or in kitchens. Of course, Stasia would go along for the ride. One thing Hank made clear, he would not drive up and down the street hollering, "Watermelons for sale." Stasia had to do that, if it was done at all. And he wouldn't go into the stores and drum up the trade.

Stasia promised. Hank drove up and down Main street, grinning broadly while Stasia went in and out of the stores, and piped in her treble voice, "Watermelons for sale."

She made one dollar and sixty cents.

Several years later, in 1914, I was asked to prepare the charter for a P.E.O. chapter in our town. This invitation came to me through a friend, Minnie Olmsted, in the nearby town of Wanoka, where there was an active chapter. Not knowing anything about this P.E.O. except that it is the largest women's organization in the world independent of a related men's organization, and is international in scope, I blithely agreed to form a chapter. I chose those members of Coterie whom I knew inside and out. There were a few other names added, and throughout all the years since then the chapter has worked and played and grown.

Oklahoma Memories

People often ask, "What is this P.E.O.? What does it mean?"

When we were organizing our chapter and I was dipping into my husband's very shallow pockets every now and then for one thing and another connected with the first meeting, he said that it meant, a "Pretty Expensive Order." Others said, when they learned that the membership of a chapter was limited to a small group, that the initials stood for "Pretty Exclusive Order." Those are as good answers as any. . . .

P.E.O. was organized in 1869 by seven girls, students at Iowa Wesleyan College in Mt. Pleasant, Iowa, and now, in the middle of the twentieth century, has a membership of almost one hundred and twenty thousand.

Our P.E.O. Chapter in Woodward, through the interest of one of its members, Myra Root, a blind young girl of our town, began a movement in the 'twenties that for a few years surprised and delighted us with the response from other chapters not only in Oklahoma, but in many of the other states.

The plan Mrs. Root presented to our chapter was not only to give reading matter to the sightless, but work to trained but idle hands. We wanted money to be paid to blind transcribers, for there were many who were skilled in transcribing, but who could not get the work to do, for lack of money in the National Library for the Blind treasury. So they sat in darkness and idleness with nothing to do and nothing to read, for they soon exhausted the scant supply of matter available. When the State Convention of P.E.O. was held in Woodward in 1927, we solicited the help of all chapters in the state. We introduced the battle cry, "Let Every Chapter Give A Book For the Blind," and many chapters in many states took up the challenge.

A committee was appointed with Mrs. Root as the chairman, and worked for five years through the various chapters and their members, and a few outside friends. In those five years, we gave work to blind transcribers who had been sitting in idle and perpetual darkness. Seventy books, besides numerous short stories and articles were given to the National Library for the sightless. Congress, importuned, raised their appropriation to $70,000.00, the Pratt Bill was passed and the Library of Congress received $100,000.00 for having books embossed.

That was a fine movement as it gave more books to be read; but it did not help those who wanted to work, and were ready to give skilled service in transcribing. Helen Keller wrote us, "Remember that the transcribing of books into Braille gives the blind a means of self-support as well as the joy of reading."

The depression may have had something to do with the discontinuance of this work through the P.E.O. Chapters but the real reason was the interest of the international, or Supreme officers, in what they considered a larger work and more in line with the policy of the sisterhood; this centered in Cottey College, which they own, in Nevada, Missouri, and the Educational Loan Fund to aid girls aspiring to further their education.

But after all, most important, the objectives had been reached; appropriations had been increased, and a consciousness had been aroused as to the need of an interest in the work for the sightless.

To jump way ahead of my story, after having served on the executive board of Oklahoma State P.E.O. I was elected State President for 1920–1921. I was overwhelmed with this honor and the duties and responsibilities it entailed, but I was fortunate in having the generous help of my predecessors, and the association of many fine women. Through this channel, my acquaintance over the state was extended and it all proved to be a most rewarding and happy experience, instead of the arduous task I had feared.

When I occasionally hear people today ridicule the "American clubwoman" I just think to myself, "You don't know what you are laughing at." Certainly, Woodward would have been a very different town—and not as good—if there had been no women's clubs, and my life, to speak only for myself, would have been infinitely poorer.

A Creek Camp Meeting

¶ *The practice of holding retreats, or camp meetings, in the summer was well established in Indian cultures long before the white man arrived. Eastern missionaries were quick to try to substitute weekendlong prayer meetings and singing festivals for the Indians' all-night dances as Christianity was layered over Indian traditions.* ¶ *As the author of this recollection noted, the description of the Creek camp meeting could easily be altered to fit a Protestant communion service among any of Oklahoma's Indian tribes.*

"ALL ABOARD for the camp meeting." It is three o'clock in the afternoon of a July day at Nuyaka Mission in the heart of the Creek country. Before one of the buildings two prairie schooners are standing ladened with camp equipage, bedding and food. Beside this in the two wagons, will soon be packed twelve people whose destination is a point fifteen miles southeast on Honey creek. The party consists of the superintendent and wife and two children, three lady teachers, four of the older pupils, staying at the mission during the summer, and a preacher. Soon all is ready and the mules start off on a slow trot with the wagons rumbling and jolting over the rough roads. The sun beats down fiercely [but] under the white canopy with a strong breeze across the prairie it is comfortable. This section of the Creek country resembles a vast park and is always beautiful. There are great stretches of prairie as green as an eastern lawn diversified by strips of cross timbers. We journey onward stopping occasionally on some rise to enjoy the magnificent prospect, or someone's attention is attracted by the flowers

From "A Creek Camp Meeting," *The Kendall Collegian* (November 1900) College Files, Worcester-Robertson Collection, McFarlin Library, University of Tulsa, Tulsa, Oklahoma.

blooming in profusion. Once we stop to catch a large tarantula by the wayside and then outspan to let the mules drink at a little pool in a ravine. About 6 P.M. we come out upon a bold bluff where the prairie breaks down and mile on mile before us lies the fertile valley of Honey Creek smiling in the sunshine. It is still several miles to the camp ground which we reach just as the day is darkening into night. While the boys unhitch the teams and lead them to water, the superintendent and preacher put up the tent and the ladies hastily prepare supper over the camp fire. Here and there through the gloom of the weeds we can see the white tents and the gleam of camp fires. Supper over we repair to the arbor where the meeting is to be held. These arbors are constructed by erecting upright supports and then laying poles across for rafters and covering the whole with prairie hay. The seats are formed by splitting logs and placing them flat side up on others laid lengthwise. These arbors will seat from two to five hundred. The pulpit consists of a small enclosed space at one end and on each side of the pulpit are seats for the communicants. Three ushers on each side of the arbor show the members of the congregation what seats they are to occupy and also wage an incessant war on the numerous dogs which desire to find a bed on the hay with which the floor of the arbor is covered. None but members in good and regular standing are allowed to occupy the seats of communicants. The men occupy one side of the arbor, the women the other, while seats are provided for visiting clergymen immediately in front of the pulpit where they sit with their backs towards the speaker. After the evening service we are glad to get to bed. The superintendent and family occupied one wagon, the preacher and two Indian boys the other and the lady teachers and the girls took possession of the tent. With my head at the end of the wagon I could look out and see the camp fires around which were gathered little groups of Indians in conversation. Gradually these groups melted away and the camp sank to repose under the silent stars. By dawn it was again astir and soon the sunrise bell announced morning prayers. After breakfast came the long morning service and then a recess of several hours during which dinner was prepared. The congregation is usually divided into different camps, each camp having its own table. We took dinner at the camp of the second chief of the tribe and he told me that they would have about three hundred for dinner at this table.

A Creek Camp Meeting

At five o'clock comes the communion service conducted by a white preacher of the denomination holding the meeting, and then there is usually a continuous service of singing, prayer and preaching during the night. Our party retired about eleven and as our slumbers were occasionally disturbed by a fight between some of the dogs we could hear the singing at the arbor as it came floating through the trees.

Sunrise is announced by the ringing of the bell and then there is a great hand shaking, a last prayer, and then all disperse for breakfast. After breakfast the camp presents an animated scene as the tents are struck, bedding and other camp equipage packed and then the wagons rumble off over the prairie and the camp ground is silent and deserted until another communion season, except when a small congregation gathers at regular intervals in the rude little church to listen to the native preacher proclaim the Word in their mother tongue.

This description of an Indian camp meeting with a slight change of details, would fit any communion service of the Methodists, Baptists or Presbyterians among the Creeks or Seminoles.

It is the custom of the full-blood churches to hold a camp meeting at their quarterly communion services. They usually go into camp Friday and continue until Monday morning. These meetings are so arranged as not to conflict. One denomination will hold one week, another the next and another the following. Then the first will conduct a meeting at some other point and the round is made again. As the three denominations among them work in harmony it is customary for all the Indians of a neighborhood to go to the nearest camp meeting to the neglect of the regular services of their own church. In the summer time some of them will move from camp to camp taking all their household goods with them. It is not unusual to find preachers of all denominations at the same meeting taking part, a white preacher of the denomination holding the meeting is usually, though not always, present to preach the communion sermon and to preside at the distribution of the elements.

Meetings are held Friday night, all day Saturday and Sunday, and all of Sunday night. The all-night meetings originated from the facts that the heathen party held their busks and dances all night, and to counteract their effect all-night religious services were inaugurated. The necessity and propriety of such meetings has ceased, but a custom once established among the Indians is hard to break up. On Sunday there are usually three services, a sunrise prayer meeting, the morning service from ten to one and the night service beginning about five or six and continuing until sunrise Monday morning. Sunrise prayer meetings are a rather recent innovation among the whites, but have been held by the Indians for many years. In one particular they differ from prayer meetings among their white brethren, they are composed almost exclusively of men; the women during this meeting are busy preparing breakfast.

The meetings are conducted with marked order and decorum and are largely attended. At one of our meetings this summer there were nearly five hundred full-blood Indians in camp from Thursday until Monday, and it is not unusual to have from two to three hundred present. They are not content with one sermon but have from two to five at one service by different preachers. There is also much prayer and singing.

A Strong Medicine Wind

¶ *As white settlers swarmed into western Oklahoma after 1889, most Indian tribal leaders recognized that resisting allotment would be as futile as opposing removal had been decades earlier. The general attitude of both the federal government and whites toward the Oklahoma Indians was a mixture of idealism and pragmatism that dates from the nation's first encounters with the continent's indigenous population. Whites desired alternately to "civilize" Indians into their system and isolate or eradicate them if they resisted. Indians also alternated between accepting and rejecting the white man's "progressive" ways.* ¶ *Ethel C. Krepps, a Miami-Kiowa who grew up to be a nurse and an attorney and serves as the treasurer of the Kiowa tribe, tells of her own family's acceptance of the white man's road. Despite all the sorrows and emotion-laden events in the Indian's history in Oklahoma, men like Grandfather Wind Goomda gave the new state a unique heritage. Many of his attitudes persist amid the burgeoning white civilization. His image and customs are more than quaint, as much a heritage of America's frontier civilization as those of the whites who displaced him.*

MY FATHER'S FAMILY were full-blood Kiowa Indians. Grandfather's English name was Wind Goomda. In the Kiowa language Goomda means Wind. His first Kiowa Indian name had been Medicine Wind. That was an appropriate name for a Kiowa warrior, and Wind Goomda was an appropriate name for a Christian rancher. Grandmother's Indian name was Kon-ta-mah, which means Ghost Woman.

Grandfather was born in the fall of 1867 during the signing of the Medicine Lodge Treaty between the United

From Ethel C. Krepps, "A Strong Medicine Wind," *True West*, 26 (March–April 1979), 7–10, 40–42.

Oklahoma Memories

States government and the Plains Tribes, in what is now Kansas. Grandmother was born in 1878 on the vast Plains which the Kiowas claimed as their territory. These are stories about their life together and how they made the transition from the free, wild life the Kiowas knew to the settled life of the whiteman.

They gave up their tribal dress of buckskin and feathers for dresses, suits and ties. They gave up their tribal ways to learn how to cook on a stove, keep house, till the land and raise a garden. They gave up their tribal religion to give their hearts to the whiteman's Jesus. Once they accepted the Jesus Road they never departed from it.

They were born in teepees on the Plains, wild and free Kiowas. They died in circumstances vastly different. They struggled to make a place for themselves in both worlds and they succeeded.

When my grandfather was a small boy he was camped with his people in Palo Duro Canyon south of what is now the city of Amarillo, Texas. The camp was attacked by General Ranald Mackenzie and his military troops at dawn. Mackenzie had found the secret entrance which the Kiowas used to enter the canyon. The Kiowa women and children ran to escape by climbing the steep canyon walls while the men stayed behind to cover, protect and conceal their escape efforts. Medicine Wind did escape from the battle raging in Palo Duro that day and at the age of six years walked back to the Wichita Mountains located in Western Oklahoma.

The Kiowas had strong medicine in their God, the Tai-Me. The Tai-Me was a small idol that was placed on public display for the Kiowas once a year at their annual Sun Dance. A Medicine Lodge was built for the Sun Dance by the entire tribe.

The Kiowas were called together for the Sun Dance by the Tai-Me Keeper. He would ride out to bands scattered over the Plains and announce that when this moon disappeared and the new moon came, all of the Kiowas should come to Rainy Mountain or some other site which had been chosen for that year's Sun dance. It was held in late summer. Afterwards the Kiowas would disperse to their favorite winter camping grounds.

A Strong Medicine Wind

During the Sun Dance the Tai-Me was tied to the center pole of the Medicine Lodge and the Kiowa dancers would stare at the Tai-Me as they danced with uplifted arms for four days and four nights without ceasing.

From 1830–1870 the Tai-Me Keeper was Anso-gia-ny or Ansote (also known as Long Foot or Old Man Foot). He died in the winter of 1870–1871. When it was time to pass the power medicine of the Tai-Me on to his successor the power was passed on to Do-Hente (also called Napawat or NoShoes). Do-Hente was the Tai-Me Keeper from 1871 to 1873. During the time that Do-Hente was the Tai-Me Keeper he had an unusual experience. It was August during the annual Sun Dance. It was especially hot and the dancers were wilting under the intense heat. The entire tribe was asking the Tai-Me Keeper, medicine man Do-Hente, for just a small rain shower to refresh themselves. Do-Hente made his power medicine for rain and clouds.

The rains came with a tempest of wind and vivid and terrible lightning. Peal after peal of thunder shook the air; the ground was literally flooded. Two visiting Cheyenne women were killed by the lightning. The next morning Do-Hente apologized for the medicine. He was a young man and had no idea of making such strong medicine. He asked the Kiowas to overlook his error in judgment. He trusted that as he grew older, he would grow wiser. The Cheyenne women were dead, not because of his medicine, but because they were wearing red blankets. All Kiowas knew that they should not wear red during the Sun Dance of the Kiowas because it might start a prairie fire. The apology was accepted, and it was hoped that all Indians who in the future might attend the great Sun Dance of the Kiowas, would remember not to wear red blankets.

In the old days the Kiowas would receive a power which would be their strength. The stronger the power the greater would be their ability to become an effective leader. The

Kiowas felt that the power could be transmitted to them through a ritual of sacrifice and prayer. They would paint their bodies and go to a hiding place in the mountains. Where their future strength and power would come from, and the rules which had to be followed in order to retain their power, usually would come to them in the form of a trance-like dream.

Do-Hente, to receive his power, went into the Wichita Mountains, called Mountains Standing by the Kiowas. After several days of fasting, prayer to the Sun and sacrifice of his own body, a voice told him that his power would come from the Cat family. Certain requirements were then given Do-Hente regarding the use and retainment of his power. One requirement forbade him to eat any meat which would be eaten by the Cat family.

The Kiowas could not choose to follow some requirements and disregard others. Each one had to be followed or their power would be weakened or lost.

After Do-Hente had become the keeper of the Tai-Me, the sacred medicine, he was selected to go with a Kiowa delegation to Washington, D.C. to meet with the President regarding tribal business. This was early in 1873.

During the trip the delegation ate their meals on the train in the dining car. One of the meals consisted of a casserole dish which contained rabbit meat. Do-Hente, careful about what he ate, asked questions trying to find out the ingredients of the casserole. However, none of the dining waiters on the train understood his questions. Do-Hente was hungry so he finally ate a small portion.

Do-Hente began to grow weak and lose weight. In order to determine what was wrong with him he returned to the spot where he had first received his power. The voice told him that he had violated one of the rules; he had eaten meat which the Cat family would eat (the rabbit meat on the train) and the penalty would be his death.

Do-Hente, still a youthful man and keeper of the sacred tribal medicine, did not want to die. He asked the voice if there was some way to avoid this penalty. The voice said that the only way to avoid his own death was to sacrifice his oldest child, a daughter by the name of Kee-some-ma, or Medicine Wind (my grandfather) who was the second oldest. Do-Hente told the voice he would take the penalty by his own death.

Before Do-Hente died he took Medicine Wind, a boy of six or seven, and led him into the waters of a mountain stream one winter morning as the first rays of morning appeared in the sky. Do-Hente prayed long and hard to the Sun to pass his power medicine on to his son, and as he prayed he took a sharp instrument and cut into Medicine Wind's chest the crescent shape moon symbols of the Sun Dance Tai-Me medicine. The blood from the fresh cut ran down Medicine Wind's chest and into the icy waters and were carried to the east in the direction of the rising sun.

However, the medicine would not pass to Medicine Wind and years later my grandfather was to say that his fate was to become a strong Christian, which was stronger medicine than the Tai-Me medicine. That was the reason the medicine would not "take," he said.

In 1873 the power of the Tai-Me was passed on to Do-Hente's brother Onkoite. However, Onkoite also fell sick and died.

There came a time for the Kiowas, a space in history, when the tribe was in constant contact with the white man's culture and had to accept it either through choice or by force. The government insisted that the Kiowas become "civilized," allotted them a plot of land, sent their children far away to a government boarding school, and forbade them to worship the Sun or hold any of their tribal dances. The new culture required the Kiowas to plant crops instead of roaming the plains on horseback in search of food. The new culture required the Kiowas to live in houses, which were built to stay in one place, instead of a teepee which they could pack up and move at will.

Today's complex society was still distant in both the Indian and whiteman's future. Inflation, credit cards, traffic lights, taxes, pollution and alarm clocks were nonexistent.

However, to the Indians it seemed as if they moved from a free world into the confining constraints and controls which modern society demands of individuals today.

These stories occurred primarily in a small western Oklahoma town in the heart of Kiowa Indian country—Mt. View. Mt. View was built on land which had been allotted to my grandmother and which she sold in 1899. My grandparents then settled on my grandfather's allotment located west of Mt. View on a bluff which overlooks the town. There they built a two-story home. Surrounding the house were a barn, a garage, a summer arbor, and other structures which make up a productive farm. There were crops in the fields, a large vegetable garden, and a fruit orchard. Herds of white face cattle and herds of horses grazed in the pastures. The restless western Oklahoma wind swept across the prairie, keeping watch over my grandparents' possessions.

Today on this same site the restless western Oklahoma wind sweeps across a vast empty space. Nothing remains on this spot where life once was so strong. Where a full-blood Kiowa man, Wind Goomda, his full-blood Kiowa wife and their sixteen children started over, and tried to respond to a new and different life. The man, his wife, and fifteen of their children now lie in a small, peaceful Kiowa Indian cemetery by Rainy Mountain, located south of Mt. View. Rainy Mountain was a favorite camping site of the Kiowas when they roamed at will over the Plains. Only my father remains now to remember how it was with his family.

Howard Goomda, my father, was born in 1915 when the prairie grasslands were just beginning to become the farmlands of this area. He was the youngest of the children. By the time he was born, other family members were already becoming a blend of Indian and white. He was named after one of the early missionaries who came to work among the Kiowas. Father also had an Indian name, after a famous Kiowa chief. In English the name would be Running Bird.

One of his childhood stories is about Big George, who

worked for Grandfather Wind Goomda. Big George told Father that there was buried treasure on the allotment of Father's grandmother. Big George would go out into the pasture at night with a lantern and dig for hours. My father would watch him out there from his window, but George was so far in the distance all he could see was the lantern. One day Big George disappeared. Later the family heard that Big George had bought an orchard in the Rio Grande Valley in Texas. Big George sent my great-grandmother a crate of oranges and wrote her that they had been grown in his orchard for her.

A Strong Medicine Wind

Father also remembers the time the family journeyed to a ranch in Burkburnett, where a movie was being produced. The Kiowas were told to come down and become "movie stars." In one scene the Kiowas were to kill a buffalo. After the buffalo was killed, Father was to be set down on top of the buffalo. Following the movie script, the buffalo was killed and then Father was set down on top of him. Things were going good, he was laughing and smiling, and then he looked down, saw the buffalo, and started to cry. It ruined his movie career.

It seemed to be the fate of my father's family to die young. Father made the remark that one year his family was dying like flies and he could not comprehend the terribleness of it. When a loved one was lost to death in battle or by sickness in the old days, the remaining family members would mourn for a full year. They would gash their skin with a knife, cut off their hair, and chop off a finger or two. As my grandparents lost their children one by one to tuberculosis they mourned deep and hard but they had put aside the old ways and had placed their belief in God's will.

My father tells of the time Grandfather sat out in the fruit orchard one hot summer day mourning for one of his little daughters. She suddenly appeared to him in the heat of the day and he heard beautiful music in the background. She spoke to him and told him she was happy and not to grieve. Several of the other little children would appear after their deaths in the house at different times. Father said he was once going up to the second floor, and when he rounded a turn on the stairs he was taken by surprise by one of his sisters who had died two years previously. She put her finger to her lips as if to silence him. He stood there transfixed, staring at her, his heart beating wildly. She gave him a radiant smile and then was gone.

Once an uncle was at the water well getting water. He was alone at the time, everyone else having gone to church. He turned to the house quickly because he thought it was on fire it was so brilliant with light. Dropping his water bucket, he raced for the house. However, upon entering, he saw his little daughter, who had died the previous spring, standing in the middle of the room. She smiled sweetly at him and walked about the rooms for a short while, then vanished as quickly as she had appeared.

The structures surrounding the house, like the family members, had the fate of not enduring. Father tells of the night the big barn burned down. The farm hands came in late one night and were putting the horses in the barn. They were talking in loud voices and woke up some of the family in the house. Someone in the house that night said they saw matches being struck as if one of the farm hands were looking for something.

Inside the barn that night, in the west end, was a new Overland touring car. My father loved that car and used to wrestle his brothers to be able to sit on his favorite pull-down seat. The night the barn caught on fire it blazed bright into the dawn hours. They couldn't save the barn or the new Overland either. The pig pen had been next to the barn and the pigs got so hot they had to shoot them the next day. The chickens roasted in the hen house. The next day the Kiowas came with pans and kettles and picked up the roasted chickens.

It seemed to be the fate of the structures on the hill to meet a fiery end. Years later the only structure still standing—though long deserted by family members—was the house on its small hill overlooking the town. The young people of Mt. View used to say it was haunted and would go there at night to break out the windows and spook themselves. Mexican migrant workers would often take shelter there. One winter night some migrant workers built a fire and it got out of control. The fire raged until it burned the big house to the ground. My father grieved for months. He would return to the hill, barren now, and say, "It's hard to come here, the place holds such sad memories for me now."

A few months after the burning he went to his cousin's house for a visit, and a mystic was there. The mystic told Father she felt as if a loved one who'd passed on was trying very hard to get a message to him. They gathered around the table and sat quietly for awhile. The mystic began to speak in a strange voice and to write on a piece of paper. She told Father that his deceased sister Ruby was saying, "Tell Howard not to grieve over the house any longer. The person who was responsible for setting the fire has been punished. He was a Mexican farm worker and he died in a fiery bus crash on his way back to Mexico. His name was Mexican Joe."

As we would stand there on the hill Father would point to the south and say, "I remember how every summer the Cheyennes used to come here and camp in that south pasture. They would come down the road in their wagons and camp in their teepees. They would camp and every day while they were here, Father would butcher a beef. They would hang the beef out in the sun to dry like in the old days. I was always anxious for them to come because I liked to play with the little Cheyenne children."

In the old Kiowa culture the mark of a powerful man was to be wealthy but also to be generous. If you could give away all you had and gain it back again then they knew you were a powerful man. This quality is considered less than wise in today's society.

Today my grandfather, Wind Goomda, would be considered generous to a fault. I can remember as a small child walking into a tent set up beside the big house and seeing fresh beef piled high on the tables set around the tent. The Kiowas would come down the dusty road in their wagons and load up with fresh beef and stay for supper. Grandfather lived to be ninety-three years old and when we would visit him I would see him put sacks of groceries in the back seat of his car and drive off to some needy Kiowa family. He did his own grocery shopping. He could tell what was inside a can by the picture on the label. I guess the store clerks were honest people when they took his money for the price of the groceries. He would say in broken English, "Maybe so how much?" and hold out some money.

My grandparents accepted the Jesus Road early in their married life. Grandmother was a charter member of the Rainy Mountain Baptist Indian Mission. Grandfather could not read the Bible but he could quote Scriptures and tell you where they could be found in the Bible.

Once after the missionaries asked the Kiowas to raise money for a new church building my grandmother wondered how she could raise her share. She had no formal education, could not speak English, and certainly had no job skills. However, she was determined to raise her part of the needed money. She would gather all her children in a wagon and start off early in the morning. They would travel over the prairie gathering up bones. She would then take the bones into Mt. View and sell them to the white people to grind up for fertilizer. The money she made she would donate to the Indian mission. The missionaries' hearts were touched by this small Indian woman who would gather up her children and ride day after day gathering up bones in order to raise her share of the church building fund. Donations began to come in for the Indian mission after her story appeared in the church paper back East.

Once the family visited a married daughter, Olive Chaney, who lived in a house that had bees living inside the walls of the house. (This house was written about in Ripley's "Believe It or Not.") My grandmother canned the honey and took it back to Mt. View and sold it for a dollar a half-gallon. She donated this money to the church fund, also.

Once after a church service the missionaries asked for a collection as they always did. The Kiowas had always given what they could and didn't say anything, but the religion was new to them and they didn't quite understand how it worked. One old Kiowa man stood up and pulled some change from his pocket and looked at it long and hard. He seemed reluctant to give up his last bit of money. Old Mokeen stood there and squared his shoulders and spoke to one of the missionaries in broken English, "Whatza matter this Jesus—He all time broke?"

A Strong Medicine Wind

There was a dining hall at the Indian mission and Kiowa families would come early Sunday morning in their wagons and bring their dinner with them. After the morning services they would eat in the dining hall and then visit until time for the evening church service. It was too long a journey to go home for Sunday dinner and then return for the evening service.

One Sunday Grandmother prepared a favorite dish of dried chokecherries, and set some down in front of an old blind man. She told him in Kiowa to eat. He felt of the dish in front of him and then put a small morsel of chokecherries in his mouth. Suddenly he cried out in a voice filled with grief for his Indian grandmother. He had loved chokecherries as a child and his grandmother had prepared them for him but he hadn't had any since her death. The unexpected treat was just too much for the old Kiowa.

The Indian church was a vital part of daily life. First the pastor, a white man, would talk in English; then a Kiowa would interpret what the sermon was about. Next a song in English; then a song in Kiowa. Then a prayer in English; then a prayer in Kiowa. The Kiowas conducted the church service this way out of consideration for the elder members who could only understand Kiowa.

Recently at a church dinner my father heard this story. A man said that, as a child of five or six years, Old Man Goomda (Grandfather was sometimes called Old Man), would stop and pick him up every Sunday and take him along to church. The Kiowas would laugh at Grandfather and ask him why he did it. He would answer, "Who knows? Maybe someday this little boy will work in the church." That little boy, now an elderly man, has been a life-long Christian and is chairman of the Board of Deacons at this church.

It was hard for the Kiowa women to adapt to new types of food and a new style of cooking that food, but they did. Grandmother learned how to use the wood burning stove and could bake excellent cakes, pies and biscuits even though she could not read a recipe or use a measuring cup. She had learned how to cook on the prairie using for a cooking pot the stomach of a buffalo. She would simmer the buffalo meat over an open fire.

However, she later won a first prize blue ribbon at the county fair for her gallon jar of plums. The plums sat on the shelf in her kitchen with the first prize ribbon attached.

Of course, sometimes things didn't turn out that well. Not only did the Kiowas think they had to adopt the whiteman's cooking and food but his holidays as well. Once when my grandparents were taking Thanksgiving dinner to a sick Kiowa family and would not be able to return in time to prepare their own, their children decided to cook Thanksgiving dinner and surprise them. My father and his brother killed the turkey, and their grandmother prepared it for the oven. Father's sister Nettie baked a pumpkin pie not knowing exactly how to bake one. She simply put the pumpkin into a pie shell without adding any spices, eggs, milk or any other ingredients which make up a good pumpkin pie.

As the story goes, the parents arrived home and all the family sat down to enjoy their holiday meal. My grandfather started to carve the turkey and they all watched in horror as parched corn spilled over the table. It seems Great-grandmother didn't take the craw out of the turkey. They had quite a time learning all the finer points of holiday dining.

When Father started to school he could not speak English, so Grandfather decided that it would be best for the children if they spoke only English at mealtime. This would encourage them to learn polite table manners and get them used to conversing in the English language. The first time it was tried, Great-grandmother was there and she was not too happy about the new table rules. She knew broken English but preferred to speak in Kiowa.

Great-grandmother used a lot of salt on her food and never began eating until she had salted everything down. That day she thought and thought, wondering how to ask for her favorite seasoning. Then obviously pleased with herself she said, "Come here, salt!"

The women in the Goomda family are accused by their spouses of being notoriously bossy. When automobiles were still a novelty, my great-grandparents got a new car. The front seat wasn't big enough for both of them. He was thin, but she was very large. She would sit in the back seat and he in the front seat, driving. Everyone said the real reason she sat in the back seat was to see in all directions at once, for she kept up a constant stream of orders for her husband regarding his driving technique. When he didn't follow her instructions to the letter she would reach up to the front seat with the cane which she always carried, and hit him over the head.

They had a little male dog "Queen" which they took with them wherever they went. They called it "Quee" because when the Kiowas first started speaking English, they could not say the letter 'n.'

A long time ago when people wanted to settle in a town they would go to the cemetery and look at the tombstones. If there weren't many recent dates or many small children's graves they would know that the water was safe to drink and that the the town was a fairly good place to live.

However, the Kiowas had no guidelines to judge how safe their family might be from the dread disease of tuberculosis. If a child became ill, it was kept at home, apart from the rest of the family and given complete bed rest. Special precautions were taken with the handling of food dishes and bed linen. Extra tasty meals were prepared to encourage an appetite. These were precautions taken to prevent other children in the family from contracting tuberculosis. However, many of my grandparents' children were victims of the dread disease, and the following story provides some insight on how the illness might have spread.

One of the boys contracted tuberculosis and was confined to his upstairs bedroom. His mother prepared his food and handled all the cleaning that was necessary. However, the children took turns carrying his food tray to him. A sister, Ruby, told of carrying his food tray to him and then returning for it a short while later. He hardly had touched his food. She picked up the tray and took it to the top of the stairs; then, before she took the food down for it to be thrown away, she couldn't resist taking a small bite because it looked so good. Just then her sick brother came out of his room with a spoon which had been forgotten. Upon seeing his little sister taste his leftover food he became so enraged that he knocked her down the stairs.

New rules were promptly put into effect among the children, and this was the last case of active tuberculosis among the brothers and sisters.

The Kiowas had a custom of having a favorite child. Usually this child was allowed to do as it pleased while the rest of the children had to toe the mark. Some of the old Kiowa parents, if their favorite child died, would continue to put up a special teepee for the child's bones, and put out food for the child's spirit to eat.

The favorite child in my father's family was his brother Joe. Joe was born on Christmas Day 1907. When he received his Indian name it was quite an honor and he received an eagle feather war bonnet.

Joe contracted tuberculosis when he was nineteen. My grandparents placed him in the Mormon Sanatorium in Oklahoma City. Joe had two friends who worked there. Every night one friend would unlock the window in Joe's room and the other friend would place a ladder under the window. Every night Joe would go down the ladder and drive off in his new Studebaker (which was garaged at the

Sanatorium) into the night life in Oklahoma City. Joe had an account with an Oklahoma City bank and every three months my grandfather would deposit $1,000 in that account.

By 1926 Joe wasn't getting any better and my grandfather wanted to take Joe and return to the original homeland of the Kiowas which was Montana and Wyoming. They started out in the Studebaker for Yellowstone National Park. In Colorado they stayed in Denver for two months to give Joe the benefit of the higher altitude. Joe entered the All State Motor Car Show in Denver and won second place in the parade. He received a silver cup.

But in Denver Joe began to get worse and when it became apparent that he would not live long, Grandfather decided to take him back to Oklahoma. Howard, my father, was only twelve years old at the time but he was commissioned to drive one of the cars back.

The young driver soon became exhausted from the ordeal of driving day and night to reach Oklahoma. He fell asleep at the wheel, the car traveled up a dirt embankment and flipped completely over, landing right side up on the dirt road. My father kept right on driving, afraid to stop the car and meet his mother's wrath, despite much honking from the car behind him. Along the way Joe's breathing became labored and he died as they crossed Raton Pass. My grandfather then took his body by train through Kansas to Oklahoma.

My brother David and I and our cousins would spend our summer months playing around the big house on the bluff. I remember the violent storms which would cross the prairie. We would all make a dash for the storm cellar while the storm raged around us. Only my father would not go. There is a tribal legend that the Kiowas made the first tornado. They gathered together a hide and the head of a buffalo and stuffed it with buffalo grass; the hide began to grow and swell and finally became a raging spinning tornado. It looked down on the Kiowas and said "You are my people.

Oklahoma Memories

When you see me coming, come out and talk to me so I will know that you are my people, the Kiowas, and I will pass over you."

My father tells the story of relatives who ran for the storm cellar one stormy night. It was still light enough to see the tornado on the ground spinning its way right toward them. They became excited and the wife said, "Stand here and talk to the tornado. You know it is our relative. Tell it to pass over us."

The Kiowa man stood his ground and emotionally asked the tornado not to destroy their farm but to pass to the south of them. His wife, standing on the steps in the storm cellar with the door open, was listening to him. She called to him in Kiowa that their boys were at the government school at Fort Sill, which was to the south of them. When he realized his error, he became frantic and told the tornado, "Wait! wait! Disregard those instructions and pass to the north of us!" The tornado veered off course and did as it was requested.

My grandmother died before I was born but I did get to know my grandfather. He saved me from many spankings when I was small. If I could run fast enough to come within Grandfather's line of vision, by Kiowa custom my parents could not and did not touch me. I would stay in his sight until my parents cooled off, and then everything would be fine. In the old days it was considered too distressing for grandparents to observe their grandchildren being disciplined, so out of respect Kiowa parents didn't correct their children in front of them.

I never did learn how to speak Kiowa and my grandfather could only speak a little broken English. However, we didn't let that stand in our way. We would sit next to each other and hold hands while he would pop the knuckles on both my hands. I would talk in English and he would respond in Kiowa or the other way round. We never knew what the other was talking about but it didn't really matter. We knew what we were trying to tell each other.

All the grandchildren are scattered now, but it seems the

strong Medicine Wind which braced us against the changing world when we were young and growing has sustained us through our own transition. We have kept alive in our hearts the influence of the strong but gentle ways of our people. As we gaze at the college degrees and honors which we have acquired in the whiteman's world we realize that in our hearts we are Indian but our minds must of necessity compete in the whiteman's world.

One cousin tells of lying badly wounded behind enemy lines in Korea, sure he would never see loved ones again. However, he had a vision. Bleeding, perhaps dying, he saw himself and our grandfather. Grandfather told Ralph that he would return home. Ralph gathered all his strength and resources and dodged enemy fire, bleeding profusely and dazed with pain, but he held that vision and those words with him until he made it back to the safety of his Airborne Unit—and later until he once again stood on the small bluff in western Oklahoma where the restless western Oklahoma wind swept over him.

The Kiowas have a legend that when a powerful Medicine dies the heavens cry. The day my grandfather died, peacefully surrounded by loved ones, he gazed at each one of us in turn. As he died a ray of sun fell across his face and a soft rain fell. In the distance a church bell tolled.

The Kiowas know it to be true, a powerful Medicine can give away all he has and gain it back again.

If You Don't Weaken

¶ *Land dominates Oklahoma history. Land had attracted thousands to the borders of Indian Territory in the late nineteenth century. The continuing desire to own land was the catalyst of radical political movements in the twentieth.* ¶ *Although Oklahomans created a political system to preserve and protect the agrarian way of life, there was never enough land. For the thousands who came in each land opening, there were only so many good homesteads. People lucky enough to stake a claim often had little or no money for livestock, seed, or implements. The penniless farmer struggling merely to hold his 160 acres faced the hardships of both nature and a complex economic system. Often the hapless farmer was forced into a debt cycle from which foreclosure was the only escape. Without land of his own, a man became a tenant farmer in order to feed his family.* ¶ *In hard times, in the best American tradition, farmers blamed economic agents like the railroad or corporations, and especially government, for their woes. The discontents that the tenant system, illiteracy, poor nutrition, drought, insects, fluctuations in market prices, and "hard times" bred were fertile soil for the growth of socialism in Oklahoma.* ¶ *Oscar Ameringer, a German immigrant who came to the Twin Territories just before statehood to enlist coal miners and building tradesmen in the Socialist party, dismissed these Oklahoma farmers as poor fuel for any Socialist bonfire. His earlier experience among midwestern farmers had convinced Ameringer that they were minor capitalists and unlikely revolutionaries. But his first visit to Harrah, Oklahoma, changed his mind. Ameringer became the leader of the Oklahoma Socialist party and for over twenty-five years published a Socialist newspaper,* The American Guardian, *in Oklahoma City.* ¶ *Socialism in Oklahoma was the logical successor to populism, the political weapon at hand for discontented farmers. The party's modified doctrines did not depart*

From Oscar Ameringer, *If You Don't Weaken, The Autobiography of Oscar Ameringer* (New York: Henry Holt and Company, 1940), 227–35.

much from the average Sooner's inherited thinking about what was necessary to achieve farm prosperity. Any belief in ideology was superficial. The existing order was at fault. The Democratic party was unresponsive, and since these desperate farmers were pathologically suspicious of the Republicans, they attacked with a Socialist vote. ¶ Oklahoma socialism was at its peak at the outbreak of the European war in 1914. With the wartime economy's insatiable demands and good weather, farm prices soared, revealing Oklahoma socialism's shallow roots. Basically, the Oklahoma farmer's flirtation with socialism was just that. The extreme, often desperate, hopes and ambitions of these last frontiersmen fortified a normal American tendency to develop strong rhetorical answers to economic distress. That mood gave a deceptively violent tone to Socialist talk. The sights Ameringer witnessed and described were true enough, but his solution was not a lasting one.

I CAME to Oklahoma City in the early spring of 1907, the year Oklahoma entered the Union as a State. On my arrival I went first to the state office of the Socialist Party of Oklahoma, on Main Street. The state secretary was Otto Branstetter, later national secretary of the party, and there were various reasons why I called on him so promptly. In the first place, I was a member in good standing of the Socialist Party. Second, the secretary should be qualified to give me the low-down on Oklahoma. Lastly, I meant to give him my opinion on the fallacy of a socialist movement almost exclusively composed of farmers. I knew farmers like a book. I had slept in their beds, eaten at their tables, had even painted farmers in the Pickaway plains of Ohio. They were fine enough people, but they certainly were not the kind to whom Marx had addressed his clarion call: "Proletarians of the world, unite! You have nothing to lose but your chains. You have a world to gain." Besides, had not Marx written about "the idiocy of rural life?"

Farmers were not wage earners. They were capitalists,

exploiting wage labor. They owned the means of production. They had a great deal more to lose than their chains. They had acres of land, thousands of dollars' worth of farm implements, fine homes and big barns to lose. And before they'd give them up, they'd fight. I explained all this to Otto Branstetter, sparing him none of my opinions on this vital point.

If You Don't Weaken

The secretary confessed there wasn't much of a proletariat in Oklahoma to build a proletarian revolution on, and with. Further east in Indian territory, he told me, there were ten thousand coal miners. A fine, fighting bunch, and a good number of them members of the Party. The conservative building-trade workers of the larger towns were fairly well organized, but on the whole, a poor crowd to work on. If anything was to be done in the line of social revolution, there was no choice but to enlist the farmers who formed the overwhelming bulk of Oklahoma's population. But was I really sure that all farmers owned large farms, and commanded the implements of production and exploitation? Above all, what did I know about Oklahoma farmers? Was I sure they were the same kind of farmers I was acquainted with back in Ohio? If not, and since I had come to Oklahoma to study its social and economic conditions, how would I like to arrange a speaking tour for me? It would give me a close-up of Southwest farmers and farm life. The Party didn't pay salaries to its missionaries. I would have to take up collections to pay my fare from place to place. However, in most instances the comrades would haul me, and in all cases entertain me at their homes. What did I think of the idea?

I thought it was a first-rate idea.

The initial speaking date which the obliging state secretary arranged for my benefit was in Harrah, a hamlet of some two hundred souls twenty miles east of Oklahoma City. I had difficulty in reaching Harrah by train. There was a flood. Creeks and rivers had overflowed their banks. Culverts and bridges had been washed out. All roads leading to Harrah were under clay-colored water. It took the train the better part of the day to make the twenty-odd miles.

The meeting was in a one-room schoolhouse, unpainted on the outside, unceilinged on the inside. I was late. The audience had already assembled and what an assemblage! All hands were soaking, sloppy wet. Puddles of water had formed on the floor. A few stable lanterns supplied the illumination. Babies were sleeping on the speaker's platform. More babies slept, nursed, or cried on the breasts of their mothers, uncomfortably wedged into school seats designed for ten-year-olds. All were wretchedly dressed: faded blue jeans for the men; faded Mother Hubbards and poke bonnets for the women. The people had trudged in soaking rain, or come in open wagons or on horseback or muleback, to hear a socialist speech—and they were farmers! This indescribable aggregation of moisture, steam, dirt, rags, unshaven men, slatternly women and fretting children were farmers! Ghost of Dan Hitler—they were farmers! I had come upon another America!

The chairman of the meeting, who looked as if he had just been dug out of a wet clay bank, apologized for the small attendance. (It wasn't a small attendance. It was an outpouring of the masses, considering the night and road condition.) The main trouble, he explained, was that most of the comrades lived in the Kickapoo country across the Canadian River, and the bridge was washed out.

Further questioning revealed that my chairman lived over the river in the Kickapoo country, too. When I asked him if he had come across in a skiff, he replied, "No, I hitched my team on the other side and swam across. I feared you might get sore, not having a chairman."

Great Jehoshaphat! He had swum the swollen North Canadian in the only suit to his name. No question but these people were American farmers, but not the kind I had known in the Pickaway plains of Ohio. These people occupied an even lower level of existence than the white and black "water rats" of New Orleans.

During the days of opulence on a rising labor scale, I had acquired a certain standard of comfort and decency. The brewery workers had been especially liberal toward me: "Don't sit up night in day coaches. Take the sleepers. Don't eat cold lunches. Eat in the diner. Don't stop at cheap hotels. Stop in good hotels and see that there is a bathroom handy. You need all your strength for the work you are doing." Such had been the advice of the officials of the Cincinnati headquarters. My weekly salary had been fifty-four dollars and all expenses, plus five dollars a day "treating money." And as I had made it a rule to stay away from saloons as much as possible during strikes, that extra five was largely mine.

If You Don't Weaken

Green as I was in my new America, I knew enough not to expect a room with bath in Harrah. As it turned out, the town contained no hotel of any kind. A comrade would entertain me in his house. The comrade was waiting. He had already loaded his wife and flock of children in the wagon bed. He and the honored guest mounted the wagon seat and started out in the pitch black night and pouring rain. The oil in his wagon lantern had given out; we jolted over blackjack stumps and roots, sumped into ruts, slushed through young lakes, had our faces caressed by wet blackjack branches. At last we came to the house, the typical tenant shack I was soon to know so well, and hate so deeply.

Actually, this was one of the better tenant shacks. The comrade was not a share cropper. He was a managing tenant. There were three whole rooms and a lean-to kitchen, as I found out the next morning. There were glass windows—with most of the panes out—in every room, but no screens on either doors or windows.

My host had replenished his wagon lantern and shown me my room and had departed with a pleasant "Good night," and an ominous admonition, "Don't let the bedbugs bite." There was no furniture in the room other than a sagging steel cot. There was not even a nail in the straight up-and-down board of the walls on which to hang my clothes. I undressed, deposited my clothes on the floor, put on my

nightgown, and lay down on the cot. I had suspected a mattress under the faded gray cotton comfort, oozing cotton from a thousand holes. There was no mattress. But there was a faded brown blanket at the foot of the cot. I was too tired from the experiences of the day to take out a book from my suitcase to read myself to sleep in the light of the smoking stable lantern.

I was lying in the dark, thinking how heartily I should kick the posterior of a certain person who had known all about American farmers the day before, when I heard the whine of an on-coming army of mosquitoes. I had encountered mosquitoes in the flats of New Jersey and the swamps of the Delta, but these Oklahoma mosquitoes were the bitingest I had met so far. Either their auger bits sank deeper, their appetite was sharper, or the hungry man-eaters had at last discovered the man of their dreams. I pulled the faded brown blanket over my rapidly swelling face. It was a horse blanket, and from the powerful ammonia odor it exuded, had served oftener under than on the back of the horse.

Presently things began biting me under the horse blanket. They seemed to care specially for my neck, wrist and ankles. At last I caught one of them and investigated. I had met bedbugs, too, before, but not these famished baby turtles.

The moon was peeping through a yellow ring of clouds. I thought I saw something like grass out of the window. It was glistening wet, but anything was preferable to that axis of mosquitoes and bedbugs!

Lying on the wet grass, I had escaped the baby turtles, but the mosquitoes still pursued me. The nightgown, wet as it was, still offered some protection for the unexposed portion of my anatomy, but now something new was feasting on me under the nightgown, something small and wingless. I was being introduced to chiggers, and they seemed to be exceedingly fond of itinerant socialists.

How I survived that long night is beyond me. When breakfast was announced I was still too full of lumps, bumps, and itches to mumble more than "Good morning." Breakfast consisted of fat meat, corn bread, molasses and black "coffee," made of chicory and minus cream and sugar. The cow had gone dry and they had forgotten to bring home sugar from town.

The home in which I was entertained the following night was not quite so luxurious. It lacked board floors and glass windows. But the mosquitoes and the bed turtles were a little bigger, hungrier, and more numerous than at the first place. I didn't try the chiggers. From the look of things they might prove to be sabertoothed tigers the size of woolly mastodons.

I am not exaggerating. As the days grew into weeks, I found worse than what I have described so far. I found toothless old women with sucking infants on their withered breasts. I found a hospitable old hostess, around thirty or less, her hands covered with rags and eczema, offering me a biscuit with those hands, apologizing that her biscuits were not as good as she used to make because with her sore hand she no longer could knead the dough as it ought to be. I saw youngsters emaciated by hookworms, malnutrition, and pellagra, who had lost their second teeth before they were twenty years old. I saw tottering old male wrecks with the infants of their fourteen-year-old wives on their laps. I saw a white man begging a Choctaw squaw man who owned the only remaining spring in that neighborhood to let him have credit for a few buckets of water for his thirsty family. I saw humanity at its lowest possible level of degradation and decay. I saw smug, well-dressed overly well fed hypocrites march to church on Sabbath day, Bibles under their arms, praying for God's kingdom on earth while fattening like latter-day cannibals on the share croppers. I saw windjamming, hot-air-spouting politicians geysering Jeffersonian platitudes about equal rights to all and special privileges to none; about all men born equal with the rights to life, liberty and the pursuit of happiness without even knowing, much less caring, that they were addressing as wretched a set of abject slaves as ever walked the face of the earth, anywhere or at any time. The things I saw on that trip are the things you never forget.

What those people needed, what they need today, is not pious soothing syrup and political Castoria. What they needed was not uplift from above, no matter how well meant, but upheaval from below that would give them a big and good enough share of God's footstool on which to work, rear their children and restore to themselves the dignity of human beings. Goethe says youth is revolutionary, maturity conservative, old age reactionary. Well, I am nearing seventy, but I still regard a social arrangement in which some possess thousands of acres of life-giving earth, while millions of children are born without enough earth to plant their little pink bottoms on, a black betrayal of democracy, and an insult to Christianity.

The Grapes of Wrath, by John Steinbeck, has shocked tenderskinned sisters and sensitive brethren who wouldn't lift a finger to wipe the foul blot off the face of America. They have called the book vile, vulgar, and indecent. It is as vile, vulgar and indecent as the condition of the people whom Steinbeck saw and I saw years before him.

For myself, the die was cast. Up to then I had been a part-time world-saver. Now I was a professional, on full time, and in every fiber of my being. This thing was too terrible to be tolerated. I would arouse these people, so much lower in the scale of life than New Orleans dock wallopers, black and white, at the end of their nine-week strike. They were worse fed, worse clothed, worse housed, more illiterate than the Chicago packing house wops and bohunks Upton Sinclair described in his *The Jungle*, and whom I had seen with my own eyes while doing my bit in one of their strikes. The Oklahoma farmers' living standard was so far below that of the sweatshop workers of the New York east side before the Amalgamated Clothing Workers and International Ladies' Garment Workers Unions had mopped up that human cesspool, that comparison could not be thought of.

But these people were not wops and bohunks. They were not Jewish needle slaves, escaped from the ghettos and pogroms of Czarist Russia and Poland. They were Americans almost to a man. Their forefathers had been starved, driven, shipped and sold over here long before and shortly after the Revolution. They were Scotch, Irish, Scotch-Irish and English with only a few exceptions. They were more American than the poplation of any present-day New England town. They were Washington's ragged, starving, shivering army at Valley Forge, pushed ever westward by beneficiaries of the Revolution. Pushed out of Tidewater Virginia, and out of the fertile Piedmont, and the river valleys of the Central Atlantic states, into the hills and mountains of the South Central states. They had followed on the heels of the Cherokees, Choctaws, Chickasaws, Creeks and Seminoles, like the stragglers of routed armies. Always hoping that somewhere in their America there would be a piece of dirt for them.

Now they had settled down in the hills of the Indian Territory, tenants of white land hogs, Indians, squaw men and Afro-American freedmen. A quarter of a century later, burned out and tractored out, they pulled up stakes for the last time until they landed in ramshackle trucks and tin lizzies in California, as ragged, hungry and shivering as their ancestors at Valley Forge.

They had hoped the Homestead Act would be applied to the Indian Territory. That Uncle Sam would have farms for them, too. Uncle Sam had presented quarter-sections of virgin prairie land to millions of Swedes, Norwegians, Danes, Germans. Why should he deny a forty-acre, two-mule farm to Americans stemming from Valley Forge and Yorktown.

The Indian Territory was not thrown open for homesteading. It had been given to the Indians under a sacred treaty, signed by the Great White Father in Washington, providing it should be theirs "as long as water flows and grass grows green." By that time the bulk of North American Indians were safely cornered. But their hunting grounds had woefully shrunken; buffalo almost exterminated and other game greatly diminished. Fire water, white man's diseases, a new, and to the Indian, unnatural mode of living, had undermined his resistance, pride and constitution.

Somebody had to support poor Lo. He could not be supported by taxes levied on the whole of the United States, all of which had been taken from him. So what more natural than to let poor Lo keep his land and the poor hillbillies work it? And so we have the interesting spectacle of white, native, Protestant Americans working as the land slaves, tenants and share croppers of the aboriginal Indian.

The Indian was not a bad landlord. He still labored under the heathen delusion that land belonged to the Great Spirit who had made air, rain and sunshine. So long as his superior Anglo-Saxon land slave could supply him with a hog or a jug of fire water now and then, in addition to the meager dole he received from the White Father in Washington, he was contented. Later on, when the Office of Indian Affairs assumed the role of rent collector, poor Lo's income went up as his white tenant's went down. Still later, when squaw men, usurers, land sharks, and Eastern insurance companies had come into possession of most of poor Lo's inheritance, to have been his "as long as water flows," the position of the tenants and share croppers hit rock-bottom. So at last they pulled out onto Highway Sixty-Six on their final journey to Gethsemane.

I wish someone would look up the names on the roster of

Washington's army at Valley Forge and trace the bloody footprints of their descendants across the North American continent until they were washed up and washed out on the shore of the Pacific. What an all-American Odyssey it would make! What a great history of the Rise and Fall of American Civilization. And I, a social worker—hell! I had a real job on hand.

If You Don't Weaken

What's the Latest from Europe?

¶ *Before 1917, many debt-ridden sharecroppers living in the tangled blackjack and post oak near the South Canadian River had joined local radical groups known as Working Class Unions. These fraternal groups, ostensibly formed to discuss ways to improve the farmer's lot, were actually secret orders with elaborate rituals involving six-shooters and Bible quotations. During World War I, leaders of the Industrial Workers of the World saw these groups as easy converts to their plans for sabotage and unrest. They encouraged the discontented farmers to resist the military draft as a protest against economic inequities.* ¶ *Because of their isolation and a long tradition of individual action, these farmers believed that direct action was necessary and justified. A ragtag group of poor whites and blacks, with some Indians, began burning railroad bridges, dynamiting oil pipelines and water mains, and tearing down public fences to protest the draft. That guerilla activity became known as the "Green Corn Rebellion," because Oklahomans believed the rebels planned to live on green roasting ears foraged from the fields as they marched on Washington.* ¶ *The march was soon curtailed, as authorities arrested leaders, and the local press demanded the scaffold or life imprisonment for the rebels. Since most of the disturbances had occurred in counties with Socialist strength, local Democratic leaders saw the chance to eradicate the troublesome "reds." Men who had joined the march as a way of expressing their economic grievances were branded as subversives, and the epithet of "slacker" plagued them the rest of their lives.*

Anonymous, from Ned DeWitt, W.P.A. *Writers Project on Oil in Oklahoma.* Western History Collections, University of Oklahoma.

ALL OF US didn't go. There was a little handful that stayed right here in the U.S. Maybe you wasn't old enough to 'member back that far but there was some of us down in this part of the country that decided we wasn't gonna fight somebody else's war for 'em, and we refused to go. We didn't volunteer and we didn't answer the draft. We had a union, the Working Class Union we called it, and there was about 5,000 of us, mostly farmers, that told 'em we was damned if we'd go. Most of us had wives and kids and we didn't wanta leave them here to do all the work of harvestin' and us have to go over there in France and fight people we didn't have anything against. We told 'em that; we ast how our fam'lies'd get along with us not here but they said go fight for democracy or our wimmen'd get raped for sure. We didn't have any bands and uniforms and that stuff down here in these sand-hills so that crap about the Germans comin' over here when they finished up the English and French didn't go over with us.

They kept after us till we decided maybe the men we'd sent to Washington didn't know as much about runnin' the country as we thought they did when we voted 'em up there, and we got to talkin' it around and decided to go up and get shet of 'em. We didn't want any trouble with anybody; all we wanted was to be let alone and go on farming. We had an idea we was just about as much 'Mericans as the men we'd sent up there that voted us in the war, but we wanted to show 'em we wasn't in'trested in fightin' over there.

The way the papers played us up you'd thought we was the wildest bunch of outlaws ever turned loose. They said there was a railroad bridge between here and Francis—a little town over southeast of here—they said we burned the bridge down to the water. That was just a plain damned lie. I walked over that bridge myself the day after they said we burned it. They had us doin' lots of things we didn't even think of; blowin' up water tanks and oil tanks and shootin' people and I don't know what all. They didn't care if we had or not; all they wanted was to stop us 'fore our anti-war idea took a big hold down here. They got the sheriffs and constables and Boy Scouts and National Guards and ever' body big enough to lift a shotgun out to hunt us. We hadn't kept it no secret that we had a meetin'-place down by Sasakwa, and the mornin' of the day we was goin' to march to Washington we split up in three armies and started out. We'd killed us a couple of beeves and barbecued them and made "Tom-fuller"—that's a kind of stew out of green corn like the Indians used to make; that's why they called it the "Green Corn Rebellion"—and we ate and talked and just sat around till time to go.

What's The Latest From Europe?

That very mornin' they surrounded us and captured the whole bunch. We couldn't shoot at 'em. The papers said we were cowards but we weren't. Some of the men in the posse were neighbors of ours and we couldn't shoot 'em down in cold blood. That's the way we felt 'bout the Germans and all the rest of 'em; we didn't have no quarrel with them a-tall. We didn't even fire a shot. They put over 500 of us in jail and kept us there a couple of days and then turned all but 74 loose. The 74 of us stayed in the state penitentiary about six weeks and then they kept about 20 of the leaders and let the rest of us go on back home on parole.

Even in jail they tried to get us steamed up to fight. The old depitty warden 'd come around ever' day, mornin', noon and night, and how he'd lay into us! He'd swear on a stack of Bibles a mile high that if we signed up to go fight we'd get off free, but we still didn't like the idea. We thought strong enough 'bout not fightin' we got thrown in the pen so one more speech didn't make such difference. I got a 2-year suspended sentence, some of 'em got from nothing at all to 5 years suspended, and the leaders got from a year-and-a-day on up to 10 years in the Federal pen. They went off laughin' and singin', but they came back old men. They really gave 'em the works. I had a friend used to live up there in the woods east of my shack; they slapped him and beat him till he went nuts. When he got out they sent him back here but he didn't know a thing and his brother finally had to ship him off to the asylum. They'd beat his brains out up there in the pen for bein' a "slacker."

I was a "slacker" too, but I didn't get my brains beat out

and didn't have to fight somebody I never had seen and wasn't mad at. But it was plenty tough. I couldn't get a job here and I had to report to the judge ever' week so there wasn't much chance of gettin' a job someplace else. My wife divorced me in 1918; she got tired of starvin' and havin' to face all the wimmen in town and know they were sayin' she was a slacker's wife behind her back. When she quit me I got a little shack back in the hills south of here and scratched around at odd jobs and managed to pull through. I'd been born on a farm, that was all I did up till I got arrested, so I knew how to raise my own feed, but I couldn't get credit for seed and no work to speak of to earn the money to buy any, and about all I could do was raise garden stuff.

I wasn't anything but a punchin'-bag for a couple of years. Ever'time the Klu Kluxers had a meetin' or when the town boys got drunk and didn't have anything else to do they'd come out and beat up on me. If I wasn't there they'd wait or maybe come back, and then it was really tough on me. I'd been a red-card Socialist all my life, since I was big enough to make my mark, so you might say I was prepared for rough stuff, and they never did make me change my mind 'bout the war.

None of my brothers or my daddy or anybody in my fam'ly belonged to the Socialists, just me. They were all farmers and didn't give a damn if there was any democracies left or not; they were gettin' $2 a bushel for wheat so to hell with agitators like me that wanted to end the war. They sung it a little different when the boys had to go to war though. I couldn't talk to any of 'em a-tall. They didn't want me 'round their houses and didn't come to see me either; they didn't care if I starved or not and prob'ly would of been glad if I had.

Sometimes I'd meet one of 'em on the street, and ever' last one would ast me the same questions the Council of Defense did: 'Why don't you wanta fight? You ain't gonna live forever, are you? You want them Huns to come over here, rapin' your wife and torturin' your kids?

When they'd ast me that I'd turn right around and put my old question to them: 'What the hell *are* we fightin' about? Russia and England and France and Italy and all the rest of the Allies ain't democracies; what the hell you so in'trested for if it ain't $2 wheat!'

Was I right or wrong? Did we save democracy? When we set it up so they could have communism and fascism and naziism and all that? Gettin' in a war's no way to save what you've got, and there's no sense of goin' to war ever' 20 or 25 years either. All this country or any other one's got to do to keep out of war and have a real democracy is give ever'body that wants it a job. If a man wants to work, let him; if he don't, let him starve. But give 'em all a chance at it, and then there won't be any reason for a man not likin' the way his country's run.

What's The Latest From Europe?

At the Old Ball Game

¶ *In April, 1903, Peter Levite and his son George, Jewish immigrants from Bessarabia in Eastern Europe, opened Levite's Handy Corner in Apache, Oklahoma Territory. George operated the store for more than seventy years. A man of many talents, merchant Levite was a civic leader, a sign painter, historian, and newspaper correspondent for the Lawton* Constitution *and* Morning Press, *the Anadarko* Daily News, *and the* Daily Oklahoman. ¶ *Life in Apache just after statehood was anything but dull. Besides the usual traveling theatrical productions, drummers, medicine shows, church socials, and school and fraternal affairs which enlivened the average week, baseball was a universal passion. Small towns and many rural communities across the country had well-equipped and colorfully outfitted teams which competed for local honors. Every old cow pasture that was transformed into a baseball diamond on Sunday afternoon nourished thousands of young boys and a few middle-aged businessmen and farmers who dreamed of "stardom in the majors." ¶ For many years, George Levite was the player-manager of the Apache baseball team. His recollections of those years are a pleasant reminder of the nature of sport before professionals edged out amateurs, and speed and violence became the spectators' new obsessions.*

"Hey! This cap is too small!"
"My socks don't match!"
"Who has a glove I can use?"

The Apache baseball team was suiting up for a Sunday game, the most important event of the week in our small town. The boys changed clothes in the back of my father's

From George Levite, *By George!* (Apache, Oklahoma: privately printed, 1974), 15–18.

store so we could keep the uniforms and our equipment from being misplaced.

It fell my lot to be player-manager for several years, and keeping the players and fans satisfied was a job with a multitude of problems.

Most small towns and many rural communities had teams that ranged from small fry and teenagers to the final jump when you were ready for the "majors" to carry the honors of the town.

Our first diamond in those days shortly after the turn of the century was in a pasture with a growth of native grass and weeds. The ninety foot square, with a semicircle for the infield, had to be skinned clean and later smoothed with a horse-drawn drag. Cleaning the area with hoes, shovels, and rakes and keeping down the growth was a tedious job, but youth with a desire for the national pastime did the job without compensation.

I never figured out why, but cattle like to hold their "conventions" on the bare ground and when they resumed grazing they left more than their tracks on our ball field. This called for more shovel work before every practice session as well as when regular games were scheduled. Occasionally we would induce some farmer to mow the outfield with a horse drawn mower, a very "modern" operation compared to our backbreaking do-it-yourself method.

Some of the players, who later became "stars" with local fans, were at first to be induced to don a uniform. One I remember in particular was a big, raw-boned, limber-jointed country lad who could knock a squirrel out of a tall tree with a rock. He liked baseball, but he didn't care for our uniforms. Well, we decided that tradition was one thing, but talent was definitely another. So there he stood in his overalls and big black farm hat mowing down batter after batter. According to an ex-league catcher who used him at a nearby town, this fellow had big league possibilities, but he couldn't be convinced to try out. Guess he was afraid that those eastern dudes wouldn't cotton to his overalls and hat like we did.

In those days only one umpire officiated. He stood behind the pitcher's mound, and at times his decisions were questionable. Shouts of "Kill the umpire!" could be heard then just as they are now, but some things have changed. The cost is one of them. The best Louisville slugger bats were $1.25 and a standard league baseball, guaranteed for nine innings, could be purchased for the same price. But back then that was a lot of money, so for economic reasons only two balls sufficed for the game. When one was lost in the tall grass or knocked into a nearby creek, time was called until the horsehide was recovered.

With sports limited in those days and no radio or television, baseball was taken seriously not only by the players but also by all their kinfolk and admirers. Grandstands were for the city folks, but without them it was difficult to control the fans at some important contests since they crowded the baselines. Some of them used at bat to lean on and some just held on to one in case an argument or fight occurred. Most of the fisticuffs were among the spectators, but occasionally players who got roughed up took to the manly art of self-defense.

With an important game in the offing, local folks, who probably bet a few bucks, would make up a pot to import outstanding individuals from other towns. Invariable these players had "off" days, and the local manager, unfortunately often me, would hear from the fans in no uncertain terms: "You should have known better," they'd tell me. "We have better men than him on the bench." And on and on and on. I soon found out that a manager had to manage much more than the team.

For years admission was twenty-five cents and later it was upped to thirty-five. Home teams would provide the balls and pay local restaurants to feed the players and their manager. Family style meals were twenty-five cents and those athletes could really put the grub away.

Gate receipts were usually divided sixty per cent to the winner and forty per cent to the loser. Most games were played in open fields with no fences. Consequently several trust individuals were stationed at strategic points to collect the fee. Most of the fans forked over the small admission, but occasionally a few refused to pay and fights resulted when they were denied admission. After the playing field was moved to the city park, freeloaders contended that they could attend without paying since the park was on city property.

On one occasion we were playing a near-by town on the 40%–60% basis. Rivalry was keen with odds against us. There was a huge crowd attending. As the game was in their home town, they hired the fee collectors. When the final out was near and Apache was leading by a wide margin, the "money man" disappeared, so we had to settle for a nominal sum.

Team trips to neighboring towns were made on horse drawn wagons and since the average speed was four miles an hour, the ball team started very early to arrive by noon. Often the trips home were after dark. Sometimes frequent stops were made so that the boys could sample watermelons, peaches, and occasionally, if time allowed, a chicken that happened to stray onto the road. Once while we were stopped at a tempting watermelon patch, the farmer caught us. He stopped his team on a one-way bridge, barring our road home. Hopping out of his wagon with a big black snake whip in his hand, he threatened to have the entire team in jail before the sun went down.

Fortunately, we had one fellow in the group who should have been a lawyer and we hurriedly elected him spokesman by shoving him to the front. He explained in his best court room manner that the boys had taken only a couple of melons and had not destroyed a lot looking for a ripe one as some ruffians might have done. He also apologized profusely for the intrusion and promised most solemnly that it would never happen again. After a pause that seemed like years, the man moved his team and let us proceed home.

Another time this same player was involved in a ruckus on a train as we were traveling to play an army team at Fort Sill. All trains had a vendor of papers, magazines, candy and fruits. These vendors were called "news butches." My sometimes lawyer friend was hit in the head with a flying banana peel thrown by a rowdy fellow-player. He quickly bought a bottle of soda pop, opened it, gave it a good shake, and pursued the peeling tosser. As he overtook him, he removed his thumb in an effort to spray his foe with the fizzing contents. But his aim was not too good and a Catholic priest was literally baptized with the sweet stuff. Since the train coaches were screenless in those days the flies swarmed all over the clergyman. The priest summoned the conductor, but the soda pop squirter hid until the train had reached its destination.

One other bit of baseball excitement occurred when the local club played the famous "Boston Bloomers" which was supposedly an all girl team; it was soon discovered that some men played the more important positions. We played them anyway. They arrived in a special white railway car that was decorated with mirrors and caused quite a stir in our quiet little town. They even brought with them a massive canvas wall that surrounded the playing field so that admission could be collected.

Before radios were a household item, Apache baseball fans were anxious to hear the world series, so R. T. Carter, a local druggist accommodated the boys by allowing them to assemble in his store to hear a radio broadcast using a head phone set. I constructed a miniature diamond of plywood with the bases and outfield marked distinctly. Each player's name was printed on a small card which was placed on the board as he came to bat.

Sitting on top of a table, I relayed each player's progress and an assistant moved the cards around the board. We were all as excited as if we had been in the grandstands.

Now folks in Apache sit in their homes and watch games from far away New York on their television sets. I wonder if they know that the same excitement was there in Carter's Drug Store in the early 1900's.

Father's 300-Room Hobby

¶ *In the first two decades of the twentieth century Oklahoma appeared destined for unparalleled growth and prosperity. While a series of oil strikes brought great riches to some, thousands more profited as oil-related industries built prosperous towns and ensured jobs for people who otherwise might have remained poor. Perle Mesta's account of growing up in her father's hotel, with wolves on the roof, lions in the halls, and bandits and oil-rich Indians in the lobby, could only have happened in Oklahoma.*
¶ *William Balser Skirvin, "a pioneer in a railroad parlor car," arrived in Guthrie on April 22, 1889. Within a few weeks he had made a considerable profit from shrewd real estate speculation. He invested those profits in an oil venture in south Texas which turned out to be the legendary Spindletop field of gushers. Grateful to Oklahoma for providing the start of his fortune, Skirvin built an ultramodern hotel just across from the Rock Island railroad depot in Oklahoma City. The Skirvin lobby soon became a bustling center of business wheeling and dealing, while the banquet rooms and nine-piece orchestra provided a sophisticated patina for the town's burgeoning social life.* ¶ *Perle Skirvin married a wealthy Pittsburgh industrialist, George Mesta, who introduced her to the world of national party politics. After his death in 1925, Mrs. Mesta became an influential Washington hostess, confidante of the great and near great, and finally ambassador to Luxembourg in 1949. Although she was the inspiration for the character Sally Adams in Irving Berlin's Broadway musical,* Call Me Madam, *Perle Mesta never forgot her Oklahoma roots. She came back often to look after various investments and to visit family and friends. She returned to familiar scenes at the Skirvin in 1974 and remained until her death, March 18, 1975.*

From Perle Mesta, with Robert Cahn, *My Story* (New York: McGraw-Hill, 1960), 17–24.

Oklahoma Memories

ABOUT A YEAR after Mother's death, Father became involved in a project that changed the course of our lives considerably. One afternoon in 1909 a Col. Ned Green called on Father. He proved to be the son of Hetty Green, the famous New York financier, and he had been sent by his mother to Oklahoma City to purchase some property. After looking all over town, Colonel Green decided he wanted four lots at the corner of First and Broadway. Father happened to own these four lots. The offer was substantial and Father was almost ready to agree to the sale when Green happened to mention that his mother planned to build the biggest hotel in Oklahoma City on the land. When Father heard this he immediately turned down the offer.

"That Hetty Green is no dumbbell," Father said to me that night. "If she thinks that's a good site for a hotel, then it probably is." Father called in his pal, S. A. (Sol) Layton, the best architect in the state of Oklahoma, and within a week they were working out plans for a six-story hotel. Early in 1910 the Governor of Oklahoma, Charles N. Haskell, helped father turn the first shovel of earth at the ground-breaking ceremony.

One night in September, Father went over to Sol Layton's office to celebrate the completion of the fifth floor framework. One drink led to another, and Sol kept insisting that at the rate Oklahoma City was growing, a six-story hotel would be far too small. By 3:00 A.M., Father thought so too, and the next day he increased his order to obtain enough of the Malakoff brick to cover eight stories.

Several weeks later, Father and Sol celebrated the completion of another two stories of framework, and that night the plans were again altered upwards. In September, 1911, when the Skirvin Hotel was ready for occupancy, it was ten stories high, had two wings and three hundred rooms, and was the biggest hotel in the state. It was also the most deluxe hotel in the entire Southwest, featuring all outside rooms, running ice water in every room, a ballroom that could hold five hundred people, and a sumptuous main dining room where every evening Professor Kachelski conducted the nine-piece Skirvin Orchestra.

Father was like a feudal baron with his hotel and didn't want to be dependent upon anyone for its operation. Finding that the local gas company had an exclusive franchise, he used his political influence to obtain a permit to build his own gas pipeline. He did the same thing with water, putting down three of his own wells. Having the water and the gas to generate steam, he put in his own electric plant. Father set up a laundry in the hotel and not only did his own but the laundry of other hotels in town. The Skirvin Hotel was almost a city in itself, and later, when Father put in his own garbage disposal plant, he was practically self-sufficient—except for telephone service. He never could get his own telephone company.

Father's 300-Room Hobby

Soon after the opening celebration, Father sold our house and we all moved into a five room suite on the ninth floor of the hotel. Marguerite and I thought living in a hotel was just about the most exciting thing in the world. We thought we were terribly sophisticated. William was less enthusiastic. He owned at that time eleven dogs, two raccoons, the one surviving monkey, an owl, and a horse. Father's rigid rule for his hotel was No Pets Allowed. But in his family's case he made a slight exception. Marguerite's poodle and Russian Wolfhound lived in the suite with us, and William built cages and doghouses on the roof for most of his menagerie, although six of the dogs and the horse were exiled to a friend's farm in the country.

There were occasional problems. One night a raccoon got loose from its pen and jumped off the roof to its death. A large hawk William brought into his aviary disposed of the owl. And guests sometimes complained about barking dogs. Father's reply was the guests were free to leave if they didn't like the Skirvin atmosphere.

One night, the room clerk awakened Father to tell him of a guest's complaint.

"The man swears he hears a wolf howling right on top of

his room," the clerk reported. Father was convinced the guest must be drunk and was all ready to have him thrown out for causing a disturbance, when he, too, heard something oddly wolflike. He put on his robe and slippers and padded up to the roof. There in a cage were three small wolves that William had trapped and secretly brought home.

Softhearted Father let William keep the wolves for a while. But as they starting growing, he became concerned, and even William realized the danger when they broke into the aviary one night and disposed of his hawk. When a rancher friend of the family offered to buy the wolves from William for five dollars each, William agreed to sell them. Not till several years later did he discover that the rancher hadn't wanted the wolves at all—that Father had paid the man twenty-five dollars to put over the deal.

Father was generally not so lenient with his paying guests

in the matter of pets. Years after the wolves departed, Katharine Cornell and her troupe came to Oklahoma City to present "The Barretts of Wimpole Street." Her manager, who had arranged her accommodations at the Skirvin Hotel, arrived a day or so before Miss Cornell. He happened to mention that the actress was bringing her two dachshunds. Father said that was all right and that an excellent kennel was provided in the basement.

Father's 300-Room Hobby

"Why, Miss Cornell wouldn't think of putting those dogs in a kennel," said the manager. "They always stay in her suite."

"Well, she'll just have to go some place else then," said Father. And she did.

But Father was unpredictable. When a family named Hutchison appeared at the hotel with a full-grown lion, Father welcomed them with open arms. The Hutchisons had picked up the lion in Africa as a cub and had raised it to be a pet. Since it was far too large for the dog kennel, Father gave the Hutchisons permission to have the lion in their room. He suggested they keep the beast in the bathroom. While the Hutchisons were out at dinner, a maid entered the room to deliver some fresh towels. There was a shriek. The maid shot out of the room, towels flying in all directions. As she went running down the hall, the lion was right behind her, thinking she wanted to play. The whole hotel was in an uproar for an hour while Father got the maids calmed down and Mr. Hutchison corralled his pet. Father used the incident to advantage. In the first place, it was fine publicity for the hotel. In the second, it gave him something to hold over the help. "Now, Rosie," he'd say to one of the maids, "you just better toe the line and do your work right or I'll get a lion after you!"

Marguerite and I were away at private school much of the time as we grew older, but we loved living in the hotel when we were back in Oklahoma. I thought it was great fun to sit in the lobby and watch all the activity, and I got my first interest in politics from eavesdropping on the lobby conversations. The official state Republican headquarters were located in a room Father donated to the Party. And at times the hotel lobby appeared to be also the unofficial Democratic headquarters. Father was a Republican, but had many Democratic friends. And although his support for local and state candidates always went to the Republicans, in national politics he was a maverick, and often sided with the Democrats.

I can almost see Father now, sitting in the lobby, usually surrounded by three or four friends, his dark brown eyes catching everything that went on. He had signals worked out with his desk clerks so that by the lift of an eyebrow he could indicate a course of action toward a prospective guest. If he saw someone he didn't like heading for the desk, Father would signal the clerk to give the "sorry, sold out" reply. On the other hand, if one of Father's oilfield cronies arrived, the clerk would be signaled to cut the price of the room in half. Often, Father would give one of his cronies a room for nothing and invite him to his suite to sample his liquor.

In 1911 Oklahoma City was still almost a frontier town. For hundreds of miles to the west, there was nothing but ranch country and a few widely separated villages. Father's hotel was a kind of melting pot: his guests included millionaires, Indians, and even the fabled Western train robber, Al Jennings, who launched his unsuccessful campaign for governor from the Skirvin lobby. Cattlemen like the millionaire Miller brothers, who owned the famous 101 Ranch, also frequented the hotel, and I loved to hear the jingle of their spurs as they walked across the gray-tiled lobby. As a gesture to the cattlemen, Father had every piece of furniture in the lobby covered with genuine cowhide leather. And he also provided numerous tall, solid brass cuspidors with wide flared tops that could hardly be missed—even at ten paces. Sometimes Osage Indians, or Cherokees or Kiowas or Pawnees, in full regalia would come into the lobby, and I was fascinated when I would see a papoose swinging from a squaw's back. When the hotel first opened, the Indians were afraid of the elevators. Father would always assign them rooms on the lower floors so they could use the stairs. And I can still picture those Indians sitting stiffly in the big leather chairs, munching peanuts, and letting the shells drop on the floor.

Father's 300-Room Hobby

One of our first guests after the hotel opened was an Osage by the name of—believe it or not—John Stink. He had been a guest at the hotel three days when the housekeeper mentioned to Father that the bed in his room had not yet been slept in. Father was ready to take this as a personal affront. He had made a trip to the Sealy factory in Texas to see exactly what was going into his box springs and mattresses. He was determined that his hotel beds would be the most comfortable in the country.

When the Indian came back to the hotel that afternoon, Father was waiting for him in the lobby.

"What's the matter, John?" asked Father. "My housekeeper says your bed hasn't been slept in for three nights. Anything wrong?"

"Nothing wrong," replied the Osage. "Bed too soft. Sleep on floor."

Oilmen like Bob Galbreath, Bill Skelly, and Walter Ramsey, who became leaders in the industry, frequently came to the Skirvin. I could always tell the oilmen by their leather jackets and laced boots, usually covered with oily mud, which they would track all over the lobby. Because of the ever-present oil and the peanut shells, Father didn't put any rugs in the lobby.

The hotel was just across an alley from the Rock Island Railroad. Father figured that by being so close to the depot, he would get first crack at all the passengers as they left their trains. Later he was to rue this decision when most of his guests arrived by automobile and there were numerous complaints about the noise from the trains.

One of the small banquet rooms, called the Green Room, was on the north side of the hotel, almost directly over the railroad tracks. There were many occasions when an after-dinner speaker had to compete with a rattling, banging freight train, and would sometimes have to stand for ten minutes waiting for the caboose to pass. Finding he couldn't do anything about the noise, Father renamed the banquet room and had an electric sign placed over the door: The Rock Island Room. People were so amused that the room then became very popular and Father dedicated it to the railroad. Father's sense of humor could turn any such liability into an asset.

The proximity to the station also made the Skirvin Hotel a favorite spot for the traveling salesmen who had to wrestle with numerous heavy sample cases. Father didn't want Marguerite or me hobnobbing with the traveling men. If he ever saw one of them talking with me, Father would refuse him a room next time he came. I wasn't supposed even to look sideways at the traveling salesmen—but I did. Even when they weren't traveling salesmen, Father resented any attentions we received from hotel guests. There was one fellow, for instance, who came to town periodically from Kansas. And I went out with him a time or two. Father saw me with him one day and then he laid down the law to me.

"I don't want you to have a thing to do with that man," said Father.

"But he's a nice man and he comes from a good family, and he knows many of our relatives in Kansas," I protested.

Father was adamant. "You will have nothing more to do with him."

"Why?" I demanded, as usual.

"Well, if you must known, your nice man was known to have had a woman in his room last night, and I'm going to put him out of the hotel."

I didn't believe a word of it. But that's the way Father was about any man in whom I took an interest. And he never let that man have a room at the hotel again. Once, shortly before Mother died, she had said to me, "I dread the day when you will want to get married because your Father will never think anybody is good enough for you."

Though Father was generally a good businessman, the hotel was mostly a hobby with him and he never worried if it wasn't making money. After his first gusher at Spindletop, Father was in on several other big oil fields in south Texas, then got in on the great Glenn Pool near Tulsa. By the time he built his hotel, he already was a millionaire.

Father's 300-Room Hobby

Father never dressed like an oilman. Even when he went out to the fields, he always dressed in a business suit and wore an impeccable white shirt and a felt hat. He saw to it that the best tailor in Oklahoma City had a shop right in the Skirvin Hotel, and he took out the rent in clothes.

Once in a while when Marguerite and I were both home from school, Father would get all dressed up in his cutaway, we would put on our best formals, and the table in the center of the hotel dining room would be decorated as if the President of the United States were coming to dinner. Even on ordinary nights, we never sat down to dinner without Father, although Marguerite sometimes would have to scout around for a couple of hours to find him, as he liked to visit friends for a few drinks late in the afternoon. Father did like his liquor, and after Mother passed on, he indulged himself more frequently.

Of course, one wonderful thing about living in a hotel was the opportunity to use the ballroom for parties. Once I wanted to have some friends in to learn a new dance, the Bunny Hug, but didn't want Father to know about it because some people thought the dance was risque. I had my friends come early so we could have the dancing over with before we ate, and thus fool Father. But just as we started dancing, the door flew open and there he stood. We were scared to death.

"So you thought you could put something over on the old man!" Father said sternly. But we couldn't keep a straight face, and broke into a laugh. Then he joined in the fun and we taught him the new dance.

Hotel life had a few drawbacks, however. My pet peeve was the lack of privacy on the telephone. The operators thought it was their mission to listen in on my calls and report to Father. I tried to win them over to my side, but they always remained loyal to Father.

The Oil Field Cook

¶ *The twentieth-century oil boom affected Oklahoma as dramatically as had the land rushes of the preceding century. Although essentially an extractive industry, oil generated feedback in refineries, filling stations, and the manufacture of oil field equipment. Oil tax revenues also brought the state new wealth. Yet however much oil as an abstraction affected the economy and society, its real importance was worked out in individual lives. While few Oklahomans actually became truly wealthy through oil ownership, the great discoveries made many landless people affluent. Oil-related industries built prosperous towns and ensured jobs for people who otherwise would have been poor.* ¶ *In the midst of all the oil booms, society often seemed a caricature of normality. New settlements erupted in the wake of each strike, and little towns near the discovery wells were changed, as if by magic, into places full of brawling, drunken, dirty humanity.* ¶ *Sadie Duggett, a poor girl from a family of nine children in Georgia, followed the oil booms from Louisiana through Texas and into Oklahoma. A shrewd businesswoman, Sadie had a sharp eye for the telltale signs of a waning boom, and she almost always managed to sell out and move on at a substantial profit. Her recollections provide an intimate view of daily life in the oil camps and are classic in the chronicles of oil industry lore.*

LOTS OF PEOPLE act like they think I'm off my nut when I tell 'em I'm in the oil game, kind of. They got the idea that the only thing there is to oil is a bunch of guys drilling a well, cussing and hollering and getting drunk payday, but it ain't. One of the most important things 'bout oil or anything else, far as that goes, is eating, and I kind of made it

From Ned De-Witt, W.P.A. *Writers Project on Oil in Oklahoma*, Western History Collections, University of Oklahoma.

my job to see that all the guys 'round the oil field get enough to eat. These smart punks that think eating ain't connected with the oil game and that the field ain't no place for a woman can go to hell far's I'm concerned; I'll back what I say by the guys that's eat with old Sadie Duggett—that's my full name, but ever'body calls me "Sade"—all these years.

And if you think I'm lying about them eating with me you oughta been here when this Oklahoma City field was wide open, and I'd just started up this eating house. Why, I've seen the time when this place wouldn't hold the men that wanted to eat with me, and this is big enough to feed a hunnerd men. They'd drive for miles to get here, and come crowding in, shoving and pushing, and all of 'em hollering at Lovie and me to give 'em personal attention, and that kind of stuff would keep up for hours, with the cash register dinging like a patrol wagon bell. Me and Lovie would be wore out by the time the noon rush was over, and before we could get the place cleaned up and new plates put on and roust the cooks up to get the food cooked, why it'd be evening again, and time for 'em to come back. But that was when there was a boom on; now it's so quiet you can hear the cockroaches walking 'round. Not that I got a lot of cockroaches, but it's just that quiet sometimes.

When I first started in this cafe business, it was good. There was boom oil towns and camps all over the country, and all I had to do was figger just which one I was going to light in and set out. The men that was working in them towns was just a-honing to set their teeth in some home-cooked meals, and they didn't mind paying for them neither. They all made good money then, too. Many's the time I've set out a platter of bacon-and-eggs, or maybe ham-and, and ring up a dollar on the cash register. But most of the time, until I got Dan to watch the register for me, I used a cigar box or whatever was handy to keep my money in. I didn't trust nobody then, or any other time either, and I always keep my money in something I can carry 'round with me. And I'd get a buck-and-a-half or maybe two for a dinner and supper, and didn't any of the boys mind paying out their hard-earned for it either. They liked my cooking so much that lots of 'em told me they'd give five dollars a platter if they had to—my cooking was worth it.

But eat! Godamighty! I never saw anything could eat like those men could then! They could set down and eat a half-dozen eggs, a side of bacon apiece, four cups of coffee, and push all of that down with a loaf of bread and a couple of pieces of pie. I run lots of family-style eating places—where all the food's on the table, and everybody helps themselves—and lots of times I had to jack my prices up to come out even. But they don't eat enough no more, not like they used to. I don't see how some of these guys can go out and work all day on what they get to eat nowadays. Most of them get married, and their wives think they can work on the same kind of food that they eat, but they can't. No man a-living can do a real day's work on the same things a woman'll fix for herself; there just ain't enough to it. But if they ain't got enough sense but to get theirselves tied down to some little fly-by-night hussy that don't know anything but toast and coffee and orange juice, then it ain't nobody's fault but their own.

You might say I was brought up on food, practically altogether. I always had plenty of it around me when I was growing up, and so it come kind of natural for me to go into running a cafe. My folks lived on a farm down in Georgia, and if we didn't have much money we always had plenty to eat. You had to have lots when there's nine kids and all of 'em working from can see to can't see—like the niggers usually say. I'd had to turn my hand to the cooking ever since I was a little bit of a thing, and I liked it, so I didn't mind at all. I was as fat as a pig, from working in the kitchen and eating so much, but I wasn't bad looking by a long sight. They marry 'em off young down there, and I had a bunch of those country boys hanging 'round the house before I was more'n twelve or thirteen. But I couldn't see 'em for the hay in their ears; I didn't like the looks of the women that had spent their lives on a farm, and I didn't want none of it.

Oklahoma Memories

We went to the county seat one Saturday, like all farmers do, just to see the sights and get in the week's buying, and so forth. I had a little money I'd made picking peanuts for a neighbor, and while the rest of the family was going around to the stores I decided to try some city cooking. I went into a cafe there and ordered a plate lunch. Well sir, that was as poor a meal as I ever tried to eat. There wasn't much meat to it, and what there was wasn't half-cooked, and the vegetables looked like they had the hookworm or pellagra, or both. The manager waited on me, and he saw me looking at the food and kind of turning it over with my fork. He ast me if there was anything wrong with it, and I said, No, nothing in particular but a lot in general. I told him that if that was a sample of the best food he could put out, it was a wonder he had any business at all. He got kind of worked up about it, and ast me how *I'd* fix the food, if I knew so much about it, I was mad, too, because I was hungry, and so I said I'd bet him a dollar to a piece of his pie that I could take the same kind of food and fix it so somebody could eat it without puking. He said he'd just take me up; for me to get behind the counter and get to work. I thought he was joking at first, and then I got mad and hopped around there and pushed the cook out of the way. He was a dried-up old man that looked like he stayed drunk all the time, so I shoved him out of my way and ast this guy what he wanted me to cook for him.

When he saw how I took hold of things he kind of laughed and said he'd give me a dollar and a half a day and my board. I thought it over a minute, just a minute, and I said all right, wait till I told my folks I wasn't going home with 'em. I went out and found my sister Laviny and told her to tell the folks for me, and for her to send other dresses in the next week. Then I went back to the cafe and started work.

I worked for that guy about six or eight months, and then I quit because he was always trying to get his hands on me. I learned a lot about cooking, though, and I worked in another cafe in that town. I got tired of that one and went to

Atlanta and worked a while, and then over to Louisiana. There was a little boom town over in Texas, and one day a feller was eating there in a cafe where I was and he said anybody that could cook like me ought to be in that boom town; I could make a million dollars. I was already tired of the place I was in, and I had some money saved up, not much of course, what with cooking in little towns, and I ast this guy all about the oil fields. Well, by the end of that week I was in that boom town, and had put me up a tent and started a cafe of my own.

The Oil Field Cook

I had to pay so much down for my tent and to rent enough ground to throw it on I didn't have a whole lot of money left for groceries. I specialized on pancakes, and those oilfield workers ate 'em up. 'Fore long I hired three girls to wait table and I did all the cooking. I worked about sixteen hours a day most of the time, sometimes all night if the boys needed lunches put up for 'em or something like that, but I cleaned up all right. Before long I had enough money to build me a shack out of sawed lumber and put in a better line of food. I still did all the cooking, but I hired men waiters; the girls weren't worth a damn in a boom town because they don't want to have to work for a living. And when I got better groceries in the boys didn't mind paying six-bits for a stack of cakes and a buck and a half for supper. The food was good, and there was lots of it, so they didn't mind at all.

I saw the boom was going to die out there, and I sold the cafe for three thousand, and followed the oil to another town. I put in a pretty good place there, and went to making money hand over fist. When that boom started to die I went to another one, but I thought at first I was going to get sunk on that one. The oil companies were putting in camps for their men; they served lots of beans and rice and potatoes, filling things, but not very tasty. I had to compete with them, so I put in a family-style cafe. I did all my own cooking and buying groceries and things like that, but I still had a pretty hard time of it. But it wasn't long till the guys working there got to know me and passed the word along, and then business started on the up. I got six-bits for breakfast here too, and a dollar and a half for dinner and supper, like the other towns I'd been in, but I had to pay my waiters thirty a week to keep 'em. I had a hard time getting any waiters at all, 'cause most of those guys wanted to be out in the field knocking off some big money, they thought, and the birds I did get drank all my lemon extract and vanilla till I couldn't make a pie or anything half the time. Couldn't get girls, and I didn't want 'em anyway after the time I'd had with the first batch of 'em.

One afternoon I just sat down on a stool, so damned tired I didn't know which end was up. We'd had a big noon rush and right in the middle of it I had to put up forty lunches for some guys working on a lease quite a ways out of town. I was hot and sweaty and feeling mad and all when in come a girl and set down close to me on a stool. The minute I saw her I knew what she was, or thought I did, I'd seen so many women 'round the booms, but it was all right with me if she wanted to eat in my place and had the price. I never barred nobody if they had the cash. This girl set down and ordered a cup of coffee, and kept looking at me. Finally I said, Been in town long? She shook her head but didn't say anything. That made me kind of mad, her not saying anything, and I said, Where you holing up? She just looked at me, kind of tired. Then she takes a sip of coffee and says, You need a girl? I laughed like hell. Me need a girl; what the hell do you think I am, a queer. I ast her.

She just kept on looking at me till I got through laughing, and then she ast me again, if I wanted a waitress. I said, No; because I didn't want any women hanging 'round my place egging the men on. She said, "I'll work for my room and board if you'll just give me a job. That kind of knocked my props out from under me. I looked her over again, and she didn't look quite so bad as she did at first. She looked tired, like she'd been out on a week drunk, and kind of dirty and draggled, but not a bad sort after all. I ast her if she knew anything 'bout hashing, and she shook her head and said, No, but she could learn easy.

Well, I gave in and put her to work at ten a week and room and board. I was saving 'bout twenty a week on her, so I couldn't lose much. That was how I met Lovie—she's the kind of thin girl back there with the short red hair, filling the salt shakers. I didn't know much about her, of course, but I thought I'd give her a chance and see if she really wanted to get away from the hotels. I ast her her name, and she said it was Dove Something-or-other, one of those foreign names. I couldn't keep from laughing again, tired as I was; a name like that, Dove, and she looked more like a sparrow that'd fell in a slush pit and had just come up. But she turned out to be a good worker and all, and it wasn't long till I got to calling her Dovie, and then after while Lovie, when I found out how she was with the men.

The Oil Field Cook

She wasn't what you'd call a bad girl, you understand, not a regular oil-field whore, but she just couldn't say no to any guy that kept in after her. She didn't want money or anything like that, but they always give her something, but that was just about the only way she knew how to get any fun out of living. That's the way I figgered it anyway, but it wasn't any of my business. All right for her, I guess, but I couldn't see it that way. But she drummed up business, not really meaning to I don't suppose, for the cafe, and I didn't care what the hell she did after she got off work anyway, just so she worked all right. And she did, I'll say that for Lovie; she always gets her work done, and she don't mind staying a while to finish up either. She's always done like that, and I just kept her on.

Well, we made just about all the oil booms there was in Texas. When I closed up a place Lovie would ast me where we was going next, and she'd pile right in the train or in the truck, if we'd got some truck driver to haul us, which we usually did to save paying money for train fare, and she'd go right along with me. There wasn't any use trying to shake her, and since she was a good worker and since I'd used all girls after I hired her and didn't want to have to put up with just any kind of girls I could find 'round a boom town, I let her come with me. She got married several times down in Texas, too; she had a husband in damned near every town we stopped in, I guess. She was kind of like a cat; she wouldn't of knowed her husband that she married three years ago if she was to serve him a lunch, right now.

She never did ast 'em to marry her or even hint at it, I never heard her lead 'em on to it anyway, but I guess they just kind of took to that red hair of hers and blue eyes and the way she kind of switches when she walks. The first thing I'd know about a new one she'd come to work one morning all pale and big bags under her eyes and say she'd gone off and got married, and more'n likely, just got in from celebrating it to go to work. The guy'd come 'round and eat at the cafe and all, but Lovie always made 'em pay cash; she didn't let her night work mix in with what she had to do, which is something you can't say 'bout a lot of people. And when we'd leave, she'd just pack up her grip and light out with me, and never say a word to her husband or anybody else.

She got caught once. I had a bean joint down in Longview, Texas, when it was booming, and she got a knockdown to a roustabout there. He was a good-looking kid, 'bout six or eight years younger than she was, but she fell for him and they was out together every minute they was off work. God knows when she got time to sleep, but there never was no complaint 'bout her work; she did that all right, all the time. And somehow 'r 'nother, she never did get 'round to marrying this guy, or maybe it was the other way, and it wasn't long till she said she was going to domino. She never had thought nuthin 'bout knocking a kid before, but this time she kind of waited 'round and didn't do anything when she was supposed to. Maybe she liked this guy better'n the rest of 'em, I don't know, but pretty soon it was too late. She up and had the kid, a boy, and course she had to lay off a couple of months.

This guy had already shoved off so there wasn't any use looking for money from him. She never did get real acquainted with him; I mean, she didn't know a whole lot about him, so it didn't make much difference anyway where he was. She didn't know anybody else and nobody else give a damn about her, just like an old cat, you see? It was up to me. I did what I could for her, paid on her bills and so forth, and when it was all over she showed up one day and put on her apron like nothing had happened and went to work. I said, Where's the kid? She looked at me and said, He's gone. Well, and you know that was about the last time she ever said anything about it. And it was about the only time we got sore at each other. I kept on at her about it for a couple of days but she wouldn't say anything. Come to find out she'd left the kid on a hospital step, and they'd had to take it in, naturally.

I give her hell about it; I said I'd of took care of the kid if she'd let me know she was intending to dump it, but she got plain red-headed about the whole deal. I got mad, too, when she started talking back to me, and I told her to go chase a rabbit—I'd got along damned good 'fore I met her and I could still do it. So she left that night, and I didn't see her for quite a while.

I kind of forgot about her after while; I hired another girl, but I had to pay her more, and got busy stuffing everything I could get my hands on in my sack. I had a pretty good wad, too. You 'member long in '29 and '30 there wasn't a whole lot doing in the oil game; well, when the Oklahoma City field come in most of the boys left from Texas and around and hit out for the new field. I'd wanted to get shet of that place I had in Texas for a long time and when I heard the good news, 'bout the new field, I made up my mind I was going to hit it. Business was poor as hell down in Texas there, and I was kind of stumped how to sell for a while. But a guy came in one night and got to talking with me. He'd heard about the town there and was looking 'round for something to put his money in that wouldn't take a whole lot of his time. He was an old buzzard, and there was just him and his wife. They thought if they could get hold of some kind of business all they'd have to do would be to sit down and in a year or two they'd be millionaires. They was from some place in Colorado; don't remember just what town it was.

Well, this old bird come by one night and stopped and give me the chin. I told him business was on the boom, but it was a lie. I had 30 tables and 26 stools, and when he was in there, it was on Friday night about eight o'clock, there wasn't but two people in there beside me and him. And one of them was the dishwasher, who'd just got off and was reading the paper on the last stool. But I saw what an old codger he was, and that he didn't know 'bout anything in an oil field, so I acted like I had a gold mine. I finally broke down and told him my husband was waiting for me in Oklahoma City, and that if I could get a good price I'd sell out and go with him.

I didn't have a husband but the old man bit on it, but he didn't like the looks of all the empty stools. I seen him looking around, just like he was getting ready to make me out a liar about all the business I had, and I said, You come 'round here 'bout nine o'clock, when the shows let out, and I'll show you what a rush there is. You can't hardly get in the door, people crowd in here so. He says, Yes? Just like he didn't believe me, but he wanted to awful bad. And I said sure, you just come 'round 'bout nine or a little after and you'll see. Course I made my pile at breakfast and at noon and night, but he didn't have to know. I only kept open at night to kind of keep my hand in.

So he moseyed on, after promising he'd be back. I knew he would, because he just had to see for himself, you know how people are; they'll believe something if they can just see it. And he wanted the place pretty bad, too. I served plate lunches and short orders and had an ice cream fountain and all that, and it looked pretty good to anybody that didn't know their way 'round. So when he went out the door I went to the cash register and got all the money out of it. I took about fifteen dollars in ones and halves and quarters and told the dishwasher to watch the place a while. I went out and rounded up all the ginks I could and told 'em to come in and drink on me, and I give those that I knew eat with me some money, so they could act like they was paying me for what they got.

Well, you know there's always a helluva lot of guys out of work in a boom town, and there was plenty of 'em in town that night, just loafing 'round on the streets. It was bad enough 'bout them not working before, but it was worse when the boom died. A lot of 'em had come in off the farms or maybe quit a pretty good job someplace else after they heard about how the guys in the oil fields was getting rich, and maybe they got in a few days or a few weeks work, and then it was all over for them. That's one thing I don't like about the game; it drags in a lot of people that ain't got no business being there in the first place, and they just clutter up things till a guy can't move 'round.

Anyway, when this old feller come back in, right around nine o'clock, he couldn't hardly get in the door; there was roughnecks, and roustabouts, and drillers, and pumpers, and bums, and women, and kids, and everybody that'd been out on the streets. Looked like half the town was there. And they was all talking at the top of their voices, and some of 'em running out and bringing their friends back with 'em, and so much noise that this old guy got so excited he couldn't hardly talk. And I'm a liar if he didn't grab hold of me and holler at me and want to close the deal right then! He just couldn't stand it when he saw all those people guzzling, and when he thought about all the money that'd roll in my register. I told him I'd think it over, and for him to come back in the morning if he was still interested, but I had to wait on my trade. I knew I had him hooked, good and proper.

Well, next morning he was there, bright and early, with his checkbook out and his fountain pen ready. I'd kind of thought about getting somebody to act like he wanted to buy the place too, only there wasn't anybody 'round that I'd trust with my roll. He'd of had to have a roll to flash around in front of the old guy. Lovie was as honest as the day's long, but she wasn't there and I didn't want a woman acting like that anyway, so I just let it go. I fidgeted 'round with this old guy like I didn't really want to sell, and finally I let him think he'd talked me into selling for four thousand, which was about twice what it was worth, with business like it was. I made him go up to the bank and get his check cashed into bills—I always like my money that way, or maybe in a cashier's check—and then I pitched off my apron and turned it over to him. I showed the old woman how to mix ice cream drinks and stuff like that, and then I left out on the next train for Oklahoma City. I rode the cushions that time, because I'd drew out all my money from the bank and had it on me. I had a little over thirteen thousand in my kick right then, and I was going to try to run it up to a million.

But I ain't much closer to that million now than I was then, when I was just thinking about it. Course, I've gone ahead a little bit, but I ain't rich yet by a helluva lot. They'd already dealt out the hands when I got up here in Oklahoma City, in the spring of '30. The town looked like a regular boom, but it wasn't. There was the usual number of leg-joints, where you could get anything from a drink of bad whisky to a swat in the puss, and whore houses, and cafes, and supply houses for the oil companies, and all the rest of the boom-town stuff. But it was run some better. What I mean was the places wasn't showy like you'd expect in a town as big as Oklahoma City is, and people acted like the boom wasn't anything so much after all; like a bunch of farmers, you know. And there wasn't so much hell-raising either.

But I knew if there was any money here I'd get my share of it or know the reason why, so I went right on the edge of the oil field, on the southeast part of town, and staked me out a lot and put up a big eating house. Prices was higher'n a cat's back for land and lumber and anything else; person'd think there never had been a stock market of a depression the way they charged for things here. And the people that'd been on the ground had first pickings, too; I'd horsed around so long down in Texas I almost let this boom get away from me.

I had a lot of friends working here, though, fellers that'd eat with me in other towns, and soon's as they heard I was here they come in and brought their friends with 'em. I got along all right after a while, right up till times got too hard for me 'r anybody else to make anything, and I kind of begin to look around for something else to put my money in. I didn't know anything but cafes, but I reckoned that if I could make money off them I could make it off something else. I looked around town, and finally I decided to give hotels a go. I got a real estate agent and we walked around the whole damned town. And you can mark me down for a liar if I didn't meet Lovie in one of 'em! Yessir, she'd followed the oil right up here to Oklahoma City, and since she didn't know nothing else either, she went to work in a hotel. She was the same old Lovie, but she didn't look quite so young as she had when she was working for me.

She ast me where I was located, and like a damn fool I told her. It wasn't more'n two days later she turned up out to my place and said she wanted to go to work. Well, I started to ast her about the kid again, the one she'd gone off and left down in Texas, and then I thought what the hell, it ain't none of my business anyway and let bygones be bygones. So I put her to work, and she's been with me every since. She's a little bit quieter than she was, but she hasn't changed so damned much that she don't size up the boys when they come in. Guess it's got to be kind of a habit with her.

I didn't buy the hotel after all. I ast around and found out what I'd have to pay for protection and all, and I decided I didn't want any of it. Lovie told me some about how they rum 'em, too. I put my money in real estate instead. Like to have lost ever damned penny I had, too, but now there's a boom on in real estate I'm going to come out in the clear with a pretty good profit. I got married, too, during the depression. Times got pretty tough in '32 and '33, and I

The Oil Field Cook

Oklahoma Memories

wasn't making everything I thought I ought to in the cafe, so I put up some beaverboards in the rooms upstairs in my place and rented 'em out to the roustabouts and workers in the supply houses. That helped out considerable. Had one fellow that lived with me ever since I first rented out rooms; he was drilling out here in the field and he got hurt. He didn't have any money saved or anything, and when they brought him here to his room I had to let him stay.

There's some kind of a damfool law says you can't move anybody that's sick out of their room, even if they can't pay. Made me pretty mad for a while to think how I was getting stuck, but there wasn't anything to do so I hadda let him stay. I got so durned used to him I didn't even notice him, except that he was crippled pretty bad. Lots of fellows always getting bunged up some way out in the fields; it's probably as hard a work and as dangerous as any kind a man can get, and there don't a day pass that somebody don't get hurt. Some of 'em pretty bad, too, like my old man. He got his tools stuck in the hole and was trying to knock 'em out with the power and pulled the whole rig down 'round his ears. Like to've killed him.

He wore a plaster cast for a year or so, and then when he got out of it he was kind of pulled over towards the front; he got his back broke, and it never did set straight or something. Well, he got all his hospital and doctor bills paid by the company, and then, just about the time he got to where he could get around all right and was helping around the place here, he got the check for his compensation. He'd had to turn his case over to the state to collect for him, and it'd taken all that time. But he got it, and showed it to me. I ast him what he was going to do with all that money; it was five thousand and some-odd dollars. He said, what would you do with it, Miss Purley? Purley was my name 'fore I was married; Sarah Purley. I said I'd use it to buy some real estate. I had my eye on a piece of ground that I just felt in my old bones was going to be worth something some day. He said, All right; you think you can make something out of it, go ahead. But there's one condition; we'll have to do it together.

I laughed, and said how would we do that; he was an oil man and didn't know nothing 'bout real estate. He said, No, he didn't, but I did, and would I marry him? If I was his wife, maybe he could learn too. That kind of floored me for a while. I'd had lots of guys try to make me, lots of times; I'm not so bad-looking, I mean I wasn't when I was a little bit younger, and there was always somebody hanging 'round trying to put his arms around me or something like that, only usually they wanted more'n that. But I always figgered they was after my wad, and I never did warm up to any of 'em much. Course I ain't no old maid, nuthing of the kind, but you understand I ain't like, well, say Lovie. I kind of pick my own man to sleep with, instead of him me. And that ain't been very often neither.

So when this old Dan Duggett ast me to marry him, I was kind of knocked off, because I seen he wanted a home and all and not just a woman. He was stove up pretty bad, but I figgered it out and finally I said, Yes. He was a nice dependable sort of a guy, and I liked him; he was easy on my nerves and all. When we got married—we run off to a little old town south of here, like a couple of kids—he had his compensation check all endorsed to me, and handed it over to me before we started. That kind of got me, too, him trusting me like that. Damned few people I'd trust, not even him for very much, and I had all my property made out in my new name the day after we was married. But he knew he didn't have so very long to live anyway, what with being crippled and all, and he knew I knew he didn't, so he just let me take care of my money and his too. That's the way we've handled it ever since; he kind of takes care of the roomers, all of 'em's men, and sees that they pay off prompt and all, and I handle the money.

I got kind of used to Lovie being around, too, and I guess I'll look after her long as she stays with me. I always kind of looked out after people, I guess I always will. Lovie's a good worker, too, and I couldn't get another girl that'd do all the work she does for her ten a week and room and board. Course her room don't cost me anything, cause this property's all clear and in my name, and if she wasn't using it, it might be empty anyway. But I wouldn't think of charging Lovie rent anyway; it's kind of nice to have a woman around that you know and feel comfortable with, like Lovie, even if she ain't so smart or anything. But she doesn't want much, and I'm willing to put up with her tom-catting around, so long's it ain't with my roomers, so neither one of us has got any complaint.

I Wish They'd Never Found Oil

¶ *Few Oklahomans attained great wealth through actual oil ownership, but the oil booms helped many landless people in other ways. Oil-related industries built thriving towns and provided jobs for people who otherwise would have been poor. Thousands of small ranchers and farmers with royalties from a single lease were able to improve their homes, travel, send their children to college, or buy livestock. The "stripper wells" that produced only a fraction of a barrel a day were to many Oklahoma farmers "what cows teats are to Wisconsin dairymen. We milk them every day."*[1] *¶ But not all farmers rejoiced in their oil profits. A Mr. Dillingham, who had blindly chosen a homestead in the run of 1889, nearly starved in those early years as a farmer with twelve children. But as the rest of the nation slipped into the depression in 1929, Mr. Dillingham's land began to sprout oil. ¶ The stories are legion about how oil wealth victimized the Osage Indians, but Mr. Dillingham recalls how his own children went "oil-crazy."*

THE MORNING of *May 2, 1889,* a stocky heavily bearded young man crawled from his blankets beneath his farm-wagon and stood looking out over his homestead. He had camped on a high knoll and from it he could see his *160* acres of brush and trees clearly, *160* acres that must be painfully grubbed and plowed. He had filed on it the afternoon before without having seen it; there were but two homesteads left in the entire county and he had blindly chosen the one to the north. Mr. Dillingham recalled his feelings that day.

I guess I was a little homesick for Pennsylvania and I chose the one nearest to it, even if it was just three miles

From Ned DeWitt, W.P.A. *Writers Project on Oil in Oklahoma,* Western History Collections, University of Oklahoma.
1. Richard Lloyd Jones, Owner of the *Tulsa Tribune,* quoted in Frederick Simpich, "So Oklahoma Grew Up," *National Geographic* 79 (March 1941): 273–74.

more to the north 'n the other farm. Some soldier 'd filed on this one the day of the Run, April 22, but they told me that when he seen how much brush there was to grub out he jumped on his horse and went back to town. That's how come it was open for filing and I got it. I'd been working on my uncle's farm up in Pennsylvania and I couldn't get hold of a wagon and team in time to make the Run so I had to take the soldier's leavings. I had $1.35 in my pocket when I got up that morning, and a wife and two kids to take care of. I'd brought a sod-buster plow along from Kansas and I left what food there was for the family to eat for breakfast and went out and got a job plowing brush for a neighbor.

I plowed for several farmers that summer and fall, clearing the brush and trees for $1 an acre, and when I got $10 I thought I could spare I went to town and talked a hardware merchant into letting me have a brush-plow for the $10 down. But that was the next year. With a regular brush-plow I got along better. When I wasn't plowing somebody's farm or clearing it off I hauled wood to town. I got $1 a rick for it and if I piled it right I could haul two ricks at a time. I pulled my family through three winters hauling wood and breaking the neighbors' land for 'em. We didn't have a whole lot to eat so I traded my team of horses the first spring for a team of work-cattle and a milk cow so we'd have milk to eat and maybe some butter to sell, and when I got able I bought two more teams of cattle and broke 'em myself to harness. I used to haul wood with 'em too, and it was sure slow hauling that 12 miles to town.

Having to work like that got me in a mind so when I did have money I put it in the bank or invested it instead of spending it on living. When they struck oil on my place I was fixed to where I could put the money in the bank and not have to spend it unless I wanted to.

We were sitting on the rear bumper of his car and through the open doorway of the garage we could look out towards the barn and the pasture. Two sleek horses were rubbing against the top bar of the corral, and around and about the barn were chickens, geese,

ducks, and almost a score of plump Hampshire hogs grunting and rooting in the lot. Mr. Dillingham waved his arm towards the huge red barn.

Everything you see out there's made out of sweat. I know to the penny what I had to pay for them pigs and horses and chickens and for that registered bull over in the back lot. I know what they cost me and I know what they'll bring on the market right now, because I've had to put out too much hard work not to know. Anytime you've got to work a half-day to get hold of a dollar you're goin' to put in in something that'll bring back your dollar and some more to boot. I never have spent money foolish. I made close to $25,000 clear off this farm since I homesteaded it besides sending all my children to school that wanted to go and us living as good as we wanted to. I didn't have to have oil-money to live on; I've always made a good living off the farm. The rest of the farmers 'round here planted cotton and corn and wheat but I put 108 acres of mine in fruit after the first three years I was here—in berries and grapes and peaches and apples and cantaloupes and watermelons—and the rest in feed for my stock. And when I had extra money I put it in land because I think that's one of the best investments a man can make.

Along in 1917 I bought 40 acres up there in the corner of section of Twenty-Ninth and South End Streets, the northeast corner. There wasn't even a street there when I bought it, just an old country road for farm-wagons and to drive cattle to the stockyards. I gave $5,000 for that 40 acres and everybody 'round here said old Dillingham'd gone crazy. I let 'em talk. I planted it in oats and barley and corn and wheat for cattle to feed on and about half or more in fruit, and before long I had it paying for itself. I could have sold that 40 acres several times but I didn't have to have the money so I held onto it. People didn't laugh at me in 1929 either. The first oil well 'round here was about three miles south and four east of my 40 acres and it wasn't a week after they found oil that men from the city were out here after me, trying to get to sign a lease. I still didn't need money so I waited, and they only offered me $15 an acre lease-money. The spring of 1929 I leased the 40 acres for $800 an acre and made 'em pay me $1,500 for my fruit trees, and then they moved the trees out on the farm here and started drilling. I didn't much believe they'd ever find oil there but I had their money so I took it and bought city real estate with it, some bungalows and little houses and rented 'em to the oil-field workers.

They drilled 18 or 20 times and got 11 good wells on my 40 acres, and there's still 5 wells making oil but not much of it. I'm not going to tell you how much they've been worth to me but it's enough for me for the rest of my life and plenty besides. I got some extra money out of the land too. People were running wild all over my land, driving trucks over it and puttin' up tents to live in and some of 'em even throwing up little sheds of places to sell whisky in without none of 'em asking me if they could or not. I got some carpenters to put up two blocks of iron sheds on the Twenty-Ninth Street side and rented them. I got two rents off of them, rent on the buildings by themselves and ground-rent for using my land to do business on. During the boom part I got as high as $300 a month from supply stores and boiler-shops and businesses like them for the buildings and an extra $100 to $150 a month for the ground-rent. And I had 5 acres nobody wanted for anything else so I rented it to an oil company to store its pipes and machinery on so they'd be near their work.

I Wish They'd Never Found Oil

Lots of people got as much as I did and some of 'em got more. Them that had big farms in the middle of the oil field were just rich overnight, but I didn't worry if they made money or not because I had plenty for myself. The only thing about me getting money was it just about broke up my family. I've got 12 children, 6 boys and the rest girls, and they all worked on the farm with me and seemed like they didn't even think about doing anything else for a living till I got oil on the 40 acres and then they all went oil-crazy. My boys got so they didn't even like their Ma's cooking. They'd rather take the oil-money and go in town and buy trash in some cafe instead of what we had here for 'em, canned fruit and vegetables and green garden-stuff like they'd always eat before. The first two years I got the oil-money I had to buy three cars. They were good ones too and I paid cash for 'em, but the boys took 'em out and wrecked 'em one at a time. Ernie got drunk and wrecked a Buick sedan I had and when I wouldn't buy another one right off he got mad and left home and didn't come back.

I put all the oil-money in Building-and-Loan stock and in city real estate. They looked like good investments to me and I thought that later on the children'd have some money to live on comfortable, but they wanted to spend it faster'n it came in. My youngest boy, Fred, didn't like the farm at all after they found oil and he didn't like me getting after him when he'd come home late at night and then not get up in time to do his chores. He kept saying he was going to have to have more rope or he couldn't stand it.

I told him: "Fred, you've got more rope now than I ever did have or you ought either. You're a man and you've got to do a man's work. I'm willing to pay you $50 a month and your room and board free if you'll stay on the farm here, but I don't want you mixing 'round in the oil fields. I'm sorry but I just can't give you more rope'n you've got. I wasn't raised that way myself and I don't want to raise you children that way."

He said he'd have to have more rope even if he had to leave and that night he wrote my name on a check for $500 and went to Texas, and I had to pay the check. Fred got in with the wrong boys or he wouldn't have done a thing like that to me. I never did teach him to steal or lie; I tried to teach him to live decent and work hard and make his own way, but he got to running around with other boys that got money from their daddies without having to work for it and he wanted to live like them. He took the money he got off the check and went to Texas and I didn't hear from him for six years, not till December 1937. He'd learned something because he was just a wild boy when he left but after he'd spent the $500 he got a job building oil derricks and saved some of his wages and paid down on a farm in West Texas. He got married to a girl down there and they've got two children of their own now.

Last fall I gave him $8,500 to finish paying for his farm and buy one next to it so he could raise more cotton. Fred turned out better'n the other boys, all but Ralph and it's not fair to count him in on it. Ralph's not right in his head. His Ma fell down in the cellar when she was carrying him and he didn't turn out right. He's the only one left of the boys at home, but there's two girls and one of them's figgurin' on getting married this month, to a driller. I couldn't even keep them home, because they were just like the boys in wanting to go to shows and dances and sneaked off when I wouldn't let 'em. That's how she met this driller. He's in Illinois now but he's due back this month to marry her.

The boys wanted me to give them money so they wouldn't have to work, and maybe I ought to've done it, I don't know. I put all the oil-money in real estate but the government makin' it so easy to buy a house for everybody has hit my property hard. I've got nine houses in town that don't rent for more'n 8 months of the year; I lose money on them. In 1937 I had 14 houses but I thought maybe if I gave the boys some money they'd come back home for awhile. I sold 5 houses and gave them the money, one house to each one. They got something around $3,000 apiece, but that wasn't enough. Joe, the next-to-the-oldest, had his all spent in a month, paying some old bills he owed and I didn't even know about, and gambling most of it away. He gets a ride out to here about once a month and wants money but I've had to quit giving it to him.

I Wish They'd Never Found Oil

All of 'em are like that except Fred. I helped Fred out more'n any of 'em because he's worked hard the last few years. He's trying to make his own way and I don't mind helping him at all. I bought Bennie a farm but he didn't want to farm after he'd kept after me till I got it for him, and so he traded it to his brother for two houses over in Crescent Hills, and then he moved out without paying the $2,300 due on 'em and would have turned 'em back to the loan company but I stepped in and paid what was due. I'd had to make the down-payments too. I got a deed from him and the loan company too and offered to let him live on in one house and take the rent money from the other one, but he didn't want to. He's talking about suing me now. Ernie, that got the farm, he moved off and left it without saying anything to me and the loan company came and took it for just a little over a thousand dollars owed on it. I don't know where he is now. I stocked that farm with horses and cows and chickens and even built a big barn and a chicken-house with electric lights in it for Bennie, but him and Ernie either one didn't want to farm anymore.

I don't like to see my own children starve or not be able to make their own way but seems like every time I try to help 'em it just gets 'em worse off and then they get mad at me and say it's my fault. Joe decided he wanted a grocery store and kept after me till I bought him one, paid $5,000 for one in a good location, but Joe married a woman that wanted more money'n he could make at running a grocery store and they turned it back to me. I only got $3,250 when I sold it and that was just a little over six months after I first bought it.

I've had good luck with the money I got from oil as far's investing it but not with my children and it too. It made them wild; they don't even want to work and every one of 'em's grown too. They're like lots of people in town; they think the oil wells'll last forever and they'll have a permanent income the rest of their life. My income's way down from what it used to be from oil and my property, but I've still got the farm here to live on. Farming's the slowest living in the world, but you always know if you can get a little rain spaced out right when the crops are growin' you'll get by, and if you watch the corners you ought to save some. I'm still working my farm, right today. I'm 76 but I get up at 4 o'clock every morning and do my own milking and all my chores and nobody to help me but Ralph. If one or two of the boys would come on home we could all live easy. If they would come back I'd deed the whole place over to 'em and leave 'em all I've got, but I don't say anything 'bout it so they won't start scrappin'.

They've been off the farm so long though, I don't guess they'll ever come back again. Joe's 51 his last birthday but he won't even look for a job; his wife works in an office. He thinks I've got more money 'n I have and he wants his share now. All of 'em do but Fred and if he wasn't gettin' along so good by himself I'd give him most of it and get it off my mind.

Oil's been a benefit to everybody, to the city and county and state and the government, because it gives jobs to people and pays big taxes, and then it pays some of us farmers money for leases and from the oil wells. Everybody gets part of the oil-money some way or other, but oil's bad for farmers. The farm boys don't want to stay home and help their folks; they want to go earn the big wages they hear about or maybe they do like mine did. I might just as well have given it to 'em if things go on like they've been doing. I can't afford to fix up my rent property because I don't get enough money out of 'em, and if I don't fix 'em up I can't rent 'em. I'd sell them right now for what they'd bring but long as the boys won't work to earn their keep I don't want to give them the money I'd get for the property to spend foolish.

There's two oil wells within a couple of miles east of the farm here, little ones but they produce steady. They've proved up this section 'round here for oil, but I haven't gone ahead and leased my land like my neighbors did. I'm not anxious either way. Sometimes I get to hoping those two wells 'd go dry so I wouldn't have to worry about anymore oil-money. I wish they never had found oil sometimes. If I hadn't got that extra money when I really didn't have to have it to live on, maybe my boys 'd stayed home with me and turned out good.

I Wish They'd Never Found Oil

Letters from the Dust Bowl

¶ *The 1930s were unhappy years in Oklahoma. Weather compounded the depression's effects, making it seem both intensely personal and blindly impersonal in scale. One bad year surprised no one; two seemed merely a longer sentence. But a long succession of dust storms inevitably affected men's spirits and ambitions, and the hopeful spirit yielded to a kind of stoicism. By 1935 unemployment had increased in the cities, and more and more marginal farmers sought a new frontier. A great exodus began.* ¶ *More than a hundred thousand people, most of them tenant cotton farmers in the southeastern counties, left Oklahoma during the 1930s, lured by the glowing advertisements offering work and housing in an ideal California climate. That exodus was never significant among the wheat farmers of the northwestern counties. Most of them managed to hold on, however dispiriting the situation, because they owned their land.* ¶ *For twenty-eight years Caroline A. Henderson and her husband had farmed at Eva, Oklahoma, in Cimarron County. In the thirties they were at the heart of the Dust Bowl. Having invested their very lives in the high plains country, the Hendersons could not "default on our task." Mrs. Henderson spoke for many of her neighbors when she wrote to a friend in Maryland, "We may have to leave. . . . But I think I can never go willingly or without pain that as yet seems unendurable."* ¶ *Mrs. Henderson's letters were published in the* Atlantic Monthly *shortly after they were written. Dorothea Lange's and Russell Lee's famous pictures recorded the history of Oklahomans on the road to California. But Caroline Henderson's letters are the record of those who remained—a vivid chronicle of one of the most pathetic and most heroic chapters of American agriculture.*

Caroline A. Henderson, "Letters from the Dust Bowl," *Atlantic Monthly* 157 (May 1936), 540–51.

Oklahoma Memories

Eva, Oklahoma
June 30, 1935

MY DEAR EVELYN:

Your continued interest in our effort to "tie a knot in the end of the rope and hang on" is most stimulating. Our recent transition from rain-soaked eastern Kansas with its green pastures, luxuriant foliage, abundance of flowers, and promise of a generous harvest, to the dust-covered desolation of No Man's Land was a difficult change to crowd into one short day's travel. Eleanor has laid aside the medical books for a time. Wearing our shade hats, with handkerchiefs tied over our faces and vaseline in our nostrils, we have been trying to rescue our home from the accumulations of wind-blown dust which penetrates wherever air can go. It is an almost hopeless task, for there is rarely a day when at some time the dust clouds do not roll over. "Visibility" approaches zero and everything is covered again with a silt-like deposit which may vary in depth from a film to actual ripples on the kitchen floor. I keep oiled clothes on the window sills and between the upper and lower sashes. They help just a little to retard or collect the dust. Some seal the windows with the gummed-paper strips used in wrapping parcels, but no method is fully effective. We buy what appears to be red cedar sawdust with oil added to use in sweeping our floors, and do our best to avoid inhaling the irritating dust.

In telling you of these conditions I realize that I expose myself to charges of disloyalty to this western region. A good Kansas friend suggests that we should imitate the Californian attitude toward earthquakes and keep to ourselves what we know about dust storms. Since the very limited rains of May in this section gave some slight ground for renewed hope, optimism has been the approved policy. Printed articles or statements by journalists, railroad officials, and secretaries of small-town Chambers of Commerce have heralded too enthusiastically the return of prosperity to the drought region. And in our part of the country that is the one durable basis for any prosperity whatever. There is nothing else to build upon. But you wished to know the truth, so I am telling you the actual situation, though I freely admit that the facts are themselves often contradictory and confusing.

Early in May, with no more grass or even weeds on our 640 acres than on your kitchen floor, and even the scanty remnants of dried grasses from last year cut off and blown away, we decided, like most of our neighbors, to ship our cattle to grass in the central part of the state. We sent 27 head, retaining here the heifers coming fresh this spring. The shipping charge on our part of the carload was $46. Pasture costs us $7.00 for a cow and calf for the season and $5.00 for a yearling. Whether this venture brings profit or loss depends on whether the cattle make satisfactory gains during the summer and whether prices remain reasonable or fall back to the level that most people would desire. We farmers here in the United States might as well recognize that we are a minority group, and that the prevailing interest of the nation as a whole is no longer agricultural. Hay for the horses and the heifers remaining here cost us $23 per ton, brought by truck from eastern Oklahoma.

The day after we shipped the cattle, the long drouth was temporarily broken by the first effective moisture in many months—about one and one-quarter inches in two or three gentle rains. All hope of a wheat crop had been abandoned by March or April.

Contrary to many published reports, a good many people had left this country either temporarily or permanently before any rains came. And they were not merely "drifters," as is frequently alleged. In May a friend in the southwestern county of Kansas voluntarily sent me a list of the people who had already left their immediate neighborhood or were packed up and ready to go. The list included 109 persons in 26 families, substantial people, most of whom had been in that locality over ten years, and some as long as forty years. In these families there had been two deaths from dust pneumonia. Others in the neighborhood were ill at that time. Fewer actual residents have left our neighborhood, but on a sixty-mile trip yesterday to procure tractor repairs we saw many pitiful reminders of broken hopes and apparently wasted effort. Little abandoned homes where people had drilled deep wells for the precious water, had set trees and vines, built reservoirs, and fenced in gardens—with everything now walled in or half buried by banks of drifted soil—told a painful story of loss and disappointment. I grieved especially over one lonely plum thicket buried to the tips of the twigs, and a garden with a fence closely built of boards for wind protection, now enclosing only a hillock of dust covered with the blue-flowered bull nettles which no winds or sands discourage.

It might give you some notion of our great "open spaces" if I tell you that on the sixty-mile trip, going by a state road over which our mail comes from the railroad, and coming back by a Federal highway, we encountered only one car, and no other vehicles of any sort. And this was on Saturday, the farmers' marketing day!

The coming of the long-desired rain gave impetus to the Federal projects for erosion control. Plans were quickly made, submitted to groups of farmers in district gatherings, and put into operation without delay.

The proposition was that, in order to encourage the immediate listing of abandoned wheat ground and other acreage so as to cut down wind erosion, the Federal Government would contribute ten cents per acre toward the expense of fuel and oil for tractors or feed for horses, if the farmers would agree to list not less than one fourth of the acreage on contour lines. Surveys were made promptly for all farmers signing contracts for either contour listing or terracing. The latest report states that within the few weeks since the programme was begun in our county 299,986 acres have been ploughed or listed on these contour lines—that is, according to the lay of the land instead of on straight lines with right-angled turns as has been the usual custom.

The plan has been proposed and carried through here as a matter of public policy for the welfare of all without reproach or humiliation to anyone. It should be remembered that 1935 is the fourth successive year of drouth and crop failure through a great part of the high plains region, and the hopelessly low prices for the crop of 1931 gave no chance to build up reserves for future needs. If the severe critics of all who in any way join in government plans for the saving of homes and the restoration of farms to a productive basis could only understand how vital a human problem is here considered, possibly their censures might be less bitter and scornful.

At any rate the contour listing has been done over extensive areas. If rains come to carry forward the feed crops now just struggling up in the furrows, the value of the work can be appraised. The primary intention of the plan for contour listing is to distribute rainfall evenly over the fields and prevent its running off to one end of the field or down the road to some creek or drainage basin. It is hoped that the plan will indirectly tend to lessen wind erosion by promoting the growth of feed crops, restoration of humus to denuded surfaces, and some protection through standing stubbles and the natural coverage of weeds and unavoidable wastes. One great contributing cause of the terrible dust storms of the last two years has been the pitiful bareness of the fields resulting from the long drouth.

I am not wise enough to forecast the result. We have had two most welcome rains in June—three quarters of an inch and one-half inch. Normally these should have been of the utmost benefit, though they by no means guarantee an abundant feed crop from our new sprouting seeds as many editorial writers have decreed, and they do nothing toward restoring subsoil moisture. Actually the helpful effects of the rains have been for us and for other people largely destroyed by the drifting soil from abandoned, unworked lands around us. It fills the air and our eyes and noses and throats, and, worst of all, our furrows, where tender shoots are coming to the surface only to be buried by the smothering silt from the fields of rugged individualists who persist in their right to do nothing.

A fairly promising piece of barley has been destroyed for us by the merciless drift from the same field whose sands have practically buried the little mulberry hedge which has long sheltered our buildings from the northwest winds. Large spaces in our pastures are entirely bare in spite of the rains. Most of the green color, where there is any grazing, is due to the pestilent Russian thistles rather than to grass. Our little locust grove which we cherished for so many years has become a small pile of fence posts. With trees and vines and flowers all around you, you can't imagine how I miss that little green shaded spot in the midst of the desert glare.

Naturally you will wonder why we stay where conditions are so extremely disheartening. Why not pick up and leave as so many others have done? It is a fair question, but a hard one to answer.

Recently I talked with a young university graduate of very superior attainments. He took the ground that in such a case sentiment could and should be disregarded. He may be right. Yet I cannot act or feel or think as if the experiences of our twenty-seven years of life together had never been. And they are all bound up with the little corner to which we have given our continued and united efforts. To leave voluntarily—to break all those closely knit ties for the sake of a possibly greater comfort elsewhere—seems like defaulting on our task. We may have to leave. We can't hold out indefinitely without some return from the land, some source of income, however small. But I think I can never go willingly or without pain that as yet seems unendurable.

There are also practical considerations that serve to hold us here, for the present. Our soil is excellent. We need only a little rain—less than in most places—to make it productive. No one who remembers the wheat crops of 1926, 1929, 1931, can possibly regard this as permanently submarginal land. The newer methods of farming suggest possibilities of better control of moisture in the future. Our entire equipment is adapted to the type of farming suitable for this country and would have to be replaced at great expense with the tools needed in some other locality. We have spent so much in trying to keep our land from blowing away that it looks foolish to walk off and leave it, when somewhat more favorable conditions seem now to "cast their shadows before." I scarcely need to tell you that there is no use in thinking of either renting or selling farm property here at present. It is just a place to stand on—if we can keep the taxes paid—and work and hope for a better day. We could realize nothing whatever from all our years of struggle with which to make a fresh start.

We long for the garden and little chickens, the trees and birds and wild flowers of the years gone by. Perhaps if we do our part these good things may return some day, for others if not for ourselves.

Will joins me in earnest hopes for your recovery. The dust has been particularly aggravating to his bronchial trouble, but he keeps working on. A great reddish-brown cloud is rising now from the southeast, so we must get out and do our night work before it arrives. Our thoughts go with you.

August 11, 1935

MY DEAR EVELYN:

On this blistering Sunday afternoon, I am, like Alexander Selkirk,

. . . Monarch of all I survey;
My right there is none to dispute.

There is no one within a mile and a half, and all day I've seen just one person pass by in an old stripped-down Ford.

Will and Eleanor went early this morning with a family of neighbors to visit the dinosaur pit in the next county to the westward—about seventy miles from here—where the State University is engaged in excavating the bones of some

of these ancient monsters, reminders of a time when there was plenty of water even in the Panhandle.

It seemed impossible for us all to leave home at once, so I stayed here to care for a new Shorthorn brother, to keep the chickens' pails filled with fresh water, to turn the cattle and horses in to water at noon, and to keep them from straying to the extremely poisonous drouth-stricken cane. We spent the better part of a night during the week trying to save two of the best young cows from the effects of the prussic acid which develops in the stunted sorghum. We thought they would die and I am not sure yet whether they recovered because of the liberal doses of melted lard and molasses or whether the poison was not quite strong enough to be fatal. It produces a paralysis of the respiratory system, and when death occurs, as it frequently does, it is due to suffocation from lack of oxygen.

Ever since your letter came, I have been thinking how different are the causes of our personal difficulties. It is hard for us prodigals in this far country, in our scarcity of all things, not to feel envious of the Del Mar Vapigs luxuriating in potatoes, peaches (and cream?), and the delicious Youngerberries. But, as I started to say, our own problems are of a quite different sort. We cannot complain of laziness on the part of our citizens. Oklahoma is one of the first states to get away from direct relief. Official reports of the administrators here emphasize the eagerness with which people accept any sort of work to help themselves and to make unnecessary the acceptance of public aid. In our county the FERA force is being cut down. Three case workers and two from the office force have been dismissed during the past week.

This progress toward more nearly normal conditions of employment occurs in the face of the most critical farm situation that we have ever encountered. For over a month we have had no rain, and the light local showers early in July had only a slight and temporary effect. All hope of an adequate forage crop has now followed into oblivion the earlier hopes of wheat and maize production. We have no native or cultivated hay crops. The cattle stay alive thus far on weeds, but the pastures are destitute of grass. Many think it can never be restored. The heat is intense and the drying winds are practically continuous, with a real "duster" occurring every few days to keep us humble. After the government erosion control project was carried through there was, for a time, a partial cessation of the dust blowing. But as the freshly upturned earth is pulverizing under the influence of continued heat and wind and entire lack of moisture, it too is ready to blow. A recently established Oklahoma law permits the County Commissioners to require the working of land that is being allowed to blow to the detriment of other farms, and I note that one such order has recently been issued in our county.

You asked about the soil erosion control programme and what could be done with an allowance of ten cents per acre. That amount just about covers actual expense of fuel and oil for listing with a large tractor. Possibly it leaves a slight margin if listing is done with a lighter outfit. In no case was any allowance made for a man's labor or the use of his farming equipment. The plan was proposed to encourage widespread and practically simultaneous working of the blowing fields, with a reasonable proportion on contour lines. Undoubtedly it has been of great benefit, and had rains followed, as everyone hoped, we should feel that we were approaching the turn in the long road. As a matter of fact, the complete absence of rain has given us no chance to test the effectiveness of the contour listing. A few people signed up for terracing as a more permanent method of conserving and distributing the longed-for moisture—if it ever comes! Will has been working early and late with one of the county terracing machines, laying up ridges on contour lines for every foot of fall. He hopes to be ready to-morrow to turn the machine over to a neighbor who will also make the experiment. Later on he would like to run the terrace lines across the pasture lands, but the future for us is most uncertain.

Everything now depends on whether a definite change of moisture conditions occurs in time for people to sow wheat for 1936. The "suitcase farmers"—that is, insurance agents, preachers, real-estate men, and so forth, from cities near or far—have bet thousands of dollars upon rain, in other words have hired the preparation of large acres of land all around us which no longer represent the idea of homes at all, but just parts of a potential factory for the low-cost production of wheat—if it rains.

A short time ago a big tractor, working for one of these absentee farmers across the road from our home, accidentally hooked on to the cornerstone of the original survey and dragged it off up the road. All these many years that stone has marked the corner of our homestead. I have walked past it hundreds of times as I have taken the cows to their pasture or brought them home again. Always it has suggested the beauty of the untouched prairie as it was when the surveyors set the stone, the luxuriant thick turf of native grasses—grama grass, buffalo, and curly mesquite—the pincushion cactuses, straw-colored and rose, the other wild flowers which in their season fulfilled the thought of Shakespeare:—

> The summer's flower is to the summer sweet,
> Though to itself it only live and die.

The cornerstone has also suggested the preparation for human occupation—the little homes that were so hopefully established here, of which so very few remain. After twenty-nine years, eight places in our township, out of the possible 136 (excluding the two school sections), are still occupied by those who made the original homestead entry. And now the stone is gone and the manner of its removal seemed almost symbolic of the changes that appear inevitable.

Letters from the Dust Bowl

We can't see why your wheat prices should be so hopelessly low. You may judge now a little of how we felt in 1931, with wheat at less than "two bits" per bushel! The price here has recently been about a dollar a bushel, several cents above the Kansas City price. I suppose the idea is to discourage shipment, as there is not enough wheat in this area now to provide for fall sowing—if it rains—and seed wheat must be shipped in.

One morning at the store, being in a reckless mood, I invested a dime in five small tomatoes and wished you might be getting something like that price for your surplus. Potatoes cost us around thirty cents a peck. I hope the protest of the Maryland growers has been successful in giving them some return for their work. Peaches are priced at four pounds for a quarter, but are not for us. So count your mercies, lady. It may surprise you to see how numerous they are.

The last sack of flour cost $1.69, and twelve-ounce loaves of good bread are still to be had for a nickel, considerably less than the price we paid during the dear old days of reputed prosperity—before processing taxes were a subject for political debate and court consideration. We feel rather proud that the proprietor of the Elkhart flour mill which we have patronized for many years has withdrawn from the group of Kansas millers suing the government for recovery of the processing tax. He explained his position by stating that, as the benefits derived from these taxes had been an actual life-saver for farming and general business interests in this section, he would not seek to embarrass the government in its attempt to collect the tax. His independent action in refusing to join in the raid seems worth mentioning in these days when individualism is supposed to be dead.

It's time to do the evening work, put the guinea pig to

bed, and begin to watch for the return of our explorers. I do hope weather conditions are favoring the growth of your crops.

January 28, 1936

DEAR EVELYN:

As I have said before, our own problems seem of slight moment as compared with yours. Yet more than ever of late "the day's journey" has indeed seemed to "fill the whole long day." As yet there are no decisive changes, no clear light on our way. Late in the summer, before Eleanor returned to her work in the medical school, she drove the tractor for her father, and with the help of the old header they worried down the scattering, scanty crop of sorghum cane and Sudan grass which had made all the growth it could through the hot, dry summer. That there was anything at all to harvest we attribute to the new planting methods encouraged by the Soil Erosion Control service, of listing on contour lines and laying up terraces to check the run-off in whatever rains might come. A shower the night they finished cutting and another about ten days later, conserved in the same way, gave us most fortunately a second cutting over the same fields, and a few loads of maize fodder from spots here and there on another part of the farm. These crops of roughage have little or no market value, but are indispensable if one plans to winter any cattle. The old, nutritious native grasses which used to provide winter pasturage are forever gone. Killing frosts happily came later than usual. In October, I drove the tractor myself and we two cut and hauled and put into the barn loft (including the earlier cutting) some twenty tons of fodder from two hundred acres, expensive feed when regarded as the entire outcome of a year's work and investment, yet essential to our attempt at carrying on.

As you know, however, wisely or otherwisely, this region has permitted wheat growing to become its main concern. The wheat situation around us is so varied and precarious as to be most difficult of appraisal. Our own acreage is fairly typical of the general condition. We have a little wheat that came up in September, made a fair start, and for a time furnished pasturage for the small calves. A part of it was early smothered out by the drift from near-by fields. Part of it would yet respond to abundant moisture if that were to come. Much of the early-sown wheat did not come up. Some of the seed sprouted and died before reaching the surface. Other portions remained dry until sprouted by a light rain in December. Most of that still lies dormant waiting for warmth to promote its growth. Large areas were drilled after the December rain, with varying results as to germination.

After the four-to-six inch snow of early January, the editor of our county paper was asked by the United Press for a candid report of actual conditions. His estimate allowed the county as a whole a 25 per cent chance; not, if I understood him, a fair chance for a 25 per cent crop, but about one chance in four for anything at all. His statement showed that fall and winter precipitation so far had been a trifle over half the normal amount for that time of year. And you must try to remember that a failure this year would mean five in succession for a large part of the high plains region. So our great problem here is production, after all. You can readily see that the conditions I have so hastily outlined promise no protection against the ravages of dust storms if the spring winds rage as in previous years.

On the whole it is not surprising that here and there some bitterness should have been felt and expressed, perhaps immoderately, over the recent AAA decision in the Supreme Court. People here, business men as well as the farmers themselves, realize that the benefit payments under the AAA and the wage payments from Federal work projects are all that have saved a large territory here from abandonment. A December statement by the Soil Conservation service reports an area in five states, including part of all of sixty-eight counties and 87,000 square miles of territory, as in need of active measures for protection and control of the dust-storm menace. Mr. Bennett, director of the service, regards this as the greatest "physical problem facing the country to-day." I was astonished to find by a little primary arithmetic that the area involved is equal to that of all the New England states, with New Jersey and Maryland and about half of Delaware added for good measure.

The desolation of the countryside would admittedly have meant the ruin of the small towns, entirely dependent as they are upon country patronage. It will also mean—if it must ever be abandoned through utter exhaustion of resources and sheer inability to hang on any longer—a creeping eastward into more settled and productive territory of the danger and losses originating in the arid wastelands. It is a problem now that no merely individual action can handle successfully.

But to return briefly to the Supreme Court decision. It has naturally been the cause of much regrettable confusion. It would probably have caused even more disturbance had there not been a background of hope that something may yet be done to compensate for the disappointments necessarily involved.

Farmers are not asking for special favors. They ask only an even chance as compared with other workers. But people don't understand.

Perhaps the many books on pioneer life with the usual successful and happy outcome have helped to give a wrong impression and perpetuate the idea that country people live on wild game and fish and fruits and in general on the free bounty of heaven. Many people have no idea of the cash expense of operating a farm to-day, or the work and planning required to keep the wheels going round, to say nothing of a decent living or suitable education for the children. This year we are keeping a separate account of expenses for car, truck, and tractor, all of which are old and frequently in need of repair. I fear we shall be horrified and discouraged by the close of the year. Not that I should willingly return to the long, slow trips of fifteen miles to town in a jolting wagon. Not that I want to take it out of the flesh and blood of horses in the hot heavy work of seed time and harvest—if they come again. But we can't combine the modern methods of work with the income of our early pioneering, when $200 used to cover all of a year's expense.

I think I told you of shipping our cattle to pasture. It proved to be a disastrous mistake. To keep in tune, I suppose we should blame Secretary Wallace or the broad-shouldered Mr. Tugwell, who likewise had nothing to do with it. Really the source of trouble was our own erroneous impression that grass is grass, and that our cattle would gain if they could have ample pasturage. Evidently other factors of acclimatization must be considered. Our experience was duplicated in that of many of our neighbors, most of whom, on finding their cattle in far worse condition in the fall than in the spring, decided to sell for whatever their stock would bring. Perhaps they were wise to do so. We shipped ours back, availing ourselves of the drouth rates for such shipments. In the spring we had paid 85 per cent of the regular rate. In the fall, to encourage reshipment and the restocking of the country if possible, the government rate was 15 per cent of the regular charge. I was quite alone here for a week while Will went after our little bunch. He had to unload them late at night ten miles from home.

That was November first, and most of our efforts and resources ever since have been devoted to trying to bring our cattle back to a normal condition. They are gaining slowly, but our home-grown feed is disappearing rapidly, and the grain feed of threshed maize which we must purchase, while about right in price for the seller at $1.10 per hundred, is piling up expenses. We have sold one mixed bunch of older cows and summer calves. That will help a little toward caring for the others, but there couldn't be much direct gain, as you will agree, in selling eleven head for $225. Still this is beter than we could have done a year or two ago, when cattle were practically without value. In general, there has been an improvement in farm prices, both absolutely and relatively, which has given us courage to keep on working, and has kept alive our hope for some

Oklahoma Memories

definite change in weather conditions that may once more make our acres fruitful and restore to us some sense of accomplishment.

At present this great southwestern plains region, most of which has been perseveringly tilled during the fall and winter so as to cut down the loss by wind erosion even if the wheat proves a disappointment, seems to be lying asleep like the princess in the fairy tale. Perhaps you can share with us the painful longing that soon the enchantment may be broken, that the deliverer may come with the soft footfalls of gentle rain and waken our homeland once more into gracious, generous life.

Perhaps it is a sin to parody anything as beautiful as Ulysses. Yet as we gray, lonely old people sit here by the fire to-night, planning for the year's work, my thoughts seem bound to fall into that pattern.

> It may be that the dust will choke us down;
> It may be we shall wake some happy morn
> And look again on fields of waving grain.

So good night, dear friend, and a happier to-morrow.

March 8, 1936

DEAR EVELYN:

Since I wrote to you, we have had several bad days of wind and dust. On the worst one recently, old sheets stretched over door and window openings, and sprayed with kerosene, quickly became black and helped a little to keep down the irritating dust in our living rooms. Nothing that you see or hear or read will be likely to exaggerate the physical discomfort or material losses due to these storms. Less emphasis is usually given to the mental effect, the confusion of mind resulting from the overthrow of all plans for improvement or normal farm work, and the difficulty of making other plans, even in a tentative way. To give just one specific example: the paint has been literally scoured from our buildings by the storms of this and previous years;

we should by all means try to "save the surface"; but who knows when we might safely undertake such a project? The pleasantest morning may be a prelude to an afternoon when the "dust devils" all unite in one hideous onslaught. The combination of fresh paint with a real dust storm is not pleasing to contemplate.

Letters from the Dust Bowl

The prospects for a wheat crop in 1936 still remain extremely doubtful. There has been no moisture of any kind since the light snow of early January. On a seventy-mile drive yesterday to arrange for hatchery chicks and to sell our week's cream and eggs, we saw more wheat that would still respond to immediate rainfall than I, with my stay-at-home habits, had expected to see. A few fields were refreshingly green and beautiful to look upon. There seems no doubt that improved methods of tillage and protection are already yielding some results in reducing wind erosion. But rain must come soon to encourage growth even on the best fields if there is to be any wheat harvest. Interspersed with the more hopeful areas are other tracts apparently abandoned to their fate. A field dotted thickly with shoulder-high hummocks of sand and soil bound together by the inevitable Russian thistles presents little encouragement to the most ardent conservationist. My own verdict in regard to plans for the reclaiming of such land would be, "Too late." Yet such fields are a menace to all the cultivated land or pasture ground around them and present a most difficult problem.

The two extremes I have just suggested—that is, the slight hope even yet for some production on carefully tilled fields, and the practically hopeless conditions on abandoned land—are indicative of the two conflicting tendencies now evident through an extensive section of the high plains. On the one hand we note a disposition to recognize a mistake, to turn aside from the undertaking with the least possible loss and direct one's time and energy to some new purpose. On the other hand we observe that many seem determined to use even the hard experiences of the past, their own mistakes and other people's, as warning signals, pointing the way to changes of method and more persistent and effective effort right where they stand.

The first attitude may be illustrated by an incident of the past week, the attempt of former neighbors to sell the pipe from the well on their now deserted homestead. This may not seem significant to you. But to old-timers in this deep-water country, so nearly destitute of flowing streams, the virtual destruction of a well of our excellent, life-nourishing water comes close to being the unpardonable sin against future generations.

The same disintegrating tendency is shown in a larger and more alarming way by the extent to which land once owned and occupied by farm families is now passing into ownership of banks, mortgage companies, assurance societies, and investment partnerships or corporations. The legal notices published in our county paper for the past week include two notices of foreclosure proceedings and nine notices of sheriff's sales to satisfy judgements previously rendered. These eleven legal actions involve the ownership of 3,520 acres of land, the equivalent of twenty-two quarter sections, the original homestead allotment in this territory. In only two cases apparently had the loan been made from one person to another. Four life insurance companies, one investment company, and one joint-stock land bank are included among the plaintiffs.

These forced sales take place just outside the window of the assessor's office, and we were told that they have now become merely a matter of routine. No one tries to redeem the property in question; no one even makes a bid on it; in fact, no one appears but the sheriff and the lawyer representing the plaintiff.

I am not questioning the legal right of these companies to take over the title of the farms for their own security or that of the people whose money they have invested. In a sense their action in pressing their claims may hold some encouragement for the rest of us, since it suggests that they look in time for a return of value to the acres which at present no one seeks to rescue. In addition to the large amount of land now owned by these corporate interests, very many farms belong to nonresident individuals. The "quarters" north and south of our own place are so held, while the one on the west has recently been taken over by an investment company. Unquestionably this remote control stands in the way of constructive efforts toward recovery.

Yet there are numerous evidences of the persevering restoration of which I have written. The big road maintainers keep the highways in excellent condition. New license tags are appearing on cars and trucks. Churches, schools, and basket-ball tournaments continue much as usual. One village church reported forty people in attendance on one of the darkest and most dangerous of the recent dusty Sundays. The state agricultural college for this section has an increased enrollment this year. More people are managing in some way—we hardly see how—to keep in touch with the world of news and markets, politics and entertainment, through radio service. A local implement agency recently sent out invitations to a tractor entertainment with free moving pictures of factory operation and the like. The five hundred free lunches prepared for the occasion proved insufficient for the assembled crowd. Within a few succeeding days the company took orders for three tractors ranging in price from around $1,200 to $1,500. Some people must still have faith in the future!

More impressive to me was the Saturday rush of activity at the small produce house where we did our marketing. Cars kept driving up and people coming with pails or crates or cases of eggs. Cream was delivered in containers of all sorts and sizes, including one heavy aluminum cooker! Eggs were bringing fifteen cents per dozen and cream thirty cents a pound of tested butterfat. No large sums of money were involved. In many cases the payments were pitifully small, but every such sale represents hard work and economy and the struggle to keep going.

At the hatchery they spoke of slow business through the extremely cold weather. The young man in charge also referred to the changes or postponements in people's plans because of their failure to receive the expected payments under the now extinct allotment plan. With spring in the dusty air, however, and renewed hope that the government contracts will later be fulfilled, orders were coming in encouragingly.

We plan ourselves for four hundred baby Leghorns about the middle of April. That will be an increase for us, but is about the safest small investment we can make to yield an all-the-year-round return. We shall have to put quite a bit of work and expense into the brooder house to keep out the dust, and the rain—if it ever comes. But we are happier to keep on trying.

This impressionistic account of conditions here and of our hope for the future would scarcely be complete without some mention of government assistance. We have had only slight contact with the Rehabilitation Service. We know that the man in charge here is taking his work seriously, trying to give definite aid and encouragement to those who have reached the end of their small resources and have lost hope and courage. He stopped here the other morning to see whether we really meant it when we promised the use of our tractor and other equipment to a young man in the neighborhood who is trying to make a new start for himself and wife and small daughter through a rehabilitation loan. In spite of seriously adverse conditions, this agent, who meets many people, spoke of a rather surprising general spirit of optimism. I suppose there is something of the gambler in all of us. We instinctively feel that the longer we travel on a straight road, the nearer we must be coming to a turn. People here can't quite believe yet in a hopeless climatic change which would deprive them permanently of the gracious gift of rain.

To me the most interesting and forward-looking government undertaking in the dust bowl centres about the group of erosion control experiments scattered over a wide area. The Pony Creek project, fifteen miles east of our home, includes all of one congressional township and parts of three others, seventy square miles altogether, or something over

42,000 acres. This is a pretty seriously damaged area, principally devoted to wheat growing, and even now blowing badly. If the methods employed succeed in checking the drift and in restoring productivity, much will have been accomplished, both of intrinsic value and of use as a stimulating object lesson. We hope some day to drive over and see how they are progressing.

We talked about this work with the young man who helped us last summer to run our terrace lines. At present they are employing 140 men from WPA rolls who would otherwise be idle and in need of relief. The work is frankly experimental. It includes such activities as surveying contour lines, laying up terraces, cleaning out fence rows piled high with drifted soil, filling gullies to prevent washing in that longed-for time of heavy rainfall, cutting down dead trees and brush, digging holes for the resetting of trees in favorable locations, testing the adaptability of different types of grass to the difficult task of reseeding wind-blown spaces, and so on. Altogether it is just such work as a provident farmer would like to get done if he had the time and means. It is done without expense to the farmers who agree to cooperate in the plan. Our young friend smiled when I asked about "regimentation." The farmers do promise to maintain for five years, I believe, the terraces built for them and to follow a system of crop rotation. But plans for planting and cultivation are worked out for each place in individual conferences, to suit the farm and the farmer. Don't worry about the stifling of individuality. "It can't be did," as one of our preachers used to say. Of course no one can predict yet the result of these experiments, but they seem to me abundantly worth while.

Our personal plans—like those of all the rest—are entirely dependent on whether or not rain comes to save a little of our wheat, to give grass or even weeds for pasturage, to permit the growing of roughage for the winter, and provide some cover on the surface and promote the intertwining of rootlets in the soil to reduce wind damage. Our terraces are in good condition to distribute whatever moisture may come. We hope we have learned a little about protecting the soil which is the basis of our physical life. In the house the poinsettia and Christmas cactus are blooming a second time and the geraniums blossom in spite of the dust. Eleanor has just sent us budded hyacinth and daffodil bulbs in little moss-filled nests. They will help us to look forward for a time at least.

March 13

We must try to get this mailed tomorrow. It has been a terrible week, with one day of almost complete obscurity, and others when only a part of the sun's rays struggled through the gloom with a strange bluish luminance. On such days each little wave of the troubled water in the stock tank glitters with a blue phosphorescent light. When I dip out a pail of water to carry to the henhouse, it looks almost as if it were covered with a film of oil. On days like this, when William Vaughan Moody's expression "dust to eat" suggests a literal danger, we can't help questioning whether the traits we would rather think of as courage and perseverance are not actually recklessness and inertia. Who shall say?

News of the 45th

¶ *Like most Americans in early 1941, Don Robinson, a reporter for the Oklahoma City Times, did not think the United States should become involved in Europe's war. But when the draft call came he joined fellow Oklahomans in training at Fort Sill. Disorganized, equipped only with World War I surplus material, and suffocating under paperwork, the Thunderbird Division survived the chaos of training, though its members often doubted the outcome. The men conducted a fencing competition with bureaucrats over such things as "Brooms, push, floor sweep, w/handle," and staged pet reviews to relieve the boredom of training in the days before Pearl Harbor. They then fought with distinction and courage on the beaches of Sicily, liberated the death camp at Dachau, and pushed toward Munich.* ¶ *Robinson's memoir is not about the heroism of the Thunderbird Division, but it offers a candid, affectionate, and doubtless accurate view of America—rather naive and a bit sentimental—clumsily preparing for a war that would change all who survived.*

IT WAS two weeks after I returned to Oklahoma that I received my draft number. It was low enough that I started packing. Then there was the first physical examination, which was given me in a clinic on the northwest side. I had never had a physical examination before in my life. I thought it was a joke.

A conscientious nurse failed in four tries to get any blood out of me for a Wasserman. A doctor had to finish it off. I had a pot belly that remained with me until Sicily, but otherwise passed all right. I was listed as "overweight but not

From Sergeant Don Robinson, *News of the 45th* (Norman: University of Oklahoma Press, 1944), 2–17.

obese," and was grateful for the concession. This over, I wrote a funny story about it for the *Times* and waited.

Meanwhile, Edith Gaylord gave me a going-away party at the Oklahoma Club. The production of lead soldiers was then roughly the equivalent of America's arms production, and kids were preparing for war faster than the country. I found the table laden with these reminders of what I would soon be experiencing, and unsurpassed food. Around the table were my closest friends. Victor Alessandro played taps on a toy bugle, forgetting his dignity as a symphony conductor. That set the tone for my going away. A few foolish toots of a toy whistle were as serious as my attitude toward the whole thing.

There was coffee later that evening at a little fried-chicken joint. The juke box played again and again a hillbilly hit of the day:

"I'll be back in a year, little darling."

Wisecracks from the news staff still in my ears, I reported to the draft board. This outfit had arbitrarily situated itself some distance from town, and young men kept appearing in cars with their families. They huddled outside the rural schoolhouse, meeting friends and joking dutifully about the coming year in the army. The ceremonies were late, of course. I ran across "Dusty" Rhodes, public relations man for the telephone company, and his wife asked me to take care of her son, Bill Dunn. Bill, in turn, had been asked to take care of someone else's son, and so it went. Before it was over, we had all been asked to look out for each other.

A bell rang, and we selectees filed into an auditorium, where the wind-lined faces of the rural draft board confronted us from behind a long table. One of the members got up and made a patriotic speech. The school children came to chime in gradually with "Columbia, the Gem of the Ocean," "America, the Beautiful," "I Am an American," and, inevitably, "The Star Spangled Banner." Then they gave the pledge of allegiance to the flag. Somebody led a prayer which left no doubt he considered God a good

American whose patriotism could be relied upon in a pinch. It was over. We piled into buses and went uptown to the armory.

There, for the first time, we met the army. It was sobering.

A lieutenant got up in the middle of the floor and asked whether any of us were felons. Nobody said he was, so he asked whether any of us ever had been arrested. The response seemed to be more satisfactory this time. Many stepped forward to confess to crimes of intoxication, speeding, and punching people who well deserved it. That was all, save that the lieutenant warned that our fingerprints were going to the FBI and that if we hadn't spoken the truth he'd find it out anyway. We went upstairs and took off our clothes. Another physical examination showed I was overweight but still not obese, in spite of the feast at the Oklahoma Club. Then I went to the psychiatrist. He asked me whether I went out with girls, what I did for a living, and how much change I'd get from a five-dollar bill if my purchase was a dollar seventy-five. I told him "yes" and "write funny pieces for the paper" and "four twenty-five." It seemed to satisfy him, even though I had short-changed him in my confusion. You see, he was fully clothed in a big office, but I was sitting there in my altogethers. I'd never had an interview under these circumstances before.

It was January, and I was shivering. So was everyone else. Teeth chattered until they almost shook the building. Finally they gave us meal tickets, told those who lived in town they could go home, those who lived out of town to go to a third-rate hotel they named, and everyone to report to the post office in the morning.

They called the roll several times at the post office and eventually got around to giving the oath of the military man. People kept telephoning me from the office to find out where I'd put things, thereby earning me the first dressing down I had ever received from a sergeant. I was a member of the armed forces. They marched us in column to a restaurant I had avoided for years, and later sent us to a movie.

I'd seen the picture in preview, but I went anyway. Back at the post office, city busses drove up, we were handed paper sacks when we got aboard, and we pulled away, passing a sign which read: "It is not too late to join the United States Marines."

A lot of women see-ers-off were at the train. The paper shot a picture of a girl kissing a soldier in a day coach from the platform. It showed off her legs to advantage. The train was late starting, but tore along at a brisk clip once under way. Bridge games started, and sessions of bawdy songs some of the men had learned in college and CCC camp were audible. Most of the boys looked out the window at the drab Oklahoma landscape; you couldn't see their faces. As it grew dark, we opened our paper sacks. Bologna sandwiches with beaverboard bread, apples, oranges, and cookies.

It was late when the train drew itself up huffily at Fort Sill. It was drizzling. We answered to our names for the twenty-eighth time since the procedure began, filed past a truck, and got overcoats that didn't fit. (We swapped around later.) Then we boarded other trucks, tried to be cheerful, and traveled over bumpy roads to our areas. The trucks would stop at an outfit, names would be called off in alphabetical order, then we would move on to the next outfit. I got off at Service Battery, One Hundred and Fifty-eighth Field Artillery, along with most of the Q's, R's, and S's.

A band played heavily, and chow was ready. There was a lot of it, and we were hungry. Everyone treated us as guests. The major made us a little speech with no hokum in it. (Maybe the army wasn't so bad after all.) Then we went through six inches of mud to the tents, which, we found, had holes in the tops. The sheets on the beds that had been made for us were folded so we could get just half-way in. And everyone laughed at my blue pajamas.

Next day it rained. We poured dripping into the trucks and went to a shed, where we were "processed." This meant a physical examination (which showed I was overweight but not obese), an intelligence test, issuance of army clothes, shots for assorted diseases, and a personal interview by a corporal. The inquest was thorough and was followed by a compulsory shower (which many needed). The general aptitude test, misnamed I.Q. by the men, was a matter of counting blocks, picking the right tools, and working problems in math. I sailed through it with 134, a fair mark. Everyone said he could have done better at it if the room had been lighter, warmer, and less crowded; if he hadn't had the shots; if he hadn't slept cold last night; and if he'd had another hour or two to devote to it. All of us conceded each other's claims.

The clothing and equipment we were issued had a certain historical value. We looked like the cast of "The Big Parade." Some of the overcoats had been cut off unhemmed for clearing barbed wire in the first World War. We found names and "1918" scratched on the aluminum of the mess kits. We drew one pair of funny slacks, one pair of breeches each. Our blouses were at least twenty years old. We looked terrible, and we felt bad. The worst came with the issuance of woolen underclothing—two pieces. The shirts were fine, but the underpants with drawstring arrangements and clinging, itchy legs were almost unbearable.

"What was your civilian occupation?" the corporal asked.

"Newspaperman."

"Can you type?" Oh, oh! Clerical work, and me with too much weight, although not obese.

"No!"

"You'll have to take a typing test."

I pounded the typewriter slowly with my thumbs. A crisis passed.

Back in Service Battery, training began. We bundled up in our motley garments and set out for a high hill. A little lieutenant, who had been a schoolteacher before he came to the Forty-fifth Division with mobilization of the National Guard, told us about "military courtesy and disCIP-line." Never heard anything so dry. He told us whom to salute,

Oklahoma Memories

but not how, which led to a clash with an unsaluted lieutenant later in the day.

We couldn't step from our tents without heavy overshoes, arctic, so we made a mile march in these things. Later a full pack was added, and we trudged many miles. Adding the full pack had come slowly. A pack had to be just so big, but must contain two blankets, complete shelter tent facilities, all toilet articles, mess equipment, first-aid stuff, pistol, and full canteen. The latter three items hung from the belt.

Only one man at a time could roll a pack, because the whole tent floor was needed. The problem was further complicated by the presence in the middle of the floor of a Sibley stove, a damnable contraption which threw out no heat to speak of and set the tents on fire every morning at reveille. Our corporal didn't know how to roll one anyway, so our packs looked terrible. Some of the boys took out the blankets and substituted stovepipes, until one day the packs were unrolled for inspection.

In those unhurried days before great training camp sprang up, established military units took on, in addition to their regular work, the job of training selectees. The training sometimes was a little absent-minded. No orders would come down for training one day, and contradictory orders the next. The men were left to find out what was going on by using their wits and the grapevine.

One sloppy February morning, when no word had come down on the uniform of the day, we fell out in fatigues with leggings. When we didn't hear what the uniform was, we decided for ourselves and all dressed the same way. The little lieutenant strutted in front of us and let fly.

Didn't we know the uniform of the day was the wool OD's with leggings? Be back in five minutes with the wool OD's. We were, but the lieutenant was gone. We stood at ease until he reappeared with an apologetic air. The uniform is fatigues with leggings. Be back in five minutes.

The best swearing I have heard in the army didn't occur when enemy planes chased us into our fox holes and snipers popped from concealed positions in the rocks. It wasn't when the boys jumped out of the landing boats and found themselves in chilly salt water up to their necks. It was that day when headquarters couldn't make up its mind about the uniform of the day. Each time we changed, we had to take off our muddy overshoes, take off our leggings, pull off our clothes, put on our clothes, put on our leggings, and buckle up our muddy overshoes.

We appeared in fatigues in five minutes. The lieutenant was gone, but an abashed sergeant was standing there. It takes a lot to abash a sergeant. He said the uniform had been changed back to woolens. Five minutes.

In tents the swearing rose to furious heights. Each change meant hauling one set of garments from the locker and carefully folding the other and putting it in. Five minutes was not enough. The top kick met us next time. Fatigues, he said. Someone told him to go to hell, but he went to division instead. Returning, he gave the final ruling, fatigues. Only corps or army or the War Department could change it now. Fortunately, they had other things to do. The swearing died down about noon.

It began all over again that afternoon. We were assembled on top of the hill when two trucks pulled up. A staff sergeant announced we would study the "normanclature" of the two and one-half ton truck. As he began to talk and his assistant to point to parts of the truck, the wind began to blow at our backs. He ate his words. We shivered and heard a monologue interspersed with wind.

"Wheel . . . water . . . carburetor . . . generator. . . ." We heard, but we couldn't get any sense out of it. This lecture was followed by one on a weapon, and the speaker had a low voice, turned inward by the wind. The only place you could have heard that lecture was from a vantage point in his stomach lining.

Next day was worse. Cannoneers' drill is a matter of coordination. You pull up in a truck, leap out, pass the ammunition, unhook the gun from the truck, and assume positions around the gun according to number. All of these things we did in a howling sand storm. I lost three pounds by erosion.

Pup tent pitching (always in the wind), study of weapons, the Articles of War, the Browning automatic rifle, and military courtesy and dis-CIP-pline. Finally, we were called to the tent theater, which bellied like a huge sail and tried to soar into the sky. On the stage were a doctor and a chaplain.

The doctor walked to the front of the platform. For half an hour he told us of the horrors of venereal diseases. He told us how to keep from getting them. Then the chaplain got up and chided us gently for having to know how to keep healthy, and suggested a way to keep from becoming contaminated that the doctor had mentioned only in passing. Next came a movie which presented both sides of the question. Sin was routed. The demon sex was branded for what it is. Some said they'd never look at a woman again. Perhaps some of them haven't.

Graduation day was cold but sunny. Colonel Grover C. Wamsley, then regimental commander, was on the rostrum of the parade ground to review us in our clumsy close-order drill. We pitched pup tents, had a full field inspection in spite of the dogs that dragged our underwear around and worried it, and assembled and disassembled our weapons. After one month, our basic training was over.

I moved boxes and crates, swept floors, and scrubbed the mess hall. One night when I was typing a letter in my tent, Captain Anderson poked his head in without saying a word. Next morning I found myself in the battalion supply warehouse counting mess kits, keeping books on outdated pants, and typing requisitions.

First, in supply, you must learn not to talk forward. It's "shirt, cotton, khaki," not "khaki cotton shirt." I hadn't learned all this nomenclature when the division moved from Fort Sill to Camp Barkeley. I had got better acquainted with the boys in the office.

There were Everett Hayes, lieutenant, and Lee Hayes, technical sergeant. They ran things, but hazily, for reasons

I learned later. It seemed that the battalion supply set-up had been changed some time before, and the band had been brought in to work on the books. They made some peculiar errors that took a year to ferret out. Every once in a while, the former regimental supply officer would come in with a case of cokes and announce we were going to work that night and straighten the books out. We'd drink the cokes and work until two or three o'clock, but we'd get a new set of errors each time.

Bill Dunn, private (now lieutenant), took three months to learn to spell "sergeant." Bill Tuttle, private (now lieutenant), was older and craftier. Clyde Klingsick, sergeant, kept the battalion fed. We got along fine, a good team. Tom White, ammunition sergeant, had no ammunition then.

The army wasn't sure of itself those days. It was like an awkward adolescent who had been given a fortune to take care of. The paper work then was fantastic, and the army regulations hadn't been learned, but it didn't matter, because new circulars were always coming out.

Once I requisitioned some paint from the quartermaster. The requisition was made in triplicate, and I had the regimental commander sign it. The QM said the paint was ordnance property. I made a new requisition on another form, and the regimental commander signed it. Ordnance said the certification was wrong. I typed a new one, with the correct certification. The regimental CO signed it. I hadn't made enough carbons. Ordnance required one more than QM. I retyped it. The regimental commander started to sign it.

"This is the fourth requisition like this I've signed today," he blustered. "What in the hell are you doing with all that paint?" I had to explain I hadn't got any yet. The requisition was perfect. The lieutenant at ordnance looked it over with approval showing in his thin face. Then he marked big zeros in the "issued" column.

"We haven't got any," he explained.

A few days later Bill Tuttle and I were thumbing through a sort of supply catalog of cleaning and preserving materials. Bill whooped. Here were some things we weren't getting, and the book said we were entitled to them. They were listed:

"Brooms, push, floor sweep, w/handle."

We made out a requisition for the number indicated and laid plans to requisition more every month. Bill climbed in a truck, stopped at a canteen and bought a coke, stopped in the warehouse and nickeled another coke out of the machine, and confronted the quartermaster lieutenant. He laid the requisition with some others on the table before him. Bill went to talk to someone who worked in the office, and waited. When the lieutenant got to the requisition, he yelled for Bill.

"What's this about 'Brooms, push, floor sweep, w/handle'?" he asked. Bill said he'd seen them in a book. The lieutenant said to show him, and produced the volume.

"Brooms, push, floor sweep, w/handle," Bill pointed out.

"Let me see that," said the lieutenant. He pored over the pages a moment, then snorted. "Those are stable brooms, and this isn't the cavalry."

"I beg your pardon, sir," Bill said softly. "It says here that these are to be issued for all permanent buildings."

"Camp Barkeley is a temporary camp, so it couldn't have any permanent buildings," the lieutenant rejoined.

"They've got concrete floors," Bill rebutted.

"Well," conceded the lieutenant, "we haven't any anyway."

Bill went off to the warehouse to draw other equipment. A darky issued him soap and other stuff. The soap situation was a funny one. They'd only let you have half the soap you asked for, so you'd ask for twice what you needed.

Bill espied a pile of cardboard boxes reaching to the ceiling. They looked like something new, so Bill, on the lookout for something to draw, asked what was in them.

"Brooms, push, floor sweep, w/handle," answered the stock clerk.

"Hmmm," said Bill. "Mind if I borrow one a few minutes?" The Negro handed him the thing, and Bill started for the lieutenant's office. On the stairway he met a lieutenant colonel.

"Where are you going with that broom, push, floor sweep, w/handle?" asked the colonel sternly. Bill explained that the lieutenant didn't think there were any and had zeroed his requisition.

"Come with me," said the colonel, taking in hand the broom, push, etc.

They trooped through the busy office, everyone looked up, and work came to a momentary standstill. When the colonel had stopped at the lieutenant's desk, everything went back to normal.

"What's this about our not having any brooms, push, floor sweep, w/handle?" asked the colonel.

"I'll take care of it, sir," said the lieutenant. The colonel having straightened everything out to his satisfaction, walked away.

Bill and the lieutenant stared at the colonel's back until that officer disappeared into the men's room. Then the lieutenant turned slowly, furiously upon Bill. He was red-faced. His was the wrath of the wronged.

"What do you mean by going over my head?" he asked Bill evenly. Bill explained what had happened, but the lieutenant listened without satisfaction.

"Just for that," said the lieutenant, "you can't have any brooms, push, floor sweep, w/handle."

Joe Stocker came around to see me often. He wasn't the editor, but he was running the Press Section and the *45th Division News* in his quiet, mildly irritated way, and he had a scheme. He had entered the Forty-fifth two weeks after I had. We talked about the current series of thefts of light bulbs which left a different tent dark each night as the bulbs were swiped and re-swiped. Then he got down to business.

"As you may have noticed," Joe began, "the *Division News* is running a big pet review. We're going to stage it after the division review and run it just like the big one. Would you like to be master of ceremonies?"

I said I wouldn't, I'd be scared stiff. But I took on the job anyway, trusting that that day, above all, I'd be witty and quick of thinking. I worked with Joe on it before the big day, and we loaded the *Abilene Reporter-News* with advance copy on the event. Joe had talked himself into a hole and knew it. If the crowd appeared and the pets didn't, we'd have a mess, and likewise if the pet appeared and no one came out from town. We couldn't find anyone discussing the project, so we lost a lot of sleep worrying about failure.

An hour before the review, Joe and I went to the reviewing stand on the parade ground and counted the house. There was nobody there but an engineer who was hooking up a microphone labeled "Texas State Network." A quarter of an hour passed, the dignitaries began to arrive and take their positions on the reviewing stand. People, admitted without passes this one great day, began to line the field. A thousand people arrived before the first pet, a punch-drunk dog, arrived with a couple of soldiers. We were frantic. An announcer was talking over the mike to his engineer. It looked as if he wouldn't have anything to describe.

The crowd swelled, and a few pets began to arrive. Soon there were enough animals to go on; others kept arriving until the minute the show was scheduled to begin. The whole thing turned out to be a success. We had no idea of the number and variety of pets to be found in an army camp. The biggest one was a great dane, aloof and not giving a particular damn for anyone, and the smallest, a turtle an inch across, held on an elaborate float by pins stuck around, but not through, his shell.

We awarded a cup for the ugliest pet to a peaceable bulldog; the one for the most beautiful to a young fawn some outfit had picked up in the woods; and that for the most unusual to a deoderized baby skunk. A fox cub was in the show, squirrels of all ages, goats, lambs, alligators, and chipmunks. Of course, there were dogs and cats of all descriptions. Most of the animals were clothed in some fashion or other; some were dressed as a little girl dresses her doll, and others had handsome blankets, their names, ranks and organizational insignia sewed to the sides.

The medics had owned and loved a Saint Bernard dog, a huge, friendly, raggedy beast a year old. His name was Mike. Mike liked to wander far afield, and one night a rancher found him in a pasture with a freshly killed lamb. No one knows to this day whether Mike killed the lamb, but the farmer had lost several sheep. He aimed his rifle and fired. The dog screamed, rolled over, and quickly died.

The regimental band played for Mike's funeral; the chaplain gave an address; and the entire regiment followed the coffin, mounted on a caisson, to the grave. Mike was mourned, for Mike was dear.

We closed our pet review with a tribute to Mike. Guilty or innocent, we didn't know, but by his own canine lights he couldn't have been guilty. We honored him with "Taps." Then there was a full minute of silence. Every man uncovered, every head was bowed. The band, with slow solemnity played: "Where, oh, where has my little dog gone."

There were even a few tears.

The Shakedown Cruise of the U.S.S. Oklahoma City

¶ *As a staff writer for the* Daily Oklahoman, *Tom Rucker worked full time in the early war years to organize the successful war bond campaign that raised the $40 million dollars needed to build the* U.S.S. Oklahoma City. *And the thousands who contributed to the fund drive read Rucker's account of the ship's shakedown voyage as the cruiser traveled through the Panama Canal to her battle station in the Pacific. Rucker's dispatches gave the home folks an intimate picture of how their "investment" was performing. And his story of the typical day in the life of Seaman First Class Ronnie Gilleland of Pawhuska helped personalize the war effort for those who stayed at home. It also must have comforted and reassured countless Oklahoma parents whose men were serving abroad.* ¶ *When hostilities ceased, the* U.S.S. Oklahoma City *had earned two battle stars. After a tour of occupation duty in Japan, the cruiser was converted to a guided-missile carrier. After four decades as the flagship of the United States Seventh Fleet based in the western Pacific, the* U.S.S. Oklahoma City *was retired in 1979.*

ABOARD THE *USS Oklahoma City* at sea—(Delayed)—Today the *USS Oklahoma City*, first fighting ship to bear the name of Soonerland's capital, weighed anchor and now is on her shakedown cruise.

The day is overcast and cold wintry blasts whip through the gear topside, but the sailors are snug in their foul weather gear.

The officers and crew, on ship since she was commissioned, already know her as the *OK City*. They like her trim, racy lines, her sweet roll, her lack of pitching and the way she handles herself in restless waters.

From Tom Rucker, *The Shakedown Cruise of the U.S.S. Oklahoma City* (Oklahoma City: Oklahoma Publishing Company, 1945), 5–6, 9–10.

Oklahoma Memories

And a slick ship she is. On this, her maiden sea voyage, she takes to rough waters as a school boy to pie, and she snakes through the seas like a fleet broken field runner does on a football field.

She does this despite what to a landlubber is her whopping big size. She is at once a city of several hundred population with fully powered and equipped plants, and a powerful sea-going fortress.

It is almost impossible to get a good look at her length, you have to back so far away. To get an idea of how long she is, stand at W. 1 and Robinson in Oklahoma City and look at the very top of the First National building. Well, she's more than 100 feet longer than that is tall.

The *OK City* skims through the seas far faster than you'd think possible for her size, and her quick takeoff racks up the knots in an amazing short distance.

Launched in February, 1944, commissioned in late December, 1944, the *Oklahoma City* is a light cruiser of the *Cleveland* class. Jane's Fighting Ships gives *Cleveland* class destroyers a length of 600 feet, a beam of about 60, and a tonnage of 10,000. All figures are approximates.

A modern light cruiser is a huge anti-aircraft platform. Her mission to protect herself, smaller and bigger craft from air attack, to bombard shores and to protect landings.

For her work, the *OK City* can produce a Sunday sock from batteries of 5 and 6-inchers and from a flock of smaller but faster guns. Besides all this fire power she carries airplanes which may be launched from catapults astern.

The question most frequently asked to date by officers and men alike is how the people of Oklahoma City feel about the ship.

They are more than pleased when you tell them the people of Oklahoma City, capital of a state which has an outstanding navy recruitment record, and flattered and honored that a fighting ship will carry their name against the enemy, and are eager to do everything possible for the ship and its crew.

Though most of the men aboard never have been to Oklahoma City, the name of their ship gives them a feeling of kinship with Oklahoma's capital. They ask all manner of questions about Indians, and want to know if there really are oil wells in backyards at home, and is everybody really rich.

Shakedown Cruise, U.S.S. Oklahoma City

The officers and crew of the *Oklahoma City* are intensely proud of their ship. They take great pains to keep her shipshape, topside and below, and practice almost incessantly to gain efficiency that is pay dirt in battle.

An estimated 60 percent of the crew is green, and many sailors are making their first voyage of any type. Even a few of the several score of officers are making their maiden trip. The purpose of the cruise is to shake down the ship, and to season and salt the officers and crew.

However, there are men aboard, both enlisted personnel and officers, who already have seen an almost unbelievable amount of action in this war. Battle ribbons and battle stars dot their blouses. Seemingly they all are there.

Most of these men fought early in the war, when we temporarily were on the short side of the ledger, and are eager to get back into the fray on more nearly even terms, and show the enemy what's been cooking.

Many of these veterans know that sickening feeling of having ships shot out from under them, and the dreamlike relief of being rescued from a watery death.

It's an odd and pleasing sensation to be so many miles from Oklahoma City and yet be hearing the name so many times a day when you're so many hundreds of miles from home and so many hundreds of miles at sea.

Tonight on the communications bridge in almost total darkness, out of the night an unseen man sang out the name, for reasons of his own or the ship's, and it was reassuring and seemed like something solid, in contrast to the sea, now beginning to boil up a bit.

Morale of the crew is extremely high. Cruiser service is known throughout the navy as good duty, and many sailors prefer it to any other, pointing out it sure beats tossing around in a destroyer.

Oklahoma Memories

As one member of the crew put it very deftly, the *USS Oklahoma City* is a fine sea billet, lacking only in two essentials: "Women and land, lots of land."

A Typical Day at Sea

Aboard the *USS Oklahoma City* at sea—(Delayed)—To Mrs. H. Gilleland, Pawhuska: This is to let you know what your son's days are like. They are about like the days of any other first class seaman aboard the *USS Oklahoma City* and will vary from the days of other seamen in the navy only by degrees.

But first, Ronnie is nut brown. The warm summer-like sun has given him a deep tan. And of all things, he's growing a mustache again. You may think 19 is still too young for that, but it isn't a bad looking mustache, either.

Well, Ronnie—Chazz as his shipmates call him—got up at 5 A.M. today, long before dawn. He partially dressed, washed, then came back to his bed—he calls it a sack—finished dressing then made up his bunk for lashing. Then he went to chow.

He ate a whopping breakfast: baked sausage, potatoes, flap jacks, cereal, milk and coffee. It's a wonder that boy doesn't get fat, but he is just a little over his fighting weight. For a few minutes he had nothing to do.

He decided to go up to his turret, No. 1 in the main battery. The sun had poked up while he was making up his bunk, and a beautiful day it was, too. The sun was slightly overcast, and a steady breeze made the day cool. It had been pretty warm lately.

Ronnie went to the handling room and began tidying up a little bit. He checked the temperatures in 4 powder magazines and reported to the proper authorities. He returned to the handling room and checked on the lubrication of the powder hoists.

Then he checked on the lights in the turret, cleaned the

turret floor—he calls it a deck—and cleaned the turret generally. He really babies that handling room, the turret and the guns. Long ago he learned that dust and dirt can really jam up a gun just when it is needed.

He knocked off working to down a couple cups of Jo—for jamoka which means coffee—and to shoot the breeze, to talk over the turret problems. The coffee pot is handy, right in the handling room. Coffee's cooking 24 hours a day, if you want it.

By this time it was getting toward 8 A.M., time to get ready for the captain's inspection. Frankly, Ronnie doesn't like inspections any too much. They take up time he'd rather spend in the handling room or the turret, pointing that big gun, which is another and very important part of his job.

When the turret is under local control he's the lad who pushes the button that shoots the shell. He likes that.

But Ronnie looks on these inspections as a sort of necessary nuisance, and he takes them in his stride. Nothing really gets him down. Must be the Indian in him. Today, the inspection orders called for wearing undress blues. You will want to know the difference between dress and undress blues, so here it is.

Dress blues have those white lines around the blouse collar and the blouse cuffs. Undress blues do not. Dress blues call for the trick neckties. Undress blues do not. That's all there is to it. Well, Ronnie, being a veteran sailor despite his youth, knew this undress blues business was coming and was prepared.

He lined up with the others on the focsle (that's the way he and other sailors pronounce forecastle) and when the gunnery boss made the captain's inspection he looked sharply to see if Ronnie's clothing were properly marked, if it were clean (and of course it was), if his shoes were shined, if his dog tags were regulation. He couldn't find anything wrong with Ronnie, and believe me he looked sharply.

As soon as the inspection was over, Ronnie went below

Shakedown Cruise, U.S.S. Oklahoma City

and changed back to his more comfortable dungarees, and back to the turret and cleaned the oil filters. He's always and forever checking or cleaning.

Just after he started painting the face plate and muzzle of the three big guns in his turret, he went below for chow and lunched on chicken fried steak, carrots, peas, bread, butter, jelly and iced tea.

Then he spent the rest of the afternoon painting the guns and turret. That is, he painted until abandon ship drill. The inspecting officer talked about things Ronnie already knew about, but some of the other fellows didn't. After that, he painted a short time, then chowed again, this time lightly. It centered around roast beef and wound up with pie.

Ronnie doesn't worry much about chow. If he's ever late, he's got a deal. That boxing he used to do comes in handy. He got acquainted with a cook, who's something of a boxer, too. Well, strictly on the q.t., this cook can fix him up in a pinch.

After chow Ronnie went back to the turret and worked on the handle of a knife he is making for himself. He also shot the breeze some more with the boys. The ones who haven't been to sea before like to get him to tell about Tarawa, the Marshalls and being torpedoed at Saipan. Your son sure has seen a lot of action in the short time he's been in the navy, but it doesn't appear to have hurt him any.

After breezing, he went to the moving picture on the fantail, then hit his sack. That was one of Ronnie's days.

All in all, it was an easy one. Not too many drills or much standing around. Some are much better because the shakedown cruise schedule of the *Oklahoma City* is a tough one. The days that Ronnie really likes are the ones that call for firing. Ronnie hopes to get a leave after the shakedown, but he's nearly positive he can't be lucky enough to get enough time to come home again. But he sure would like too, though. Meantime he sure likes to get letters from home, sweet home.

Guess Who's Coming to School?

¶ *The economic progress that began during World War II touched most of Oklahoma in the postwar years, but fundamental social attitudes predictably resisted change. Of predominantly southern origins and attitudes, most Oklahomans shared the racial prejudice of the day.* ¶ *Although formal segregation was not included in the state constitution, the first legislature promptly enacted a set of segregation codes for schools, public facilities, and transportation that resembled those of the Deep South. Formal segregation was especially rigid in the public schools and seemed unsuited to the social changes so clearly transforming the state after 1945.* ¶ *George Lynn Cross, at that time the president of the University of Oklahoma at Norman, recalls the events leading to the United States Supreme Court's rulings that ended segregation in state-supported graduate schools. The public response revealed a new level of maturity in the Sooner State. Segregation ultimately ended without violence in Oklahoma. On the whole, the acceptance of the inevitability of desegregation was proof of how much both the power structure and the people of Oklahoma had changed in a generation.*

"ONE NICE THING about Norman is that you will never have to worry about a nigger problem here. We have an unwritten law that niggers can't be in town after sundown." The time of this incredible remark was late August, 1934. The place was an appliance store in Norman, Oklahoma. The speaker was a salesman who was attempting to explain to a new member of the University of Oklahoma faculty some of the advantages of the community. I was the new

From George Lynn Cross, "Guess Who's Coming to School?" *Oklahoma Monthly*, 2 (September 1976), 42-51.

faculty member, my appointment was assistant professor of botany and bacteriology would be effective September 1.

The man made the remark with obvious pride. He told me that the restriction on blacks in Norman had been in effect since the settling of the city during the land rush of 1889. He explained that, while blacks could work in the city during the day, they had never been permitted to live there because their residential areas would certainly become slums that would destroy the value of adjacent property owned by whites. He mentioned a few Oklahoma cities in which this had happened, where the citizenry had lacked the foresight shown by the Normanites. When I asked how the Norman law was enforced, he replied that there had never been any need to enforce it; the "niggers" understood the situation, he said, and knew better than to remain in town after the sun went down.

Coming from South Dakota, I knew only vaguely of the segregation laws in the southern states, but after being named to the presidency of the University of Oklahoma in 1944, I soon found it necessary to become familiar with them. Because late in the summer of 1945, following a meeting of the National Association for the Advancement of Colored People held in McAlester, Oklahoma, Thurgood Marshall, a distinguished black leader and attorney who had come from his home in New York City to attend the meeting, announced to the press that a decision had been reached at the meeting to test Oklahoma's segregation laws in the courts. He said that an attempt would be made to enroll students at the University of Oklahoma who needed courses at the graduate level, or in professional programs, not offered at Langston University.

A quick exploration of the legal problems that would be involved with this effort revealed that the Oklahoma constitution provided for the maintenance of separate schools for blacks, and the statutes of the state made it a misdemeanor for a school administrator to admit blacks to a white school, for a teacher to instruct classes composed of mixed races, or for students to attend classes composed of mixed races. The law provided that the president of a university or college who permitted mixed enrollments was subject to a fine not to exceed $500; a teacher who taught a mixed class would be subject to a fine not to exceed $50; and a white student who attended a mixed class would be subject to a fine not to exceed $20. Each day would be a separate offense for all involved, and accordingly, each day could bring an additional fine. It was clear that a formidable financial problem faced anyone who might be inclined to experiment with the enforcement of the law.

Marshall's announcement from McAlester caused great excitement throughout the state, especially in educational circles, and there was a flurry of newspaper speculation concerning what would happen next. It seemed unlikely that a black would attempt to enroll at OU for the fall semester, but the second semester, beginning in January, was a distinct possibility. I received a great deal of advice concerning what I should do when a candidate for admission arrived on the campus, including the suggestion that if a graduate of Langston University should apply, admission should be refused because Langston was not an accredited university. The latter didn't make much sense because the university had in its student body numerous white students who had transferred from unaccredited schools.

The regents of the university discussed the approaching problem thoroughly at their meeting in September 1945, but they were unanimous in deciding that the institution had no alternative but to follow the state laws. They passed a resolution instructing me to do this; however, during the discussion of the motion it appeared to be the consensus that a majority of them had little enthusiasm for the state laws.

Weeks passed with no further word from the NAACP concerning the test case or cases Marshall had mentioned in his release at McAlester. Then, one morning, my secretary informed me that Roscoe Dunjee, editor of the *Black Dispatch* in Oklahoma City was calling me by telephone. Dunjee, in a crisp but courteous manner, reminded me of Mar-

Guess Who's Coming to School?

shall's announcement, and asked for an appointment as early as possible. He wanted me to meet a graduate of Langston University who had been selected to test the state's segregation laws, one who wished to apply for admission to the law school at OU. An appointment was set up for the morning of January 14, 1946.

Dunjee appeared promptly for the 10 o'clock appointment that morning, and he had with him Dr. W. A. J. Bullock, of Chickasha, regional director of the NAACP. With him also was a young woman whom he introduced as Ada Lois Sipuel Fisher, the Langston graduate who wanted to study law at OU. The young woman was charming and well poised; she acknowledged the introduction with a pleasant smile which recurred frequently during our visit. I remember thinking that the Association had made an excellent choice of a student for the test case.

The sharp featured, articulate Dunjee led the conversation. Without hint of belligerence, he explained that Mrs. Fisher was the wife of Warren W. Fisher, whom she had married during her junior year at Langston University. She was an honor graduate of Langston University, and she now wished to study law, a field not included in the Langston curriculum. She had her transcript from Langston, and she wanted a form on which to apply for admission to the University of Oklahoma.

After listening to Dunjee's opening statements, I reminded my visitors that the constitution of Oklahoma and the statutes of the state prohibited officers of the university from admitting blacks to the institution. I mentioned some of the details of the law, especially the provision that made it a misdemeanor for the president of the university to admit a black and the cumulative fine that could develop from such action. I told my visitors that, while I did not approve of the law, I was not financially equipped to experiment with its enforcement.

As I spoke, I noticed a tinge of amusement form on Dunjee's previously impassive face. When I had finished, he said, "President Cross, we know about the law. We have studied it far longer than you have. We know that you cannot legally admit Mrs. Fisher to the University of Oklahoma, or permit her to be admitted. What we want from you, is a refusal of admission in writing—stating that she is academically qualified for admission, but cannot be admitted solely because of her race." A letter of this kind was needed, he said, because refusing her admission without giving race as the sole reason, would handicap them in their efforts to test the state laws in the courts.

Guess Who's Coming to School?

I was greatly relieved to hear Dunjee's comments. I sent Mrs. Fisher's transcript immediately to Roy Gittinger, dean of admissions, for evaluation. While we were awaiting the dean's report, we continued our conversation, with Dunjee doing most of the talking, but occasionally turning to Mrs. Fisher for corroboration of what he had said. Dr. Bullock took no part in the conversation.

Within a matter of minutes, a report came from Dean Gittinger's office that Mrs. Fisher was academically qualified for admission to OU. I then asked my secretary to join our group to take the letter refusing admission. But the name on the transcript was Ada Lois Sipuel; the name Fisher had not been added after she had married during her junior year at Langston. I asked to whom the letter should be addressed, to Miss Sipuel or Mrs. Fisher. Dunjee suggested, and Mrs. Fisher nodded in agreement, that the application be made under her maiden name as on the transcript, and the letter refusing admission should be addressed to Ada Lois Sipuel. Within a very few minutes, the requested letter was prepared by my secretary, signed and handed to Miss Sipuel, with an extra copy. My visitors then expressed their satisfaction and appreciation of the visit, and as the trio left my office, they were invited to lunch by members of the university's YMCA–YWCA Race Relations Committee.

Miss Sipuel's denial of admission was widely publicized by the news media of the state, and one of the articles in a local paper stated that Thurgood Marshall, the NAACP's chief counsel, would come to the state on February 15 to file a test suit—that he would be assisted by Amos Hall, a black attorney from Tulsa. But the court test was delayed until April 6, 1946, when Hall, acting as attorney for Miss Sipuel, filed a petition for a writ of mandamus with Judge Ben T. Williams of the District Court of Cleveland County. The petition listed the Board of Regents of the university, the president, and other officers of the institution, as defendants. I well remember receiving my copy of the writ, and the strange feeling I had, when I realized that I was a defendant in the first legal action initiated to end segregation in Oklahoma's educational system.

The regents of the university asked the Office of the Attorney General of Oklahoma to handle the case for the defendants. Fred Hansen, assistant attorney general, was given the responsibility of preparing the defense, with the agreement that Professors Maurice Merrill and John B. Cheadle, of the School of Law, would assist him.

After many conferences and delays, the attorneys involved with Judge Ben Williams finally set July 9, 1946, as the date of the hearing.

Court convened at 10:30 that morning. Hall, representing Miss Sipuel, argued that, in denying Miss Sipuel admission to the university, the Fourteenth Amendment of the Constitution, which requires the states to furnish equal educational facilities for black and white races, had been violated. Hansen based his defense on the state laws that made it a criminal offense for those in charge of an educational institution to permit mixing of the races in a classroom. At 7:45 that evening, Judge Williams ruled to deny the writ of mandamus on the basis that the laws of the state of Oklahoma prohibited the university from admitting Miss Sipuel. A couple of days later, Hall filed a motion for a new trial, but Judge Williams overruled the motion late in July. As I read Roscoe Dunjee's report of these happenings in the *Black Dispatch*, I noticed, with interest, that his approach to the situation was not based on the state's failure to provide "separate but equal" facilities for blacks. He rejected this concept with the statement that "separate but equal" was a myth. He argued that the only equal education for the races would be the same education.

The Sipuel case was then appealed to the Oklahoma Supreme Court, and oral argument there was heard on March 4, 1947. Two new attorneys were named for the plaintiff, Thurgood Marshall and Robert L. Carter. Marshall presented the plaintiff's case at the hearing and argued brilliantly that segregation was a violation of the Fourteenth Amendment. He also elaborated on the theme earlier set forth by Dunjee, namely that there could be no equality under segregated systems, and that such equality could be only "legal fiction and judicial myth." But despite Marshall's impressive presentation, the Oklahoma Supreme Court, not unexpectedly, sustained the ruling of the Cleveland County District Court in an opinion filed on April 29, 1947.

Guess Who's Coming to School?

The attorneys for the plaintiff then filed a petition with the United States Supreme Court. The court accepted the petition and heard the arguments on January 8, 1948. The justices, acting with unprecedented speed, gave a decision on January 12, ordering Oklahoma to provide a legal education for the petitioner and provide it as soon as it would be provided for the applicants of any other racial group. But the court did not declare Oklahoma's segregation laws unconstitutional. It appeared to be the reasoning of the members of the court that, since enrollment at the university for second semester classes would begin on January 29, it would be necessary either to permit Miss Sipuel to enroll, or not to enroll any white students in the school of law. They apparently assumed that it would be impossible for the state to provide facilities for her in seventeen days.

But the Supreme Court obviously underestimated the evasive capabilities of the Oklahomans involved with the problem. While Miss Sipuel and those sympathetic to her cause were rejoicing in her apparent victory before the supreme court of the land, the Oklahoma State Regents for Higher Education, with assurance from Attorney General Mac Q. Williamson that the court's decision did not invalidate the segregation laws of Oklahoma, decided to establish a Langston University School of Law in the State Capitol Building—a branch of Langston University. A dean for the new law school, and two additional faculty members were employed to instruct Miss Sipuel. All of this was accomplished in approximately one week.

Understandably, Miss Sipuel and her attorneys would have nothing to do with the new law school. They announced that they would go to court again in an effort to establish that the intent of the Supreme Court of the United States had not been met by the creation of the new institution. During the course of her appearance in Washington, it came to light that Miss Sipuel was married to Warren Fisher, and her married name was used in subsequent legal action initiated on her behalf.

But, not wishing to wait for the results of further court action taken on behalf of Mrs. Fisher, six blacks saw opportunity to profit from the supreme court's stipulation that the state of Oklahoma must provide a legal education for Mrs. Fisher and "provide it as soon as it does for applicants for any other group." On January 28, 1948, the last day of enrollment for the second semester of the school year, the six appeared in my office to apply for admission to the university. They sought programs not offered at Langston—architecture, commercial education, social work, and graduate programs in zoology and education. Included in the group was George W. McLaurin, a member of the faculty at Langston University. The six applicants obviously had reasoned that, although the state had been able to accomplish a minor miracle in establishing a school of law associated with Langston University in less than a week, it would require a major miracle to create the programs they needed overnight. The OU regents went into called session the next day and, acting on the advice of the attorney general of Oklahoma, finally decided that the six should be denied admission on the grounds that the state laws still prohibited mixing of the races in classrooms. The attorney general took the position that the six had not made known to the state their need for the requested programs of study in time for the state to set up programs for them.

Guess Who's Coming to School?

Students at OU have never been hesitant in expressing their views about any issue, and the regents got an interesting sample of student opinion the morning of their meeting. Approximately one thousand students, with a sprinkling of faculty, assembled north of the Administration Building to protest the denial of admission of blacks to the University of Oklahoma. Several speeches, all loudly cheered, were made. The meeting ended with the shredding of a copy of the Fourteenth Amendment. The torn paper strips were placed in a cookie can, doused with lighter fluid, and set on fire. The ashes were then carefully emptied into an envelope addressed to President Harry S Truman, whereupon the group marched to the campus corner Post Office to mail the letter, singing the Battle Hymn of the Republic as they went along.

In the meantime, Mrs. Fisher's attorneys had petitioned the United States Supreme Court for a writ of mandamus alleging that the state of Oklahoma had failed to comply with the court's mandate of January 12, 1948, and requesting the court to compel the state to comply. The court denied the petition, on the grounds that the County Court of Cleveland County had retained jurisdiction in the matter, and it was up to the local court to decide whether the state had complied with the Supreme Court's mandate.

So, after nearly two years had passed, Mrs. Fisher and her attorneys found themselves back where the case had started—the District Court of Cleveland County. After several delays, the hearing finally was held on May 24 through 27, 1948, inclusive.

The plaintiff's attorneys had arranged for an impressive list of witnesses including deans and professors of law from the University of California, the University of Wisconsin, Harvard Law School, the University of Pennsylvania, Cornell University and the University of Oklahoma.

Dr. John Hervey, former dean of the OU School of Law and, at the time, legal advisor to the Council on Legal Education and Admissions of the American Bar Association, was the principal witness for the defendants. Hervey testified that a legal education at the Langston University Law School would be equivalent to one available at the University of Oklahoma.

The witnesses for the plaintiff testified impressively that this was not the case. All emphasized the importance of a substantial student body in modern methods of teaching law. Perhaps the most colorful testimony given during the court session was that of Dr. Henry H. Foster, Jr., former attorney with the National Labor Relations Board and a member of the law faculty at the University of Oklahoma. Foster charged state officials with "cheap political chicanery." He branded the Langston School of Law a "fake, fraud and deception." When asked specifically if it were not possible that the two schools could afford equal educational opportunities for students, Foster shouted, "only a prejudiced or an academic mind could conceivably find the slightest substance to say that the two schools are at all comparable, let alone substantially equal or equivalent."

After the hearing was concluded, Presiding Judge Justin Hinshaw took the case under advisement. He didn't get around to rendering an opinion until August 2, when he denied Mrs. Fisher a writ of mandamus that would order the University of Oklahoma to admit her. He held that the Langston Law School was "fully qualified" to offer the training, and he added that the library of the new school was equal "in all respects" to the library on the Norman campus.

In the meantime, three of the six blacks who had applied for admission to OU on January 28, including George W. McLaurin, had petitioned the local Cleveland County Court for a writ of mandamus forcing the university to admit them. But McLaurin, perhaps advised by the NAACP attorneys, decided in July to drop his suit in the Cleveland County Court and file instead a complaint in the District Court of the United States for the Western District of Oklahoma. The District Court accepted jurisdiction, and with Judges A. P. Murrah, Edgar S. Vaught, and Bower Broaddus presiding, ruled on September 29, that McLaurin must be admitted to the University of Oklahoma or that the university must discontinue for white students the course of study leading to a doctor's degree in education—the program in which McLaurin sought to enroll. However, the district court did not strike down Oklahoma's segregation laws. In clarifying its opinion with respect to this issue, the court stated, "This does not mean, however, that the segregation laws of Oklahoma are incapable of enforcement. We simply hold that insofar as they are sought to be enforced in this particular case they are inoperative."

Guess Who's Coming to School?

The attorney general of Oklahoma interpreted the district court's ruling to mean that McLaurin must be admitted to the university, but in accordance with the state's segregation laws. His academic activities would need to be on a segregated basis—separate classrooms, separate instructors, and separate extracurricular facilities. Knowing that several, perhaps many additional blacks would soon be attending the university as a result of court action in the McLaurin case, university officials realized that the problem of providing segregated facilities would be formidable. The space needed was not available; neither was the money.

But after much discussion, and several conferences with the regents of the university, the Oklahoma State Regents for Higher Education, and the attorney general of Oklahoma, a possible solution to the problem was developed. We would divide each classroom involved with the instruction of mixed races into two areas, and regard each area as a separate classroom. The blacks would be seated in one "classroom" and the whites in the other. Separate eating, library and sanitary facilities would be arranged for the two races. Following this decision, McLaurin was admitted to the university and all of his classes were scheduled in a room on the bottom floor of the old Carnegie Library, located to the northeast of the Administration Building. He was seated at a desk in a small alcove just off the room, where he had a clear view of the blackboard and the instructor.

A toilet was reserved for him in the same building, a table in the library was labeled "for Negroes," and he was served lunch under segregated conditions in the Union Building—an incredible situation made necessary by the state laws. The following semester, several additional blacks enrolled, and other classrooms were divided to accommodate them. In some instances, ropes were stretched dividing the rooms; in other cases wooden railings were installed to accomplish the division.

Understandably, McLaurin and his attorneys, especially Thurgood Marshall, were not satisfied with the arrangement. An appeal was made to the district court to end the discrimination, but the court rejected the appeal.

The absurdity of the situation was further complicated by the fact that, despite the district court ruling, the state laws still prohibited the admission of black students to white colleges. The laws had neither been declared unconstitutional nor amended. In hopes of clarifying the situation, an effort was made to persuade the 1949 legislature to amend the state laws and bring them into conformity with the order given by the district court. The legislature did pass a bill which permitted the admission of black students to white colleges when the programs they desired were not available at Langston, but at the last moment a member of the senate managed to insert a clause in the bill which provided that instruction should be given under strictly segregated conditions—separate classrooms and separate instructors. A great deal of effort expended to get the law passed had produced little by way of results.

In the meantime, McLaurin and his attorneys had decided to appeal his case to the United States Supreme Court. The court accepted jurisdiction, but spent many months arriving at a decision. It was not until June 1950, that the Supreme Court ruled unanimously in favor of McLaurin. The court ruled that the restrictions imposed upon him at the University of Oklahoma did "impair and inhibit his ability to study, to engage in discussion, and exchange views with other students, and in general to learn his profession." The court ordered all such restrictions removed.

The long awaited decision was hailed with enthusiasm by the administration, the faculty, and most students and alumni of the University of Oklahoma. The enthusiasm was heightened by the realization that the decision did not apply solely to the University of Oklahoma; but meant that, in the future, blacks would be admitted to graduate study in all state-supported colleges and universities throughout the country. Desegregation had been accomplished in the nation for at least a portion of higher education.

The Supreme Court's decision represented one step forward. Desegregation was accomplished, and the legal barriers to integration of the races were removed. But many problems, some of them seemingly insurmountable, remain. Their solution probably cannot be accomplished through further court action.

Because, while desegregation can be legislated, integration cannot. Integration, like morality and ethics, involves personal attitudes not subject to legal control. These attitudes can come only from education and the realization that all individuals are ultimately interdependent, and of equal worth in the overall scheme of things.

Integration has not yet been achieved within any race. Class and group distinctions prevent this. Integration between races is much more difficult to achieve, and efforts to bring it about through the forceful application of regulations will only increase the difficulty.

But the fact that there has been some improvement in a difficult situation provides hope for additional betterment in the future.

Guess Who's Coming to School?

Behold the Walls!

¶ *The civil rights movement that began in Oklahoma at the end of World War II gathered momentum in the late fifties. A year before the national press reported the sit-ins at Greensboro, North Carolina, the Oklahoma City NAACP Youth Council, under the leadership of Clara Luper, staged the first of a series of lunch counter sit-ins and other demonstrations that were to last nearly six years.* ¶ *These protests were significant not only for integrating Oklahoma's public eating places, but also for being the first major demonstrations in the sit-in movement of the 1960s. They were also the longest nonviolent, concentrated effort in the black Oklahomans' struggle for equality.* ¶ *The sit-ins that Clara Luper recalls helped create a climate for interracial progress. They changed hiring practices and housing patterns, exposed hidden segregation, and helped focus national attention on the struggle for civil rights.*

THE SAME GROUP of NAACP Youth Council members had congregated at my house located at 1819 N.E. Park in Oklahoma City, Oklahoma. It was August 19, 1958. The long hot summer's heat seemed unendurable in the small five-room, white frame house, but the mosquitoes were in complete control outside and the youngsters remained inside where they, with sweat on their faces, held their weekly meetings. Gwendolyn Fuller, president of the Council, was presiding. Ruth Tolliver and I were in the kitchen preparing grape Kool-Aid and lunch meat sandwiches.

There was no advisor–youth council membership relationship then. It was a far deeper feeling that I had for the NAACP Youth Council members. I had watched them

From Clara Luper, *Behold the Walls* (Oklahoma City: Jim Wire, 1979), 1–15.

grow up from infancy. I had seen their minds develop and the values which they would carry through their lives change. I knew their parents and knew how much their parents loved them. I knew how unpopular it was to have your children involved in the NAACP Youth Council activities. It was even more difficult to get adults involved in the Council.

This was not the first NAACP Youth Council to operate in Oklahoma City. Mrs. Lucille McClendon had worked untiringly with a group some years before. Non-participation and non-support had spelled doom for the youth council. Through the leadership of John B. White and the insistence of Mr. and Mrs. D. J. Diggs and others, I had decided to take over the responsibility of reorganizing the Oklahoma City NAACP Youth Council. The fact that I was teaching American history at Dunjee High School in Spencer, Oklahoma and was a member of the Fifth Street Baptist Church furnished me with an ample number of young people who would become the nucleus of the Youth Council. William Miles, a student from Dunjee School, had been elected as the first president.

Each year at school, I'd present plays during Negro History Week, as it was called then. In 1957, I presented "Brother President," the story of Martin Luther King, Jr., and the nonviolent techniques that were used to eliminate segregation in Montgomery, Alabama. The cast consisted of 26 students that were talented, ambitious and dedicated. The leading characters were William Miles, Joseph Hill and Maxine Dowdell. This play had filled the auditorium at Dunjee High School and drew tremendous turnouts all over the state.

In 1957, it was presented at the East 6th St. Christian Church, where Herbert Wright, the National Youth Director of NAACP, was in attendance. He was so impressed with the play that he invited me to present it in New York City at a "Salute to Young Freedom Fighters Rally."

The cast, most of whom had never been out of Oklahoma City, stopped in St. Louis for dinner and experienced their first integrated lunch counter service. This they continued to enjoy and appreciate on the trip. Words are inadequate to describe the expression and action of young people who, by tradition and custom, had been separated by the strong Visible Walls of segregation.

Behold the Walls!

The group stayed at the Henry Hudson Hotel in New York City and the play was presented in both Manhattan and Harlem. The youth met freedom fighters from the south and the excitement and adventure of such a trip had a permanent effect on their lives.

In planning the trip, we decided to go the northern route and return by the southern route. On our return trip, we stopped in Washington, D.C. and visited the top historical spots including Arlington National Cemetery. As we stood in the Cemetery and watched the change-of-the-guard, each youth had an opportunity to think about Freedom. One asked, "What do you think would happen in this country if the Unknown Soldier's casket was opened and they would find out that he was black?" Joan Johnson said, "I don't know."

Barbara Posey, the secretary of the Youth Council, told the group that since all of these people had died for our freedom, we need to really get busy and do something for our country. Yes, these people that are buried at Arlington Cemetery did all they could for freedom. I don't think the color of the unknown soldier's skin is important. I think it's what he did, and we have to do something.

Silently the group left Arlington Cemetery, after pledging that they'd do something for their country, and loaded on the Greyhound bus. As the bus headed southward, the walls of segregation became so visible. In Nashville, Tennessee, the bus driver admitted that he did not know of any place where blacks could sit down and eat. So paper-sack lunches became the order of the day through Tennessee, Arkansas, and into Oklahoma.

John White's words, "The Sooner State, The Sooner we get rid of segregation, the better off we'll be," were repeated by the group. "True, you know segregation just doesn't fit in with my personality," William Miles said with a quick smile that faded back to a face of solemnity. The group applauded with loud outbursts of "Freedom Now! Freedom Now!"

Back in Oklahoma City, the group decided to break down segregation in public accommodations for all time and pay any price for it. "That will be our project—to eliminate segregation in public accommodations," the group said.

A strategy was worked out, where the public accommodations' owners and managers would be approached directly by a small delegation. There was never to be over three in the delegation and Mrs. Caroline Burkes, a stately freedom-loving white woman, was to accompany the groups on all occasions. This she did with a dedication that was followed up with letters and personal visits. This campaign was followed by a direct private approach to the city manager and city council which told the groups, "We are sorry, we do not have the power to interfere in private businesses. We don't tell the businessmen who to serve and they don't tell us how to run our city government." The campaign turned into a letter-writing campaign to churches—the white church leaders turned a deaf ear as their beautiful buildings stood as monuments to their dedication to Christianity. The black churches did not want to get involved at this time and told us that we could meet in their churches. They would take up a collection for us and make announcements concerning our worthwhile activities.

The meeting continued with a warm-up chanting rally. The group was chanting:

> We want to EAT—eat!
> We want to EAT—eat!
> NOW! NOW! NOW!
> We don't want any more excuses!
> We want to E-A-T—eat!
> We want to E-A-T—eat!
> NOW! NOW! NOW!

Gwendolyn Fuller leaned back in her chair and looked at the group as the singing and clapping grew louder and louder. Barbara Posey, the spokesman for the Public Accommodation Committee made her report. "The owners of all public accommodations in Oklahoma City say they will not serve blacks. Now, what are we going to do?" Marilyn Luper spoke out, "I'll tell you, Barbara. I move that we go down to Katz Drug Store and sit down and drink a Coke." "I second the motion," said Areda Tolliver. The motion was carried unanimously by the group.

"When shall we go?" the group asked as if in a choir. "Gwen, let me tell you, you know that I made the motion to go, and I feel that I should have the privilege of deciding when we should go," said Marilyn Luper.

A silence fell over the meeting and after a few minutes with Marilyn staring into the future, she said, "Tonight is the time and as I read in Mr. Wisener's typing book, 'Now is the time for all good men to come to the aid of their party.'" "That doesn't mean that we will have to go tonight!" shouted Calvin.

A brother-sister debate occurred and in a high-toned voice, Calvin said, "Don't you ever think that I'm afraid to go!"

Barbara Posey said, "We have waited for over fifteen months, and Oklahoma has waited fifty years. Let's go down and wait in front of the manager so that people can see our problem."

Portwood Williams Jr. said, "The men in the NAACP Youth Council are ready to go right now and we are able to take care of any situation."

"We wouldn't doubt that," Gwendolyn said, and a bit of laughter sparkled in the air and echoed back into moments of silence.

Barbara Posey was recognized by the president, Gwendolyn Fuller, and she said, "We had better see what Mrs. Luper thinks. After all, she is the Youth Advisor."

I could feel the eyes of the members on me. I thought for

Behold the Walls!

a brief moment and traced the steps that we had taken. We had been patient and I saw in the children's eyes reflections of my restless childhood when I wanted to do something about a system that had paralyzed my movements and made me an outsider in my own country. Yet, these were children whose ages ranged from seven to fifteen years old.

I thought about my father who had died in 1957 in the Veteran's Hospital and who had never been able to sit down and eat a meal in a decent restaurant. I remembered how he used to tell us that someday he would take us to dinner and to parks and zoos. And when I asked him when was someday, he would always say, "Someday will be real soon," as tears ran down his cheeks. So my answer was, "Yes, tonight is the night. History compels us to go, and let History alone be our final judge." We had another problem, we didn't have any transportation. Ruth Tolliver and I discussed the situation and decided to call three people that we knew wouldn't turn us down. Portwood Williams Sr., Lillian Oliver, and Mary Pogue were selected.

I called Portwood Williams first. He lived in the next block. Mr. Williams was a talkative man with a sharp tongue, quick wit, and an adequate supply of words. He said, "I want to volunteer to drive car number one down to Katz Drug Store. My car is clean and ready. I don't blame you. I shined Mr. Charlie's shoes, and my mother washed Miss Ann's clothes. Now, I'm an upholsterer, the best in town, and my car is ready. I'll be there."

My next call was to Mrs. Lillian Oliver, a quiet, dignified, tall school teacher and one who had served as an assistant NAACP Youth Council Advisor. I had known her since 1940 and through the years. We had been very close friends. I told her that I needed another car to take the NAACP youths down to Katz Drug Store. She didn't ask any questions. She said, "I'll be there in a few minutes. If you all are crazy enough to go, I'm crazy enough to take you!"

Lillian Oliver's cousin, Mrs. Grace Daniels, had related some of her experiences in Phoenix, Arizona, to the group and as I put the telephone down, I thought about Grace and how proud she would be of us. Lillian would have to call and tell her that we had started a direct-action campaign. I walked out on the porch where the kids were singing, "I want to be ready to sit for Freedom, just like John."

Behold the Walls!

I hurried back into the house and called Mary Pogue, the mother of two of the youth. I knew that she would make me explain everything to her in detail . . . and she did! After I had finished, she said, "I'll be there in a few minutes."

I put the telephone down and heard it ring again. I had a feeling that it was my mother and I knew that it was not the proper time for me to tell her what we were going to do. I picked up the telephone and she said, "I just called to see if the NAACP Youth meeting was over." I said, "No, mother, it is not over. In fact, we are just beginning." She said, "Well, Clara, don't keep the kids up too late. You know tomorrow . . ." I said, "Yes, Mother, I'm going to take you downtown to eat for your birthday, which is only two days away." She said, "Clara, you aren't going to take me anywhere tomorrow. I'm not thinking about those white folks. What day is tomorrow, anyway. Well, Clara, we won't worry about it for tomorrow is just another day." I said, "Yes, Mama, tomorrow is just another day."

I rushed out of my house and on a still, hot, August night, August 19, 1958, we headed to Katz Drug Store in the heart of Oklahoma City. I went to the three cars and called the following names, Richard Brown, Elmer Edwards, Linda Pogue, Lana Pogue, Areda Tolliver, Calvin Luper, Marilyn Luper, Portwood Williams Jr., Lynzetta Jones, Gwendolyn Fuller, Alma Faye Posey, Barbara Posey, Goldie Battle and Betty Germany.

Are we ready to behold the walls, non-violently?

All the way downtown, I wondered if we were really ready for a non-violent war.

So non-violently, we were on our way to Katz Drug Store.

Katz Drug Store was located in the Southwestern corner of Main and Robinson in downtown Oklahoma City. It was a center of activity with its first-class pharmacy department, unique gifts, toys, and lunch counter. Blacks were permitted to shop freely in all parts of the store. They could order sandwiches and drinks to go. Orders were placed in a paper sack and were to be eaten in the streets.

This was the kind of wall that the older people should have undertaken years ago instead of financing this type of treatment. This was the kind of wall that the white Christians or the Jewish brothers should have fought. Maybe, this is the kind of battle that the atheist should have fought and now these thirteen little children could be enjoying an evening at home with their parents.

As I was thinking about what should have been done, Lana Pogue, the six-year-old daughter of Mr. and Mrs. Louis J. Pogue, grabbed my hand; and, we moved toward the counter. All of my life, I had wanted to sit at "those counters and drink a Coke or a Seven-Up." It really didn't matter which, but I had been taught that those seats were for "whites only." Blacks were to sweep around the seats, and keep them clean so whites could sit down. It didn't make any difference what kind of white person it was, thief, rapist, murderer, uneducated; the only requirement was that he or she be white. Unbathed, unshaven—it just didn't make any difference. Nor did it make any difference what kind of black you were, B.A. Degree black, Dr. Black, Attorney black, Rev. Black, M.A. Black, Ph.D. Black, rich Black, poor Black, young Black, old Black, pretty Black, ugly Black; you were not to sit down at any lunch counter to eat. We were all seated now in the "for whites only territory." The waitress suffered a quick psychological stroke and one said in a mean tone, "What do you all want?"

Barbara Posey spoke, "We'd like thirteen Cokes please."

"You may have them to go," the waitress nervously said.

"We'll drink them here," Barbara said as she placed a five dollar bill on the counter. The waitress nervously called for additional help.

Mr. Masoner, the red, frightened-faced manager, rushed over to me as if he were going to slap me and said, "Mrs.

Luper, you know better than this. You know we don't serve colored folks at the counter."

I remained silent and looked him straight in the eyes as he nervously continued. "I don't see what's wrong with you colored folks—Mrs. Luper, you take these children out of here—this moment! This moment, I say." He yelled, "Did you hear me?"

"Thirteen Cokes please," I said.

"Mrs. Luper, if you don't move these colored children, what do you think my white customers will say? You know better, Clara. I don't blame the children! I blame you. You are just a trouble maker."

He turned and rushed to the telephone and called the police. In a matter of minutes, we were surrounded by policemen of all sizes, with all kinds of facial expressions. The sergeant and the manager had a conference; additional conferences were called as different ranks of policemen entered. Their faces portrayed their feelings of resentment. The press arrived and I recognized Leonard Hanstein of Channel 9 with his camera and I sat silently as they threw him out and a whole crew of cameramen.

The whites that were seated at the counter got up, leaving their food unfinished on the table and emptied their hate terms into the air. Things such as "Niggers go home, who do they think they are? The nerve!" One man walked straight up to me and said, "Move, you black S.O.B." Others bent over to cough in my face and in the faces of the children. Linda Pogue was knocked off a seat, she smiled and sat back on the stool. Profanity flowed evenly and forcefully from the crowd. One elderly lady rushed over to me as fast as she could with her walking cane in her hand and yelled, "The nerve of niggers trying to eat in our places? Who does Clara Luper think she is? She is nothing but a damned fool, the black thing."

I started to walk over and tell her that I was one of God's children and He had made me in His own image and if she didn't like how I looked, she was filing her complaint in the wrong department. She'd have to file it with the Creator.

Behold the Walls!

I'm the end product of His Creation and not the maker. Then, I realized her intellectual limitations and continued to watch the puzzled policemen and the frightened manager.

Tensions were building up as racial slurs continued to be thrown at us. Hamburgers, Cokes, malts, etc., remained in place as pushing, cursing, and "nigger," became the "order of the day."

As the news media attempted to interview us, the hostile crowd increased in number. Never before had I seen so many hostile, hard, hate-filled white faces. Lana, the six-year-old, said, "Why do they look so mean?"

I said, "Lana, their faces are as cold as Alaskan Icycles."

As I sat quietly there that night, I prayed and remembered our non-violent philosophy.

. . . I looked up and saw a big burly policeman walking toward me. When he got within two feet of me, another officer called him to the telephone. I wondered why the policeman had to stand over us. We had no weapons and the only thing that we wanted was 13 Cokes that we had the money to pay for.

Amid the cursing, I remembered the words of Professor Watkins, my elementary principal and teacher in Hoffman, Oklahoma. He told us to "consider, always, consider the source."

There were some blacks entering the drug store. I saw some of the cooks and janitors. I opened my purse and wrote,

> "When the time comes for cooking the food, blacks are all right;
> When the time comes for washing the dishes, blacks are all right.
> But when the time comes to sit down and eat, the blacks are all wrong and that's not neat."

My daughter, Marilyn, walked over and pointed out a big, fat, mean-looking, white man, who walked over to me and said, "I can't understand it. You all didn't use to act this way; you all use to be so nice."

We remained silent and as he bumped into me, the police officers told him that he had to move on. An old white woman walked up to me and said, "If you don't get those little old poor ugly-looking children out of here, we are going to have a race riot. You just want to start some trouble." I remained silent. "Don't you know about the Tulsa race riots?" the woman asked.

I moved down to the south end of the counter, then back to the other end. This was repeated over and over. As I passed by Alma Faye Posey she burst out laughing and when I continued to look at her, she put her hands on the counter and pointed to a picture of a banana split.

It had been a long evening. Barbara, Gwen and I had a quick conference and we decided to leave without cracking a dent in the wall. Mr. Portwood Williams, Mrs. Lillian Oliver and Mrs. Mary Pogue were waiting. We loaded in our cars and left the hecklers, heckling.

We passed our first test. They pushed us, called us niggers and did everything, the group said.

"Look at me, I'm really a non-violent man," Richard Brown yelled. "Look at me. I can't believe it myself."

Small details of events were written out by Goldie Battles and it was not easy to make plans for the next day because of the large number of obscene telephone calls and threats that I was receiving. The call that really caught me unexpectedly came from a black man who would not tell me his name, but he told he how good the white folks had been to him and I was disgracing my race by taking those poor innocent children downtown.

"Sir, do you have any recommendation on what we can do to eat downtown?"

He said, "No, I do not."

Then I said, "I have one for you sir."

"Okay."

I said, "Sir, since the white folks are so good to you, where do you urinate when you are dressed up in your fine suit downtown?"

He said, "I take my can with me."

"Then, sir, I feel that it is time for you to go and empty your can."

Another black caller said that she was so embarrassed that she could hardly hold her head up. One black lady said she was working out in Nichols Hills and the lady told her to look and see what those people were doing. "Do you know them?" She said that she said no. She continued to do her work and when she got home she called me and I had never talked to my friend when she was in such a state of fright.

To my surprise, my mother and Mary Pogue came up to the house and explained to me all the dangers that I had gotten "all of us in." Mary had taken us downtown, but she said, "Oh! It was awful. Those people mean business. You should have heard the things that they were saying about you." The conversation continued and finally they went home.

As the crowd left my house, I hurried to bed, slept as soundly as a log. The robins reminded me that it was another day. The telephone started ringing, mostly hate calls. Then, Mary Pogue, my mother, Mrs. Pearl Chiles and Ruth Tolliver called. They were all saying, "Be careful, Clara—please, be careful."

As the calls continued to come in, I wondered if the kids would return. What are their parents saying? Will the parents be afraid of reprisals? Will there be violence today?

"Well," Reverend W. K. Jackson said in a sermon, "If you believe that you are right, go on and God will take care of you. Let His will be done."

I couldn't believe the kids were all back with new ones, including Edmund Atkins, Robert Lambeth, Elmer Smith, James Arthur Edwards, Carolyn Edwards, Henry Rolfe Jr., Leon Chandler, Willie Johnson, Arnetta Carmichael, Thomas Taylor, David Irving and Theresa Scruggs. Cars were lining up in front of my house. I had calls from Rolfe Funeral Home, Temple Funeral Home and McKay Funeral Home. They sent cars over to take the children downtown. Blanche, the owner of Blanche's Drive-In, called to say,

"Clara, I'll send some food and anything you need." We all started jumping up and down for truly, "This was the beginning, oh no, it was not the beginning, it was the continuation of man's desperate struggle to be free and Oklahoma City would never be the same." I joined the freedom band and we all began to sing:

Behold the Walls!

"I want to be ready,
I want to be ready,
I want to be ready,
To walk for freedom
Just like John!"

In two days, the walls had fallen, not only at Katz in Oklahoma City, but Katz, billed as the world's leading cut-rate drug store, announced that its 38 outlets in Missouri, Oklahoma, Kansas, and Iowa would serve all people regardless of race, creed or color.

No longer could anyone go to Katz Drug Stores and say, "Behold the walls!"

We had to talk about "our yesterday" at Katz Drug Store. Yesterday, when Gregory Pogue became the first black to eat at Katz. (His order was delivered first. Some of the children had waited so long that they had forgotten what they wanted.)

"This is just great, it's not the food, it's the feeling. I just feel good inside." Theresa Scruggs said.

The "Humane and Lenient Treatment" Begins

¶ *Colonel Robinson Risner had been in combat in South Vietnam less than a month when the North Vietnamese captured and imprisoned him. He remained their prisoner for seven nightmarish years. When Risner failed to write a "confession" after his capture, he was punished by being locked in legstocks and fed on bread and water. Though physically ill, abused, and losing strength and weight rapidly, Risner determined not to lose heart. He occupied the time as best he could with elaborate mental schemes for his oldest son's education. He relived trips. He plotted and executed field exercises in his head.* ¶ *As Thanksgiving Day approached in the fall of 1965, Risner realized that he might be in the stocks indefinitely; perhaps he would die chained like an animal. Earlier he had tried not to think of his parents and of his childhood in Oklahoma. The emotional strain was too intense and he feared that he might give in to his captors. But as thoughts of the turkey dinner and family festivities overcame him, Risner realized that these memories would sustain him. Slowly he began to grow stronger emotionally and mentally. Recalling Oklahoma had helped him in passing the night.*

AS THANKSGIVING DAY began to approach, I kept thinking about spending it with my feet in stocks and on bread and water. Thanksgiving had always been a special day at home, not only because it was a holiday but also because it was the annual family reunion for the Risners. We would have a packed house—a lot of food, singing and horseplay, just good comradeship. We would get together a quartet and sing some of the old-time songs like "Here comes the man with a sack on his back; Got more crawdads

From Robinson Risner, *The Passing of the Night: My Seven Years as a Prisoner of the North Vietnamese* (New York: Random House, 1973), 85–89.

than he can pack," or maybe "Salty Dog." Sometimes we would sing religious songs which Dad, who was a good bass, loved to join in on. Mother or one of my sisters would play the piano. There would be a lot of picture taking, pranks played, laughter, noise and confusion, plus plenty of good food, and visiting.

I thought about them more and more as Thanksgiving neared. Though it made me more lonesome, I somehow felt much closer to them.

We moved to Sapulpa, Oklahoma, when I was six. Then, after only six months, we moved to Tulsa, where Mother and Dad lived in the same house until his death in 1962, and where Mother remained until a couple of years before her passing. During most of those years Dad continued trading livestock, and even though we lived in town, I had a spotted horse that I kept in the backyard.

It was here that I came under the influence of the church. I began going regularly to the First Assembly of God in Tulsa. I formed lasting friendships in its youth group. We did everything together, from church activities to buying and riding cycles.

At age sixteen I got a part-time job as stock clerk for the Chamber of Commerce, and had an occasional job welding as a result of vocational training in school. Dad had also gone into the used-car business now. So on Saturdays I washed and waxed cars.

Dad was a short Dutchman with a fiery temper. He had two forbidden topics: criticizing his children or President Franklin D. Roosevelt. One day my sister was teasing him about thinking too highly of FDR. He looked at her dead serious and said, "Mary, if you ever vote Republican, I hope to live to see the day that you go hungry!"

These and other memories flooded my mind and made me more lonesome than ever. Yet when no hint of release was forthcoming, I forced my mind to adjust to it. I repeated mentally several times, "Okay, I'm going to be here through Thanksgiving. I will just have to make the best of it."

When Thanksgiving morning came, it was like any other morning. But around two o'clock, at about the time Kathleen and the boys would be sitting down to Thanksgiving dinner, I began thinking about them eating with my place empty and not knowing if I was dead or alive. I was not even sure where they were, but I imagined they had returned to the States. I wondered which one of them would say grace. We were such a close family, I doubted that they would make it all the way through the blessing. The more I thought about it, the more choked-up I became.

That afternoon when they brought my meal, it was the same bread and a cup of water. I said a prayer of thanksgiving for the blessings that had been mine. And even though I was imprisoned and in stocks, I was glad to be from a country like America. Then I said a prayer for each of the boys and Kathleen, and closed by asking God to "Bless their food. Bless their lives. And protect them." It was a prayer I prayed thousands of times.

"Humane and Lenient Treatment" Begins

First Impressions of Newcomers to Oklahoma City, 1978

¶ *The recent population growth and economic expansion in the Sun Belt have had an enormous impact on Oklahoma and promise greater changes for the future. After four decades of losing population, the trend of outward migration has been reversed. For the first time since the end of the oil boom of the twenties and thirties, large numbers of people from other parts of the country are finding jobs and opportunities in Oklahoma. Even more important, younger Sooners with many talents are electing to stay.* ¶ *As new residents settle in modern Oklahoma, they have to adjust to the environment just as the first settlers did. Interviews with recent newcomers to Oklahoma City reflect their expectations of life in the Sooner State and their adaptations to southwestern living.*

NEW RESIDENTS—many from big cities across the country—are coming to the greater Oklahoma City area at the rate of nearly 700 newcomers per month.

In most cases, they are coming to the metropolitan area because they have landed jobs.

"It's still open out here. There are jobs to be had and good jobs too," said one newcomer.

After the newcomers get settled, they start noticing the character of the Southwest and, more specifically, Oklahoma City. One of the first things they sense is a "slower pace of life."

They welcome the clean air and "easy living." On the other hand, they say there's less to do here.

What they bring to the city is an "image" unknown to long-time residents, because the newcomers make compari-

From Mick Hinton, "First Impressions of Newcomers to Oklahoma City," *The Sunday Oklahoman*, Discussion Page, December 17, 1978, p. 37.

sons between what they encounter here and what they have experienced elsewhere.

In recent interviews, seven out-of-staters who have lived in metropolitan areas as big or bigger than Oklahoma City, offered their views about living in their newfound home. Their lengths of residence vary from three months to a year and a half.

Diane Stroup, 26, former airline stewardess retraining as a hairdresser. Native of upstate New York, lived in Albany, N.Y., Puerto Rico and Atlanta before marrying an Arkansas native and moving to Oklahoma City.

"When people back home talk about 'going west' they mean west of Syracuse," said Mrs. Stroup. "I never would have believed anyone if they told me I'd live in Oklahoma. It just never occurred to me."

Mrs. Stroup said she hopes to work in the downtown area after finishing school.

"I like the concourse and the people—the activity," she said, noting her northside suburban neighborhood is a nice place to live, "but you don't have anything to talk about with the neighbors if you don't have kids."

Unlike the East coast, "the buildings are new; everything here is new. My father's a builder and when he visited, he was amazed at all the new houses, most of them brick. He asked if everybody here is rich."

"And there's more building all over, and low unemployment. But it will be interesting to see how everyone reacts when General Motors or some large employer has their first strike," she said.

"OU football—is there anything else? The first time I walked into a department store, they were going at it over a loudspeaker. I thought these people are nuts, crazy."

Mark Lester, 25, single, geophysicist with Union Oil Company of California. Born in Michigan, he grew up at Fort Wayne, Ind., lived in New Orleans, and Lafayette, Ind., for six years before coming to Oklahoma City this past summer.

Six months ago, Lester chose to locate in Oklahoma City over Houston, New Orleans, Dallas, and Tulsa.

"It's a good place for people in the oil industry to get a start," he said. In 1975, Lester spent a summer in Oklahoma City, interning with an oil firm. However, in a few years he intends to move on to "some place like Denver because I like the mountains."

He senses a growing community in Oklahoma City, evidenced by all of the highway work.

"I'm amazed at the Street Department, closing a main section like the 39th Expressway until 1980. Every place else I've lived, they might close down one lane of traffic at a time," but not the whole highway.

Familiar with Tulsa, he says Oklahoma City's downtown "is about 10 years behind" in development. He also chides natives who put up with the smell from the stockyards and packing plants, "especially on a hot summer day driving along the interstate. I'd like to see the stockyards move out of town."

Larry Cuff, 38, assistant comptroller at new General Motors assembly plant. Native of Dallas, worked for GM in Detroit and Framingham, Mass., before moving to Norman in May, 1977.

"It's like coming home," said Cuff, who detects little difference between his native Dallas and Oklahoma City.

"Sure, the New England landscape is beautiful, especially in the fall," Cuff said. "I spent all summer trying to keep alive my two trees in Norman. But I see the flat land, red clay and dust, and I know I am home.

"I dressed up in a leisure suit and cowboy boots for a farewell party in Massachusetts. That's what a lot of people expect to find out here."

Cuff said the schools here are as good or better than those in Massachusetts.

"My kids got A's in Framingham; and here they're getting A's and B's, so I think the schools might be harder here."

Waunita Nelson, 30, homemaker and mother of four,

Newcomers to Oklahoma City, 1978

raised in Minneapolis, lived for seven years at Colorado Springs and at Tulsa two years before moving to Oklahoma City in June, 1977.

"I didn't leave the house all summer the first year we were here," Mrs. Nelson said. "But I'm getting used to the heat."

She finds Oklahoma City residents "are more friendly than Tulsans. Most people don't agree with me, but the Tulsans I met more or less stayed to themselves. My new neighbors here came over and greeted us immediately."

The Village homemaker said she would never go downtown shopping in Oklahoma City, although she frequently did in her native Minneapolis. "Minneapolis has hundreds of different shops, while Oklahoma City has only a few specialty shops."

Mrs. Nelson said her family still considers Colorado Springs their home, and would move to Minneapolis if job opportunities were equal to here.

"My husband I both grew up there. But we like it here; don't get me wrong. It's an easy place to live."

Pearl Lonian, 31, junior college counsellor lived in Detroit, Cleveland, New York City, Rochester, N.Y., Boston, and Worcester, Mass., before locating in Oklahoma City in July.

Mrs. Lonian said she moved here with her family because her husband, a physician just starting his practice, is an Oklahoma City native.

"My husband was impressed with the school systems and we think this is a good place to raise a family."

The New Orleans native said she thinks "Oklahoma's clean air is probably its strongest selling point."

Her family misses "going for walks, one of our favorite pastimes in Massachusetts. On Sunday afternoons, we would often do that. But here, nobody goes for walks. There's something nice about mingling with people in parks, along walkways."

Mrs. Lonian finds "less hustle and bustle here" and people initially more friendly. Oklahomans display a trust on first encounter, where they're more suspecting in the East. She attributes that to a less cosmopolitan atmosphere.

The junior college counsellor said there is less to do here as far as entertainment. "Maybe it's just because we're new. Everybody talks about going to Dallas and Tulsa for a big weekend."

Bill "Hoge" Hogaboam, 29, plays center for the new Oklahoma City Stars hockey team. Grew up in Saskatchewan, Canada. Lived in Omaha, Atlanta, Virginia Beach, Detroit, Minneapolis, and Fort Worth.

Hogaboam moved here around the first of October and got an apartment for his family, who joined him two weeks later.

"I'm enjoying the late fall nice weather. I played golf and it was in the 80s a couple of weeks ago. I don't miss the harsh winters of the north."

Hogaboam notes the availability of day-care centers here. "In Minneapolis it's much harder to get child care. My wife can get out and go to the hockey games."

"People dress more casually here. But the landscape is similar to where I grew up in Saskatchewan—on the prairies, but the mountains weren't that far away."

Bill and Jane Morilak, both 49, lifelong residents of a Polish neighborhood in Cleveland until 1974 when they moved to Hammonton, N.J., an Italian community midway between Philadelphia and Atlantic City.

First-generation Americans, Bill, from Russia, and Jane, who is Polish, say they miss ethnic identity here. They're accustomed to shopping in neighborhood stores.

"Someone told us there is a Polish community in Harrah," Mrs. Morilak said. "Well, we drove out there looking for businesses with Polish names, but we didn't find any."

They say they thrive on the clean air in Oklahoma. In Cleveland, the pollution was so bad the river caught on fire one time, the pair says.

"The sun shines here most of the time, but I can't get used to the drinking water," Morilak said. "That Lake Hefner water tastes muddy; it tastes like dirt."

Oklahoma Memories

The Morilaks say they find most people avoid the downtown area and do their shopping in malls.

"We drove around downtown for three nights looking for the big department stores, until our realtor told us there aren't any."

The Morilaks say they were pleasantly surprised to see "so much green here. Our daughter keeps sending us towels with cactuses on them. She thinks we're living in the desert."

Morilak said they also were surprised with the stockade fences and small lots without sidewalks here "where there's supposed to be plenty of wide open spaces."

"Neighborhood associations there all adopted a certain tree and everybody planted them on their easements between the sidewalks and streets. But the easements are in the back yards here."

CITY LIFE CHECKLIST

Are Oklahoma City residents genuinely friendly?

The newcomers all agreed they're really friendly, but had a hard time explaining just why they thought so.

Cuff: Maybe you could call it trust. When I bought my house, we made the deal with just a handshake. The papers came later. I didn't have to go through all the rigamarole.

Mrs. Stroup: These are Southern people here. More relaxed. If a restaurant is busy, people aren't quick to take offense. Slower pace—not much going on.

The Morilaks: Clerks take time to say hello. It's not a "keep your nose to the grindstone" attitude.

GETTING AROUND

Mrs. Lonian: This city has the worst public transportation system I've ever encountered.

Hogaboam: You don't have to worry about rush-hour traffic here. There really isn't any.

Bill Morilak: I rode the bus in Cleveland, a very nice set-up. But it's easy to get all over the city. People go by the honor system. At a four-way stop, you take your turn; everybody does. It doesn't work that way in Jersey.

Mrs. Stroup: Roads are horrible in the far Northwest. There isn't even a major highway to get downtown.

Lester: Public transportation? I've never seen a bus.

Newcomers to Oklahoma City, 1978

COST OF HOUSING AND TAXES

Cuff: There's no comparison. My real estate taxes in Massachusetts were $2,000, and I sold the house for $57,000. My home in Brookhaven cost $76,000, and the taxes were $400 less. This home is 25–30 percent larger.

Hogaboam: Our apartment is $100 cheaper than a similar one in Fort Worth, where we played last season.

DINING OUT

Mrs. Stroup: Most of my friends entertain at home, and I like that. I've seen better restaurants, but there's the usual chains where you can't get a bad meal. But you can cook a good steak and potato at home.

The Morilaks: We're cafeteria nuts, and the cafeterias are excellent here. We miss the real ethnic restaurants.

ENTERTAINMENT

Lester: I've never seen a city so liberal with its topless, bottomless places, and so conservative about liquor.

Mrs. Stroup: There isn't a centralized place for entertainment. It takes a half-hour to get anywhere, and everybody heads in a different direction.

We used to go downtown in Atlanta to the big hotels, eat out at a good restaurant, then go to a good show. I think this will come to Oklahoma City. It's still a growing city.

Index

Agencies, Indian: 70–71, 73
Alessandro, Victor: 246
Ameringer, Oscar: 163
Anadarko, Oklahoma: 57–60, 65, 96
Anso-gia-ny or Ansote: 147
Apache, Oklahoma Territory: 181, 185
Apache baseball team: 181–85
Apache Indians: 55, 57
Arapaho Indians: 93, 94, 96, 97, 104
Arkansas City, Kansas: 70, 74, 101, 106
Aunt Tenah (mission cook): 11, 12
Ayahkombee, Gipson: 33
Ayahkombee, Selina: 30

Barnard, Evan G.: 83
Bartlesville, Oklahoma: 110–12
Bass, Althea: 93
Battles, Goldie: 289
Beadle, J. H.: 37, 38
Bell, Mr. (neighbor): 19
Bennett, Mr. (director of Soil Erosion Control service): 235
Biedler, G. A.: 75
Big Turkey Creek: 85–90
Blackburn, Mr. (neighbor): 19
Boudinot, Elias: 53
Boudinot, William: 53
Branstetter, Otto: 164–65
Broaddus, Judge Bower: 275
Brown, Richard: 189
Bryce, the Reverend J. Y., Sr.: 32
Buffalo hunt: 97–100
Bullock, Dr. W. A. J.: 268–69
Burkos, Mrs. Caroline: 282
Buskirk, Van: 90–91
Byrd, Mrs. William: 31

Caddo, Oklahoma: 31, 58
Call Me Madam (Broadway musical): 187
Carter, R. T.: 185
Catoosa, Oklahoma: 23
Chadick, E. D.: 80
Chamberlain, Charles: 77
Chaney, Olive: 154
Cheadle, Professor John B.: 270
Cherokee Indians: 18–20, 25, 40, 52–54, 171, 192
Cherokee Strip, opening of: 127–30

Cheyenne Indians: 97–103
Chickasaw Indians: 25, 50, 171
Choctaw Nation: 21, 25–27, 37, 49, 51–54, 171
Christian, Emma Ervin: 26
Cimarron County: 223
Civil War: 7, 19, 25–28, 30
Claremore, Oklahoma: 109–110
Colbert, Pitman: 35
Collins, Brad: 49
Collins, Jim: 19
Comanche Indians: 57–58, 65
Cornell, Katharine: 191
Creek Indians: 7, 41, 46, 47, 50, 54, 141–44
Cross, George Lynn: 265
Cuff, Larry: 299, 302–303

Dalton, John: 108
Daniels, Mrs. Grace: 284–85
Darlington, Oklahoma: 96–104
Darlington, Brinton: 95
Davis, William: 61–62
Desegregation: 265, 277
Diggs, Mr. and Mrs. D. J.: 280
Dillingham, Bennie: 219
Dillingham, Ernie: 217, 219
Dillingham, Fred: 217–19
Dillingham, Joe: 219–20
Dillingham, Mr. (oil-rich farmer): 213–21
Dillingham, Ralph: 218
District Court of Cleveland County: 270, 273–74
Do-Hente (Napawat or No Shoes): 147–49
Dorsey, Roll H.: 80
Dowdell, Maxine: 280
Duggett, Dan: 211
Duggett, Sadie (Mrs. Dan Duggett): 197
Dunham, Arthur W.: 67
Dunn, Bill: 246, 253
Dunjee, Roscoe: 267–70
Durant, Oklahoma: 27, 58
Dust Bowl, the: 223–44

East Cache Creek: 58, 61
El Reno, Oklahoma: 59, 102, 108, 115
Eva, Oklahoma: 223

Ferber, Edna: 214
Ferguson, Elva Shartel: 113
Ferguson, Thompson Benton: 114
Five Civilized Tribes: 15, 25, 37, 127
Flynn, Dennis: 115–16
Fort Gibson, Oklahoma: 8, 15, 51, 52
Fort Reno, Oklahoma: 71–73, 123
Fort Sill, Oklahoma: 57–65, 160, 184, 245, 252
Fort Smith, Arkansas: 17, 19, 20, 31, 51
Fort Towson, Oklahoma: 27, 31
45th Division: 245, 255
Fourteenth Amendment: 270, 273
Franklin, Dave: 19
Frazier, Robert: 30
Freedmen: 15, 22, 38, 44
Fuller, Gwendolyn: 279, 283

Galbreath, Bob: 193
Gaylord, Edith: 246
Gerlach, Margaret: 133
Gibson, George: 69
Gilleland, Mrs. H.: 262
Gilleland, Seaman First Class Ronnie: 259, 262–64
Gittinger, Roy: 269
Glenn Pool near Tulsa: 195
Goodman, Peper: 20
Gore, Oklahoma: 23
Grapes of Wrath, The: 170
Green, Colonel Ned: 188
"Green Corn Rebellion": 175, 177
Griffith, "Uncle Jeff": 59
Guthrie, Oklahoma: 70, 80, 106, 110, 187

Hall, Amos: 270
Hansen, Fred: 270
Harrah, Oklahoma: 163
Haskell, Governor Charles N.: 188
Hayes, Everett: 252
Hayes, Lee: 252
Henderson, Caroline A. (Mrs. Will Henderson): 223
Henderson, Eleanor: 224, 229, 234, 244
Henderson, Will: 229
Henrietta, Texas: 58, 59
Hervey, Dr. John: 273–74
Hildebrand, Nancy: 23
Hildebrand, Steve: 23
Hill, Joseph: 280
Hogaboam, Bill "Hoge": 301, 303
Holt, George: 16
Homestead Act, the: 171
Honey Springs, Oklahoma: 19–20

Indian doctors: 32–35
Indian Territory: 7, 25, 26, 37–39, 49–50, 55, 58, 71, 73, 83, 105, 108, 163, 165, 171–72

Industrial Workers of the World: 175
Ingram, the Reverend Job: 116

Jackson, President Andrew: 7
Jackson, the Reverend W. K.: 290
Jennings, Al: 192
Johnson, Joan: 281
Jungle, The: 171

Katz Drug Store, Oklahoma City: 284–85, 291, 293
Kiamichi river: 29–31
King, Martin Luther, Jr.: 280
Kingfisher, Oklahoma: 108, 115, 116, 122
Kingsbury, Cyrus: 28
Kiowa Indians: 57, 145–61, 192
Klingsick, Clyde: 253
Krepps, Ethel C.: 145

Lange, Dorothea: 223
Langston University: 266–68, 272, 274
Laune, "Nonie Russell" (Mrs. Sidney Laune): 131
Laune, Sidney: 132–33, 135
Layton, S. A. (Sol): 188
Lee, Russell: 223
Lester, Mark: 298–99, 303
Levite, George: 181
Levite, Peter: 181
Lonian, Pearl: 300–301
Lovie (waitress): 203–205, 207, 209, 211–12
Luper, Clara: 279, 283, 286–86, 291
Luper, Marilyn: 283, 288

McAlester, Oklahoma: 58, 266–67
McClendon, Mrs. Lucille: 280
McEachin, Joe: 110–11
McGee, Lizzie: 22
Mackenzie, General Ranald S.: 146
McLaurin, George W.: 272–76
Marguerite (sister of Perle Mesta): 189, 191, 194–95
Marshall, Thurgood: 266–67, 269, 276
Medicine Lodge Treaty: 99, 145
Medicine Wind: *see* Wind Goomda
Merrill, Professor Maurice: 270
Mesta, Perle Skirvin (Mrs. George Mesta): 187
Miles, Agent: 100
Miles, William: 280, 282
Mixed bloods: 15, 25; and land speculation, 38
Moody, William Vaughan: 244
Morilak, Bill and Jane: 301–303
Mulhall, Zack: 106
Munger, W. H.: 116
Murrah, Judge A. P.: 275
Muskogee, Oklahoma: 38, 41–44, 48, 51, 58, 109
Muskogee Indians: *see* Creek Indians

Index

National Freedman's Bureau: 22
NAACP (National Association for the Advancement of Colored People): 266, 269, 274; Youth Council of, 279–85
Nelson, Waunita: 299–300
Norman, Oklahoma: 70, 74, 108, 265–66
Nowata, Oklahoma: 109

O'Brian, Hank: 137
Oil: 213–21
Oklahoma, University of: 265–67, 273, 275, 277
Oklahoma City: 67–69, 71, 77–81, 102, 106–108, 112, 158–59, 164–65, 187–88, 191–92, 195, 198, 206, 208–209, 260, 279–80, 282–83, 291, 297–304
Oklahoma run of 1889: 76–78, 83–91, 213–14
Oklahoma State Regents for Higher Education: 271
Oklahoma Station: *see* Oklahoma City
Oklahoma Territory: 131–32
Oliver, Lillian: 284–85, 289
Olmsted, Minnie: 137
Osage Indians: 192, 213

Payne, Captain David L.: 84
Perry, Oklahoma: 70
Pin Indians: 19–20
Pogue, Mr. and Mrs. Louis J.: 286
Pogue, Lana: 286, 288
Pogue, Mary: 284–85, 289–90
Ponca City, Oklahoma: 70
Posey, Barbara: 281, 283, 286
Powless, Hattie: 96
Prettyman, W. S.: 127
Pryer, J. W.: 105
Purcell, Oklahoma: 70, 72, 74, 108
Purington, A. S.: 46

Railroads in Oklahoma: 37–39, 41, 48–49, 58, 67, 80
Ramsey, Walter: 193
"Ranicky Bill": 85–91
Red River: 21, 25, 49, 58, 64, 65
Reese, Roddy: 22
Risner, Colonel Robinson: 293–95
Robertson, the Reverend W. S.: 46, 47
Robinson, Sergeant Don: 245
Root, Myra: 138
Rucker, Tom: 259

Sands, George L.: 76
Sapulpa, Oklahoma: 110, 294
Scott, Sterling: 22, 23
Scruggs, Theresa: 293
Segregation: 265, 275
Seminole Indians: 25, 171

Sheppard, Caesar: 16
Sheppard, Easter: 16
Sheppard, Joe: 15, 16, 19
Sheppard, Morris: 15
Sheppard, Wash: 22
Sipuel, Ada Lois (Mrs. Warren Fisher): 268, 270, 272–73
Sit-in participants at Katz Drug Store: 285, 290, 291
Skelly, Bill: 193
Skirvin Hotel, Oklahoma City: 188–95
Skirvin, William (brother of Perle Mesta): 189–90
Skirvin, William Balser: 187
Slaveholders and slavery: 15, 25
Slaves: 5, 19, 22, 25, 43, 46
Sneed, General R. A.: 57
Snyder, Lieutenant Colonel: 75
Socialism in Oklahoma: 163–73
Soil erosion control: 226–27, 231–34, 243–44
Somers, Captain C. F.: 71
Starr, Tom: 19
Stewart, Carrie: 37
Stiles, Captain D. F.: 75
Stillwater, Oklahoma: 106
Stine, Len: 136
Stink, John: 193
Stocker, Joe: 255–56
Stroup, Diane: 198, 302–304
Suggs, Carl: 59
Sutton, Jim: 19
Sweezy, Carl: 93

Tahlequah, Oklahoma: 52
Thunderbird Division: *see* 45th Division
Tolliver, Ruth: 279, 284, 290
Tuttle, Bill: 253–55
Turner, Avery: 76

U.S.S. Oklahoma City: 259–62

Van, Captain ("Rich Joe"): 21, 22
Van, Joe ("Little Joe"): 21, 22
Vaught, Judge Edgar S.: 275
Vinita, Oklahoma: 38, 58, 108
Vore, Major J. G.: 45

Wagoner, Oklahoma: 109
Walker, Tandy, Esq.: 49, 51
Wamsley, Colonel Grover C.: 252
Watonga, Oklahoma: 114–17, 120
Webbers Falls, Oklahoma: 15, 16, 20–23
White, John B.: 280–81
White, Tom: 253
Wickmiller, C. P.: 108
Williams, Attorney General Mac Q.: 271–72
Williams, Judge Ben T.: 270
Williams, W. G. ("Caddo Bill"): 58

Williams, Portwood, Sr.: 284, 289
Wind Goomda: 145–46, 150–53, 159–61
Woodward, Oklahoma: clubs in, 131–39; library in, 132–39
World War I: 175, 245, 249
World War II: 265
Wright, Herbert: 280